Palgrave Macmillan Studies in Banking and Financial Institutions

Series Editor: **Professor Philip Molyneux**

The Palgrave Macmillan Studies in Banking and Financial Institutions are international in orientation and include studies of banking within particular countries or regions, and studies of particular themes such as Corporate Banking, Risk Management, Mergers and Acquisitions, etc. The books' focus is on research and practice, and they include up-to-date and innovative studies on contemporary topics in banking that will have global impact and influence.

Titles include:

Yener Altunbaş, Blaise Gadanecz and Alper Kara
SYNDICATED LOANS
A Hybrid of Relationship Lending and Publicly Traded Debt

Yener Altunbaş, Alper Kara and Öslem Olgu
TURKISH BANKING
Banking under Political Instability and Chronic High Inflation

Elena Beccalli
IT AND EUROPEAN BANK PERFORMANCE

Paola Bongini, Stefano Chiarlone and Giovanni Ferri *(editors)*
EMERGING BANKING SYSTEMS

Vittorio Boscia, Alessandro Carretta and Paola Schwizer
COOPERATIVE BANKING:INNOVATIONS AND DEVELOPMENTS

COOPERATIVE BANKING IN EUROPE
Case Studies

Roberto Bottiglia, Elisabetta Gualandri and Gian Nereo Mazzocco *(editors)*
CONSOLIDATION IN THE EUROPEAN FINANCIAL INDUSTRY

Alessandro Carretta, Franco Fiordelisi and Gianluca Mattarocci *(editors)*
NEW DRIVERS OF PERFORMANCE IN A CHANGING FINANCIAL WORLD

Dimitris N. Chorafas
CAPITALISM WITHOUT CAPITAL

Dimitris N. Chorafas
FINANCIAL BOOM AND GLOOM
The Credit and Banking Crisis of 2007–2009 and Beyond

Violaine Cousin
BANKING IN CHINA

Vincenzo D'Apice and Giovanni Ferri
FINANCIAL INSTABILITY
Toolkit for Interpreting Boom and Bust Cycles

Peter Falush and Robert L. Carter OBE
THE BRITISH INSURANCE INDUSTRY SINCE 1900
The Era of Transformation

Franco Fiordelisi
MERGERS AND ACQUISITIONS IN EUROPEAN BANKING

Franco Fiordelisi, Philip Molyneux and Daniele Previati *(editors)*
NEW ISSUES IN FINANCIAL AND CREDIT MARKETS

Franco Fiordelisi, Philip Molyneux and Daniele Previati *(editors)*
NEW ISSUES IN FINANCIAL INSTITUTIONS MANAGEMENT

Franco Fiordelisi and Philip Molyneux
SHAREHOLDER VALUE IN BANKING

Hans Genberg and Cho-Hoi Hui
THE BANKING CENTRE IN HONG KONG
Competition, Efficiency, Performance and Risk

Carlo Gola and Alessandro Roselli
THE UK BANKING SYSTEM AND ITS REGULATORY AND SUPERVISORY FRAMEWORK

Elisabetta Gualandri and Valeria Venturelli *(editors)*
BRIDGING THE EQUITY GAP FOR INNOVATIVE SMEs

Kim Hawtrey
AFFORDABLE HOUSING FINANCE

Otto Hieronymi *(editor)*
GLOBALIZATION AND THE REFORM OF THE INTERNATIONAL BANKING AND MONETARY SYSTEM

Munawar Iqbal and Philip Molyneux
THIRTY YEARS OF ISLAMIC BANKING
History, Performance and Prospects

Sven Janssen
BRITISH AND GERMAN BANKING STRATEGIES

Kimio Kase and Tanguy Jacopin
CEOs AS LEADERS AND STRATEGY DESIGNERS
Explaining the Success of Spanish Banks

Alexandros-Andreas Kyrtsis *(editor)*
FINANCIAL MARKETS AND ORGANIZATIONAL TECHNOLOGIES
System Architectures, Practices and Risks in the Era of Deregulation

M. Mansoor Khan and M. Ishaq Bhatti
DEVELOPMENTS IN ISLAMIC BANKING
The Case of Pakistan

Mario La Torre and Gianfranco A. Vento
MICROFINANCE

Philip Molyneux and Eleuterio Vallelado *(editors)*
FRONTIERS OF BANKS IN A GLOBAL WORLD

Simon Mouatt and Carl Adams *(editors)*
CORPORATE AND SOCIAL TRANSFORMATION OF MONEY AND BANKING
Breaking the Serfdom

Anastasia Nesvetailova
FRAGILE FINANCE
Debt, Speculation and Crisis in the Age of Global Credit

Anders Ögren *(editor)*
THE SWEDISH FINANCIAL REVOLUTION

Dominique Rambure and Alec Nacamuli
PAYMENT SYSTEMS
From the Salt Mines to the Board Room

Catherine Schenk *(editor)*
HONG KONG SAR's MONETARY AND EXCHANGE RATE CHALLENGES
Historical Perspectives

Noël K. Tshiani
BUILDING CREDIBLE CENTRAL BANKS
Policy Lessons for Emerging Economies

Ruth Wandhöfer
EU PAYMENTS INTEGRATION
The Tale of SEPA, PSD and Other Milestones Along the Road

The full list of titles available is on the website:
www.palgrave.com/finance/sbfi.asp

Palgrave Macmillan Studies in Banking and Financial Institutions
Series Standing Order ISBN 978–1–4039–4872–4

You can receive future titles in this series as they are published by placing a standing order. Please contact your bookseller or, in case of difficulty, write to us at the address below with your name and address, the title of the series and the ISBN quoted above. Customer Services Department, Macmillan Distribution Ltd, Houndmills, Basingstoke, Hampshire RG21 6XS, England

---

EU Payments Integration

The Tale of SEPA, PSD and Other Milestones Along the Road

Ruth Wandhöfer

palgrave
macmillan

First published 2010 by
PALGRAVE MACMILLAN.

Palgrave Macmillan in the UK is an imprint of Macmillan Publishers Limited, registered in England, company number 785998, of Houndmills, Basingstoke, Hampshire RG21 6XS.

Palgrave Macmillan in the US is a division of St Martin's Press LLC, 175 Fifth Avenue, New York, NY 10010.

Palgrave Macmillan is the global academic imprint of the above companies and has companies and representatives throughout the world.

ISBN 978–0–230–24347–7 hardback

This book is printed on paper suitable for recycling and made from fully managed and sustained forest sources. Logging, pulping and manufacturing processes are expected to conform to the environmental regulations of the country of origin.

A catalogue record for this book is available from the British Library.

Library of Congress Cataloging-in-Publication Data

Wandhöfer, Ruth, 1976–
EU payments integration: the tale of SEPA, PSD and other milestones along the road/Ruth Wandhöfer.
p. cm. — (Palgrave Macmillan studies in banking and financial institutions)
ISBN 978–0–230–24347–7 (hardback)
1. Finance—European Union countries. 2. Payment—European Union countries. 3. Euro area. I. Title.
HG186.A2W35 2010
332.1'78—dc22

2010027570

10 9 8 7 6 5 4 3 2 1
19 18 17 16 15 14 13 12 11 10

Printed and bound in Great Britain by
CPI Antony Rowe, Chippenham and Eastbourne

Contents

List of Tables

List of Figures

Foreword

Gertrude Tumpel-Gugerell
Member of the European Central Bank's Executive Board

It is a great pleasure to write this foreword to an important contribution concerning the Single Euro Payments Area. This book delivers a very timely reflection on the evolution of the European payments landscape and its role as a building block for the Single Market. Readers from Europe and outside may benefit from learning about one of the biggest integration initiatives in Europe that has ever taken place.

The European Single Market forms the largest domestic market in the world, with a population of roughly 500 million people and accounting for about 21 per cent of world GDP. The road to integration, involving the free movement of people, goods, services and capital is removing many obstacles to intra-European trade. An integrated EU market is more competitive and offers more opportunities than a market divided by national borders could ever do. It provides opportunities for economies of scale and scope, innovation and entrepreneurship.

A vital component of the Single Market is the area of payments. Payments are an essential ingredient of all economic transactions. The introduction of the Euro, which in itself has significantly improved trading and financial transactions for both companies and private citizens, has not led to a fully integrated payments market yet. Retail payments especially have long remained fragmented along national lines. This is not entirely surprising, given the very different evolution of the payments industries and of user habits within individual countries. Yet the Single Market and especially the common currency should also enable its users to make payments in one 'domestic' way, no matter where the payer and the payee are situated.

This is why two landmark initiatives were launched: the creation of the Single Euro Payments Area (SEPA) and the introduction of a harmonised legal framework through the Payment Services Directive (PSD). This book provides an essential descriptive analysis of these initiatives, exploring the design and implementation of the new European landscape for payments.

The SEPA project was started by the banking industry in 2002. Once SEPA is completed, all Euro payments will become truly domestic, allowing us to fully reap the benefits of the single currency. With one set of payment instruments, citizens will be able to make payments throughout the Euro area as quickly and easily as they make national payments today. This will make payments more efficient and will bring cost savings for all payment users in Europe.

The harmonised legal framework, as defined by the PSD and by now implemented in national legislation, plays a key role in providing the legal basis for SEPA. The PSD also harmonises consumer protection rules across all adhering countries. For example, the PSD significantly reduces transaction times for payments to a maximum of one day by 1 January 2012. It provides a clear and concise set of harmonised information requirements. These must be fulfilled by all payment service providers, regardless of whether they offer SEPA products or existing national payment products. This will improve transparency for customers. It also provides clarity and certainty with regard to the core rights and obligations of both users and providers of payment services.

Harmonising the European retail payment markets will also promote new sources of competition. Payment services may now be provided by new non-bank players, called payments institutions, in addition to the services offered by banks and e-money institutions. This creates a level playing field with enhanced competition, which will also help foster innovation.

Based on the new common payment instruments, rulebooks and frameworks, the providers of payments infrastructure (for instance, clearing houses, card schemes and payment networks) are able to evolve in a way that promotes higher levels of efficiency, quality and security and supports the necessary reach across the newly integrated market. The use of modern information and communication technology and international standards are key essentials of Europe's new payment strategy. There is significant potential for the provision of new innovative services such as e-invoicing, e-payments and mobile payments.

Thanks to the united efforts of the European banking community, legislators and the central banking community, SEPA has made a successful start with the introduction of the SEPA credit transfer more than two years ago and the SEPA direct debit last year (2009). But, of course, SEPA is far from complete. The full migration to SEPA credit transfers and SEPA direct debits will take some time. The European Commission has just published a paper discussing a SEPA migration end-date for SEPA credit transfers and SEPA direct debits. In the world of payment cards, card schemes and processors need further to adapt to the expectations set out in the SEPA Cards Framework. I believe that Europe should develop at least one additional SEPA-wide cards scheme. Despite the financial crisis, cashless payments increased on a global basis by almost 9 per cent to 250 billion transactions per year in 2008. Of this growth, card payments were the strongest driver. In the European Union, card payments reached a total of over 29 billion transactions in 2008, also growing at a rate of almost 9 per cent. This shows the immense potential of this payment instrument for the financial industry and demonstrates that without the success of SEPA for cards, the project will not be complete.

One question I am frequently asked is whether the financial crisis has had an impact on the SEPA project and the pace of migration. During the financial crisis, the retail payments business of banks has proven to be a solid and stable source of revenue. Combined with the fact that the aim of SEPA is to make payments in Euro more efficient, not just for customers but also for banks, this would rather strengthen the case for investments in the SEPA project.

To conclude, I would recommend this book to anyone looking for a comprehensive and stimulating insight into the forces and events that have shaped – and are still shaping – the story of EU payments harmonisation. I very much welcome this effort to educate and inform at a key moment.

About the Author

Ruth Wandhöfer is well known in the European banking industry for her in-depth knowledge of the regulatory, market and competitive landscape and in particular is acknowledged as one of the foremost authorities on SEPA and the PSD. She holds a number of influential positions, including the chairmanship of the European banking industry's PSD Expert Group, membership of the Plenary and Co-ordination Committee of the European Payments Council (EPC), chairmanship of the EPC's Information Security Support Group and membership of the EU Commission's Payment Systems Market Expert Group.

Ruth is currently responsible for Market Policy & Strategy within Citi's EMEA Global Transaction Services business. As such, she has external responsibility for engaging with and influencing the evolving regulatory and market/standards environment on a wide range of established and emerging topics, as well as driving and coordinating the business response within Citi GTS. In a SEPA and PSD context, this has included responsibility for Citi GTS PSD implementation project as well as the product evolution and thought leadership in relation to all aspects of Citi's response to SEPA.

Prior to joining Citi, Ruth worked for the European Banking Federation where amongst her other responsibilities she was closely involved with the EPC in developing the SEPA Credit Transfer scheme rulebook, as well as being a high profile and influential lobbyist in the negotiation of the PSD and other relevant legislation with the European Commission, Council and Parliament.

Previously, Ruth worked in financial management in the banking sector as well as in the European Commission DG Economic and Financial Affairs. She speaks five languages and has completed studies in various countries, including an MA in Financial Economics in the UK, an MA in International Politics in France and an LLM in International Economic Law in the UK.

Acknowledgements

First of all I would like to express my thanks to Gertrude Tumpel-Gugerell, Member of the Executive Board of the ECB, who honoured me by agreeing to write the foreword to this book.

I am also indebted to my colleague and friend Simon Newstead, who provided editorial assistance throughout the creation of this saga.

Also a big thank you to Akinbo Akinwunmi, Madhadevan Balakrishnan, Charles Bryant, Gerard Hartsink, Harry Leinonen, Michael Montoya, Liz Oakes, Eric Sepkes, Joleen Young and the EPC Rulebooks(!).

Finally, I wish to thank Paese who supported me with constant patience, warm meals late at night and his valued opinions.

Commonly Used Abbreviations and Acronyms

ACH	Automated Clearing House
AML	Anti Money Laundering
AOS	Additional Optional Service
ASEAN	Association of Southeast Asian Nations
ATM	Automated Teller Machine
B2B	Business-to-Business
B2C	Business-to-Consumer
BIC	Bank Identifier Code
CEMAC/ EMCCA	Economic and Monetary Community of Central Africa
CMA	Common Monetary Area
CMF	Creditor Mandate Flow
COMESA	Common Market for East and Southern Africa
COR	Committee of Regions
CSD	Central Securities Depository
CSM	Clearing and Settlement Mechanism
DD	Direct Debit
DMF	Debtor Mandate Flow
EAC	East African Community
EACB	European Association of Cooperative Banks
EBA/ABE	Euro Banking Association
EBF	European Banking Federation
EC	European Commission
ECCAS	Economic Community of Central African States
ECB	European Central Bank
ECOWAS	Economic Community of West African States
ECON	Economic and Monetary Committee of the European Parliament

ECOSOC	Economic and Social Committee
ECSA	European Credit Sector Association
EEA	European Economic Area
EMI	e-Money Institution
EMV	Europay MasterCard Visa programme to implement CHIP and PIN security for card transactions
EP	European Parliament
EPC	European Payments Council
ESBG	European Savings Bank Group
ESSC	European Community for Steel and Coal
EU	European Union
Eurosystem	European System of Central Banks
Euratom	European Atomic Energy Community
Euro Area	16 EU countries using the euro as legal tender (as of 2009)
FATF	Financial Action Task Force
FSAP	European Commission's Financial Services Action Plan
GCC	Gulf Cooperation Council
GDP	Gross Domestic Product
IA	Impact Assessment
IBAN	International Bank Account Number (ISO 13616 norm)
ICP	Interbank Convention on Payments
ICSD	International Central Securities Depository
IPF	International Payments Framework initiative
ISO	International Organisation for Standardisation
JASDEC	Japanese Securities Depositary Centre
MBP	Multilateral Balancing Payment
MENA	Middle East and North Africa
MEP	Member of the European Parliament
MIF	Multilateral Interchange Fee
NCB	National Central Bank
NFC	Near Field Communications
NLF	New Legal Framework

NPCI	National Payments Corporation of India
P2P	Person-to-Person
PE-ACH	Pan-European Automated Clearing House
PEDD	Pan-European Direct Debit, the original working title for what would become the SEPA Direct Debit Scheme
PI	Payment Institution
PSD EG	European Banking Industry's PSD Expert Group
PSMEG	European Commission's Payment Systems Market Expert Group
PSP	Payment Service Provider
PSU	Payment Service User
RTGS	Real Time Gross Settlement
SADC	Southern African Development Community
SCF	SEPA Cards Framework
SECA	Single Euro Cash Area
SEPA	Single Euro Payments Area
SEPA B2B DD	SEPA Business to Business Direct Debit
SEPA Core DD	SEPA Direct Debit
SEPA CT	SEPA Credit Transfer
SMEs	Small and Medium-sized Enterprises
STP	Straight-Through Processing
SWIFT	Society for Worldwide Interbank Financial Telecommunication
TARGET2	Eurosystem's Trans-European Automated Real-time Gross settlement Express Transfer system
T2S	TARGET2 for Securities
WAEMU/ UEMOA	West African Economic and Monetary Union
WAMZ	West African Monetary Zone
WATCH	Worldwide Automated Transaction Clearing House initiative
XML	Extensible Mark-up Language

Title I
The Opening Act: The Beginning of the End ... or Just the End of the Beginning?

(1) Prelude

All books need to have a moment of conception, a moment when a story or a character jumps into your mind demanding to be written down.

In some cases this can apparently happen during an interminable railway journey. In my case I can trace my inspiration for this book to a moment of pure theatre I witnessed during an otherwise interminable debate in the European Parliament(EP).

The democratic event in question was the final Parliamentary debate on the proposed text for the Payment Services Directive (PSD), prior to the vote due the next day. From my viewpoint in one of the best seats in the house, it gradually became clear that what was expected to be the usual and somewhat ritualistic exchange of party positions, followed by endorsement of the legislative proposal, was in danger of being overshadowed by a simmering row over a quite separate issue – fundamental concerns around the fact that the US Government's demanded access to EU financial messaging data passed over the global messaging network (SWIFT) on the grounds of terrorist finance concerns.

The signs of the gathering storm went entirely unnoticed by the tourists in the public gallery. Even to the cognoscenti, the threat was barely perceptible at that stage – the first indications being the tiny whispers of bilateral conversations rising above the Plenary debate.

Acutely conscious that the stakes were high, the key protagonists – the European Commission (EC), the German Presidency of the EU Council and the Parliamentary Rapporteur for the PSD – then sent out their agents across the floor of the Parliament for a flurry of heated conversations. Shortly after this, a formal request was made for a statement from the German Presidency on the data transfer issue, followed by a threat to table a last minute amendment to the PSD – which would have significantly endangered the first reading adoption and consequently delayed the launch of the Single Euro Payments Area (SEPA) project by months, if not years.

The culmination of these events was an image I shall never forget. A trilateral meeting was hastily convened at the back of the Parliamentary hemicycle – amidst the Member State flags that represent the EU ideal – with the participants looking for all the world like conspirators behind the arras during a great Shakespearian drama. In the end, the meeting under the flags did the trick, and a compromise was reached allowing the Parliament to satisfy its desire to register outrage about this issue by including a strong sounding reference in its formal resolution that would accompany the PSD, rather than by amending the Directive text itself.

An interesting footnote to this story is that this data transfer row between Europe and the US was to continue right up to the current time (a good three years later!), with issues being raised over EU consumer protection; questions of EU citizens' rights of appeal to US authorities; and concerns over the US failing to provide reciprocal access to its data. The fact that the EU was to go as far as stopping to share Terrorist Finance Tracking Program related data with the US Treasury Department in January 2010 signalled the urgency for a new formal deal to be reached between the two sides. Following a series of negotiations an agreement was finally struck between the US Treasury, EU Member States and the European Parliament on 24 June 2010 under which 'scrutineers' appointed by the EU are to become part of the US Treasury's operations that examine the financial transactions of terror suspects and the European Commission has been asked to prepare a framework for the extraction of data on US soil, with a view to setting up an EU equivalent to the American Terrorist Finance Tracking Program.

Anyway, returning from this more recent story to the one I was relating before, on the day after I had witnessed this high drama in the Strasbourg hemicycle all the excitement had clearly ebbed away and I was instead watching the Parliament very quietly (and rather too rapidly for my taste) formally adopting the PSD – a law that has thus far robbed me of a good four years of sleep (and I dare say I'm not the only one).

With this event, Act I of the PSD, the official adoption of the final text was now over, and about to give way to Act II – the implementation process – which as I later found out would, in its own way, turn out to be equally full of drama. To be continued ...

(2) Overture

It is a truth universally acknowledged that a Single Market in possession of good fortune must be in need of harmonisation. Certainly this truth has tended to be acknowledged by the European Union (EU) when approaching legislation in the field of financial services.

In the context of the massive regulatory armoury that strives to achieve a competitive and integrated Single Market, the PSD stands out as a landmark measure. Among its panoply of impressive objectives, the PSD is intended to provide the legal framework for SEPA, the latter in turn marking the third and final stage of the introduction of the euro with the creation of a euro-currency based payment system for Europe.

This book provides a comprehensive assessment of the EU's legislative activism in the field of payments, focused particularly on the PSD and SEPA, but including impacts and interactions with the broader set of payments related legislation in the overall context of the radical reshaping of the payments landscape that is currently happening.

On the path to assessing the origins, intentions and implications of this stretch of the great river of financial market integration in Europe, this book also examines a range of related topics and issues, such as the identification of various ambiguities, shortcomings and key concerns for competition, consumer protection and the future of payment services, while at the same time keeping an eye on global developments and implications in this space.

Divided into seven main parts, or more appropriately 'Titles' – in the spirit of European legislative terminology – our story begins right here with Title I, the opening remarks.

Title II will follow shortly, with a background analysis of the EU lawmaking process. In doing so, it will take a close look at the internal workings of the EC Services and the process of legislative conception, followed by a glance at the lengthy gestation period involved in reaching final agreement within the triumvirate of decision-making EU institutions – the Commission, Parliament and Council. Building on this introduction, we then briefly explore key measures that form part of the growing web of payments related legislation since the 1980s.

Title III examines the many interactions between EU regulators and the financial industry, which among other things lead to the creation of the banking industry's 'self-regulatory' SEPA initiative. The origins of SEPA and the inherent challenges of achieving political consensus between a varied range of competing interests within the payments industry – even in the face of a significant and obvious common threat – are described from the standpoint of an eyewitness to these events.

Within Title IV, the PSD, formally known as New Legal Framework for Payments (NLF), is explored in detail – from the very early ideas and drafts of the EC up to the final text, including an assessment of its implications in the context of SEPA.

Title V then turns to the considerable challenges that were encountered following the final publication of the PSD at the end of 2007. It is fair to say that despite the many years of negotiation and crafting of this EU legislation leading up to that point, the real challenges in terms of translation, interpretation and applicability only truly began at that stage.

In parallel to the evolution of the PSD, the SEPA schemes and the Cards Framework have also gradually evolved and are discussed in detail in Title VI. This section offers a critical review of the success so far of the SEPA Credit Transfers and the SEPA Cards Framework, both launched in January 2008. In addition, the challenges and opportunities around SEPA Direct Debits, the third SEPA pillar, introduced to the market in November 2009 are assessed.

Finally, Title VII provides an evaluation of the success so far of the PSD and SEPA in meeting their combined objectives of harmonisation, increased efficiency, consumer protection and the integration of the EU financial market to enhance competition. It is made clear that to achieve the full benefits of SEPA, an effective switch-off date for local schemes and a rationalisation of clearing and settlement mechanisms across the Eurozone is essential. Furthermore, this final section addresses the potential implications, and lessons to be learnt from this major European payments landscape change project by other regions around the globe, including the global spread of XML and the ISO 20022 as well as the interest shown by a number of communities in the legal harmonisation exercise reflected by the PSD and other regulatory measures in Europe.

I wish you all an informative, thought provoking and hopefully enjoyable reading experience!

Title II

EU Financial Regulation Explained: 'The Powers and the Pitfalls'

Introduction

Once upon a time, the Member States of the European Union chose to place their national legislative powers around financial services into the hands of the European Community – an act that was motivated by the decision of Europe to start growing together and to create a Single Market.

The foundations of the Single Market – which lies at the heart of the European Union (EU) and promotes the free circulation of people, goods, services and capital – can be traced back to the establishment of the European Economic Community in 1958. For many decades the EU has actively promoted the Single Market mantra and several important pieces of legislation were enacted to assist the integration of the market, fostering a peaceful neighbourhood policy in Europe.

The fact is that European legislation, in the context of the sheer size of the European market, has over time become a very important influence on the global markets, making a critical assessment of the European process of law creation and regulatory output an important part of being able to understand not only European but also global regulatory trends.

The practical challenges of creating laws in such a way that they address genuine market failure and provide solutions that improve market integration and enhance efficiency are many and complex. This Title describes and evaluates the current procedural framework within which EU financial services legislation is created and adopted. Particular attention is given to the key legislative instruments that are at the disposal of EU lawmakers, the negotiation process that goes into their construction and the steps that need to be taken in some instances to weave EU requirements into domestic legal systems. The challenges of enforcement and supervision will have to be left to fill another book.

(1) Single Market legislation: origins and architecture

The saga of a united Europe started with the ECSC Treaty, which established the European Coal and Steel Community.[1] Nowadays, environmentalists might be suspicious about this title, however, as we all know it was one of the first key attempts after World War II to bring an exhausted Europe back to its feet by enhancing trade between these countries in respect of those (at the time) popular goods.

Signed in Paris in 1951 as the result of diplomatic brilliance, the ECSC is considered as the foundation of what was destined to become the European Single Market (albeit in truth this is still a work in progress). Article 2 of this Treaty makes a clear statement to the effect of creating a common market for coal and steel with the objective of forming a key foundation for economic expansion, growth of employment and enhancement of living standards, including working conditions, competitive prices and the free movement of such goods. As such, the ECSC is the precursor of all that was to follow in terms of the integration of a group of European countries with the aim of jointly increasing competitiveness in the light of growing international trade.

The legal basis of what we call today the 'Single Market' is primarily anchored in Articles 3c, 14 (formerly 7a) and 18 (formerly 8a) of the European Community Treaty. The first time the term 'market' was used in the context of the EU was with the creation of the common market, defined by the Treaty of Rome when it came into force on 1 January 1958 – one of the many treaties to follow the initial Paris Treaty. The common market had the concrete mission of doing away with trade barriers that countries within Europe had maintained for many centuries. This was of course a measure with a double objective, delivering economic growth and prosperity while at the same time tying the countries ever closer together.

Moving forward from the economic miracles of the 1950s to more challenging times with the oil crisis of the 1970s, the progress of the common market objectives, namely the removal of trade barriers between Member States, again became the focus. While some development had been made with the introduction of the customs union (1968), the abolition of quotas, some tax harmonisation with the introduction of general VAT in Europe (1970) and the introduction of free movement for employed persons, there was still a significant Member State practice of maintaining frontiers – physical, technical and tax-related. Instead of quantitative restrictions, national technical rules for products had spread out, leading to continued protectionism. People still could not move freely and had difficulty establishing themselves in other countries, at times clashing with national regulatory provisions that had not been abrogated. Indeed, some public authorities had used state aid and other means to actually limit free trade of goods with their neighbours.

The Cecchini report, prepared for the European Commission (EC) in 1988 estimated that the cost of non-completion of the Single Market would be as high as 4.25 per cent to 6.5 per cent of EU GDP (Gross Domestic Product). The reason for the slow advancement in completing the common market was mainly attributed to the method of decision-making, which required unanimity of the European Council to actually decide legislation. However, in reality Member States were also partly shying away from the prospect of increased competition and limited abilities to subsidise or discriminate in favour of their local industries. This failure of achievement, however understandable (Member States had to get used to the idea of joining forces rather than sticking to national agendas), led to the setting of revised objectives and deadlines for integration measures under the Single Market Program.

In 1985, the European Council decided that the continual dragging out of deliverables was unacceptable and thus set a date for Single Market completion – the end of 1992. The EC was asked to prepare a clear programme and timetable working towards this goal and provided this deliverable in form of the famous 1985 White Paper, which listed no fewer than 300 ideas for legislation, covering the elimination of the three types of remaining frontiers (physical, technical and tax-related). This proposal also tried to remedy the bottleneck created by previous attempts to harmonise national rules (apart from the areas of security and health) and instead settle for the famous 'mutual recognition' principle, essentially that (non-EU-harmonised) goods and services lawfully sold in one part of the Single Market cannot be excluded from being marketed in another Member State, even if they do not comply a 100 per cent with the technical rules of that Member State.

When the Single European Act, revising the Treaty of Rome, entered into force in 1987, the Single Market was specifically defined as an area without frontiers where people, goods, services and capital can move freely. This Single European Act, commonly referred to as the European Community Treaty, also introduced the relevant changes in the legislative system that would allow for the development of further measures (that is, laws) needed for completing the integration of European markets.

Amazingly, a stocktaking exercise conducted in 1992 against the items on the EC's White Paper laundry list revealed a 90 per cent plus success rate in terms of legislative coverage. What had been achieved, at least on paper, was the full liberalisation of capital flows, the abolition of customs checks on goods at the frontier and the free circulation of people within Europe (the Schengen agreement of 1985). Freedom to establish one's business in another Member State via mutual recognition principles leading to the opening of public markets, the possibility to change country under regulated professions, recognition of diplomas as well as the provision of key services such as banking and insurance were all facilitated by law with the goal of creating a frontierless Europe.

Despite these positive efforts, there were still some remaining legislative gaps – areas where more legislation was needed to effectively break down the remaining barriers that existed. More importantly, there had also been serious failures by Member States, either by having omitted to have transposed legislation at all, or by having implemented legislation in a 'bad' way by overlooking or wrongly interpreting the relevant EU legal texts. Redress procedures for consumers and businesses were still burdensome, and no common rules for out-of-court redress procedures existed as of yet. All of those failures were meticulously listed in the 1992 Sutherland Report commissioned by the EC. During this period, the EC became as strict as a nineteenth-century school teacher and started preparing regular reports on Member States' performance. By 1997, the *Action plan for the Single Market* listed a set of 62 actions to be completed according to a strict timetable, along with bi-annual monitoring of Member States' efforts on a 'name and shame' basis. This radical measure was seen as the only effective means of getting Member States onto the same page.

At the same time, in areas where political pressure and public monitoring would not suffice, the EC made more extensive use of its powers under Article 226 (formerly 169) of the European Community Treaty in terms of prosecuting Member State infringements relating to delays in transposing Directives, incorrect transpositions, or 'bad' implementation scenarios. Under a gradual escalation approach, starting with an initial 'default notice', progressing to a 'reasoned opinion' and finally a referral to the European Court of Justice, stage one of this process has been used on average about 200 times a year since 1995, with a clear peak of around 400 in 1997.

The next big phase in the grand design of the Single Market was motivated by the creation and introduction of the Euro, the common currency for Europe. With a common currency in place it became almost a necessity to harmonise the tax system, integrate infrastructures (transport, energy, telecom), finally complete the freedom of movement for people and provide legal instruments to support businesses operations across Europe in what was now intended to become a true 'home market'. All of those steps were envisaged to be fulfilled by the time Euro banknotes and coins entered our pockets as legal tender in 2002.

We know of course today that 2002 did not even come close to marking the year of full market integration in Europe. Instead, a new set of priorities and needs emerged following the introduction of the Euro, with a strong focus on infrastructure harmonisation in the payments system space that would lead in turn to additional requirements for harmonisation of consumer protection, stimulation of competition and alignment of practices and rules – all with the goal of fully integrating the Euro within Europe.

In the pages to come, this book will examine the extraordinary journey that was to commence with the creation of this common currency.

What is the Single Market for financial services?

The Internal or Single Market of Europe, as explained above, is constructed on the basis of the free movement of people, goods, services and capital. As such, there are four distinct aspects that can be described in themselves as Single Markets: the Single Market for People, the Single Market for Goods, the Single Market for Services and the Single Market for Capital.

The importance of the financial markets in Europe (as well as their occasional instability) is undeniable and their integration across the EU has potential to significantly improve capital allocation and long-term economic performance. Achieving a Single Market for Financial Services was – and still is – therefore a top priority of the EU.

The below figure (see Figure 2.1) attempts a simple overview of the different elements of the Single Market, with specific emphasis on the Single Market for Capital that is the key focus area of this book.

The Single Market for Capital is among other things the birthplace of the Single Market for Financial Services. This market segment is composed of three key elements: banking, insurance and securities. Over time a number of additional areas have been added to the scope of the Single Market for Financial Services in the context of its continued

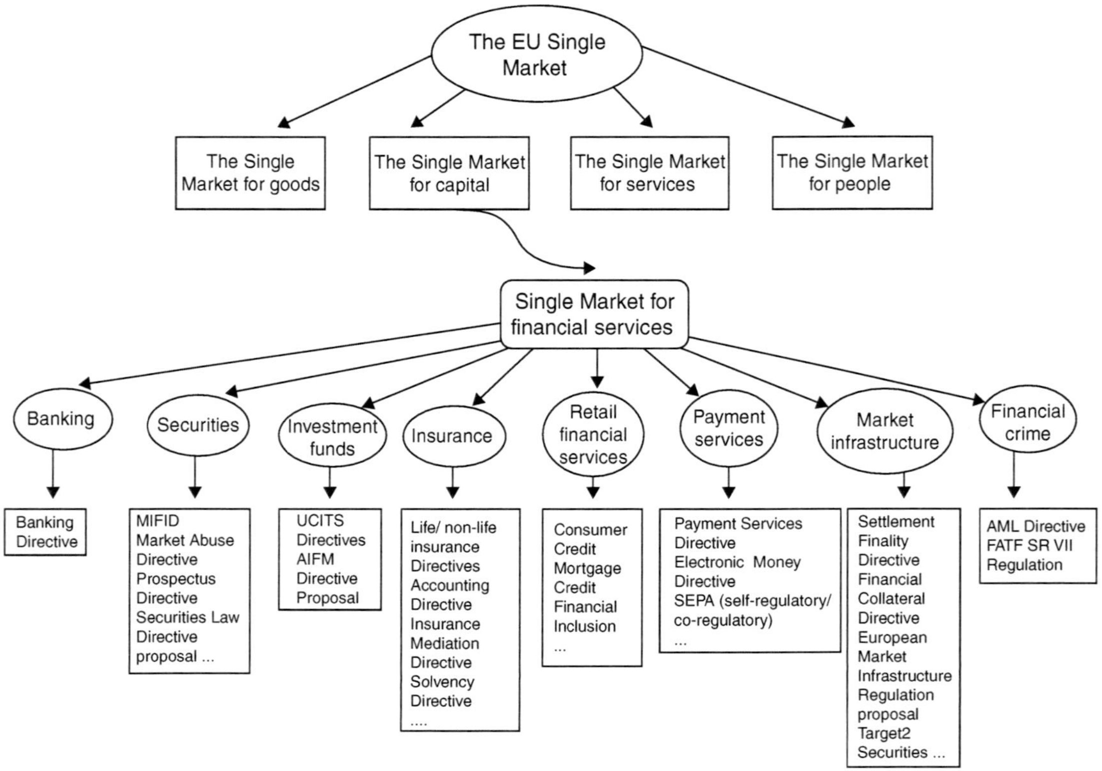

Figure 2.1 The key elements of the Single Market

evolution. One of these is the area of payment services, which as a consequence now itself has a comprehensive set of legislation.

The emergence of specific payments legislation goes back in time more than 20 years and has evolved around five key building blocks:

1. Legislation to protect and sustain payment systems;
2. Legislation of actors in a payment system – the payment service providers;
3. EU Competition principles and rules;
4. Consumer/User protection legislation; and
5. Ancillary legislation around anti-money laundering and prevention of terrorist financing.

When we later explore some of the key legislative developments including the Payment Services Directive and how these measures are starting to cause the reshaping of the entire European payments landscape, we will refer back to some of the above elements to highlight how this whole web of legislation ties together.

(2) The institutions, instruments and regulatory processes

On the 1 December 2009, Europe took a major further step towards integration and unification. After eight years of discussions, drafting, negotiation, adoption, rejection, rewriting and a lot of nerve-straining, the Treaty of Lisbon finally came into force as the 7th Treaty of Europe. When looking at the framework of the EU with all its institutions, committees, working groups and legislative action, the picture can be quite confusing. The following paragraphs will try to shed some light on how the overall construct of Europe evolved since the 1960s and on what basis decisions are taken on a pan-European level, which ultimately impact citizens and government bodies in Europe.

I will start with an overview and brief analysis of the key bodies that make up the EU.

We then take a look at the different sources of law as well as the principles of legal harmonisation before turning to an overview of the various types of legal instruments used by the EU to regulate the Single Market, and in particular the Single Market for Financial Services.

To complete the landscape, we of course need to examine the legislative decision-making process of the EU, which not surprisingly is complex and full of exceptions (rather like almost everything to do with EU legislation in fact!).

The European institutions and relevant treaties

The key bodies are the European Parliament (EP), the Council of Ministers (Council) and the European Commission (EC). Let's see where they come from and what they do.

All three institutions have undergone various transformations in terms of their role, name and degree of institutional power since the start of Europe in 1952. To understand the way they function today, a little background on the way each has evolved is important.

We begin with the European Parliament, one of the oldest EU institutions, which started its life in 1952 as the 'Common Assembly' for the ECSC that we mentioned earlier. In those days it was merely a consultative committee composed of members of national parliaments (78 at the time – larger by a multiple of nearly 10 these days) with no legislative powers whatsoever. However, the ECSC Treaty already hints towards the idea of democratic legitimacy, characterising this Assembly as representative of the people and a body that should be elected directly.

When in the following years the ECSC was enlarged by the European Economic Community (EEC) and the Atomic Energy Community (Euratom), the 'Common Assembly' was re-named the 'European Parliamentary Assembly' in 1958 and re-named again in 1962 when it finally became known as the 'European Parliament', or EP for short. With the merger of the three Communities (under the Merger Treaty signed in 1965) the EP served this growing structure of Communities from 1967 onwards and was directly elected for the first time in 1979. As an aside, the Parliament was the first institution to adopt the European Union flag in 1983 with the other institutions following only three years later (so interestingly it turns out that this flag has already existed for 27 years).

The EP is, on paper at least, the most democratic body of the EU, with currently 736 directly elected members (the maximum number of members is capped at 751 by the Lisbon Treaty) and with elections conducted every five years under universal adult suffrage. The EU's electorate is the second biggest worldwide after India and certainly unique in terms of the number of languages it operates under – currently 23 in total!

To facilitate targeted work on the many different subjects the EP is involved with in terms of legislative decision-making and other positioning, it has 20 standing Committees, each of which is supported by a dedicated chair, bureau and secretariat. Each Committee is also composed in a way that mirrors the overall political composition of the full Plenary. While Committees are empowered to propose and adopt amendments to legislative proposals, in many cases the final adoption of a legislative text by the Council can only occur when the EP gives its consent by an absolute majority (that is, a simple majority) of its members.[2]

One of the perceived shortcomings compared to national parliaments in Europe is the fact that the EP has no right of legislative initiative. Essentially, it cannot do anything without having a bill on the table in front of it, and such bills are always drafted by the EC. Still, as one of the most recent EP Presidents argued, the Parliament nevertheless has quite substantial *de facto* powers because it can ask the EC to draft legislation and through the years of collaboration the EC has become more inclined to follow the EP's proposals. With regard to the EC, the EP is empowered to elect the Commission as a whole – a process that is repeated every five years. While it also has the power to reject the entire Commission (as happened in 1999 with the Santer Commission), it has no power to propose a new one, which arguably rather weakens the democratic nature of the whole process.

The EP's legislative powers have grown steadily over the years from mere consultative functions to co-operation and eventually the power of joint decision-making with the Council – the so-called 'ordinary legislative procedure' or 'co-decision'. The Lisbon Treaty further enhanced the powers of the EP by adding another forty subject-matter fields to the joint decision-making process. Key fields that have been added are in the area of justice and home affairs, while other matters such as tax, social security, foreign policy, defence and police co-operation remain for the Council alone, requiring a unanimous decision from Council members. Additionally, the EP now has power over the entire budget of the EU, putting it on an equal footing with the Council, whereas in the past the EP was only allowed to exert its influence on certain budgetary matters. Interestingly, the EP is now also empowered to adopt the budget alone if disagreements between itself and the Council cannot be solved via the conciliation procedure.

Giving the EP the power over the entire EU budget was very important as the more democratic the institution controlling and approving/discharging the budget, the more this should provide legitimacy, in turn giving credibility to the EU in general. There is only one problem with this theory. The EP in practice still suffers from a lack of interest in its workings by European citizens. This has been the case for the last 31 years and can be explained partly by the influence of domestic politics, as the apparent driver of all legislation (this is of course not true as such, as decisions on most legislation is taken jointly within the EU community). Additionally, the fact that the EP is physically remote and that national representatives are not always very visible within their own constituencies does not help bringing the EP closer to the citizen.

While citizens mostly understand that they have the right to vote for a Member of the EP (MEP), many are not aware of the significance of this act, which might be one of the factors explaining an electoral turnout of less than 50 per cent in EP elections since 1999. The President of the EP even set up a special working group on parliamentary reform in 2007, to look at improving the efficiency of this process and more importantly the EP's image. However, the lack of a 'true' European electorate – no one really considers him/herself as a European voter still – makes it difficult to get the same traction as with Member State domestic elections.

Conscious of some Member State governments' perception of the EU as something of a law factory, the Treaty of Lisbon actively aims at increasing their early involvement by allowing national parliaments to examine draft European legislative acts for eight weeks with the ability to oppose the text. This move is expected to create more pressure on the EC to review or potentially even withdraw a proposal, and national parliaments will also be able to bring a case in front of the European Court of Justice if a proposal is considered to be in opposition to the (almighty) principle of subsidiarity.[3]

There is also an overall lack of public awareness around the fact that legislation is often made in Brussels/Strasbourg but then implemented at a domestic level – as for many on the receiving end it looks and feels just like more national legislation. Citizens are therefore also directly encouraged by the Lisbon Treaty to push the EC into submitting a legislative proposal if they are able to come up with a petition signed by one million citizens (not really a small number!).

Let us now turn to the Council of the European Union (*Lat. Consilium*). The Council is the second legislative body after the EP and is composed of appointed representatives of the 27 national governments. Its origins also relate back to the ECSC where the Council was first known as the 'Special Council of Ministers'. Obviously at the time it was solely focused on coal and steel, giving its consent to any decisions taken by the so-called High Authority (the executive, and the forerunner of the European Commission in that domain). With the creation of the other two Communities – atomic and economic – the Council suddenly had competition, as each of those also had their very own Councils, a situation that finally harmonised itself in the form of a merger between the three to create the Council of the European Communities in 1967.

As late as 1993, and following the implementation of the Maastricht Treaty, the Council was re-named the Council of the European Union, the title by which we know it today. (Note: the Council should not be confused with two other rather similar-sounding bodies: the European Council, which is the assembly of EU heads of state/government, and the Council of Europe, an organisation of 47 states, seeking to develop throughout Europe and beyond common and democratic principles based on the European Convention on Human Rights and other reference texts on the protection of individuals, and which also happens to have its seat in Strasbourg).

The EU Council, even though a single entity, can appear and act in various configurations, as defined by Article 16(6) of the Treaty of the European Union, depending on the subject matter at hand. There are overall ten subject matter areas and when discussing or deciding financial market legislation, the Council appears in the form of the Economic and Financial Affairs Council (ECOFIN), which is made up of national ministers of finance and economies.

The presidency of the Council rotates at an interval of six months between individual Member States with the agenda for each period being determined by the Member State that is in charge. The only exception to this is in the context of the Foreign Affairs Council, which has its own separate president that chairs the meetings.

Further, the Council is administered by its Secretary General, which has a secretariat apparatus responsible for ensuring the whole infrastructure, physical and intellectual. And all of it, just like in the case of the EP, is done in the 23 official languages of the EU!

The Council has the power to amend and adopt legislation proposed by the EC, either alone or increasingly often together with the EP under the already mentioned 'ordinary legislative procedure'. It also has the right of legislative initiative, unlike the EP, but this is limited to certain sensitive areas such as defence and foreign policy. Because there are still some areas not subject to the 'ordinary legislative procedure' requiring to be handled under the 'special legislative procedure' (what else!), the Council is a very powerful body, as in those instances the EP as well as the EC have practically no influence.

Voting in Council is done on a qualified majority basis with Member States having different weightings according to their population size. This will change, however, with the Lisbon Treaty, which from 2014 will require the majority of decisions to be made under the 'double majority' voting system, which put simply means that individual country weightings will disappear – they are considered undemocratic – and a decision can only be taken if voted for by 55 per cent of the Member States that at the same time represent at least 65 per cent of the EU's population.

The Council is a very political body representing the interests of national governments, which can be rather different to the interests of citizens that are being 'looked after' by the EP. There are not many comparable set-ups – the nearest specimen of comparison is the German Bundesrat, which in a way is a smaller version of the Council as it represents the different governments of the states of federal Germany. Similarly, members of the Bundesrat never give up their state role and can return to local politics once their term is ended. Also, the Bundesrat has a rotating presidency and different weightings for voting depending on the size of the local governments.

With the Lisbon Treaty coming into play, some significant changes have been introduced to the institutional set up of the Council. Firstly, the European Council (heads of state/government) now has a president, elected by the very same and in office for a two and a half years on renewable terms. This is currently (2010) Herman van Rompuy, who up until recently was the Belgian Prime Minister. The president has the key role of maintaining continuity of the Council's work, alleviating the potential confusion arising from the six-month rotating presidencies, as well representing the Union externally in the context of the Common Foreign and Security Policy (CFSP). He is of course not allowed to hold any other office, which marks quite a significant evolution towards a real identity for Europe in terms of its institutional construct and governance.

The other main innovation is the role of the High Representative of the Union for Foreign Affairs and Security Policy, a role that consists of three elements and involves being the Representative for the CFSP, the President of the Foreign Affairs Council and also the Vice-President of the EC. Baroness Catherine Ashton currently holds this role, having been appointed by the European Council (and approved by the EP in the context of its consent to the new EC) and will serve a term of five years. The role is designed to enhance the EU's unity and international presence on matters of external policy and in support of this the Lisbon Treaty also introduced a new European External Action Service, a body consisting of Member State diplomats and representatives of the General Secretariat of the Council and of the EC.

And now we turn to what is arguably the most powerful body in the EU – the European Commission. Its origins also date back as far as 1952 where it first appeared as a small club of nine members, called the 'High Authority', acting as the executive of the supranational administration of the ECSC. With the emergence of the EEC and Euratom, two additional executive bodies, this time called 'Commission', were added to the landscape and finally collectively merged in 1967 into one EC following implementation of the Merger Treaty.

The EC stands out as the 'European Executive' by virtue of the Lisbon Treaty, with powers that actually exceed any other institution, as it is the only body that can propose, execute and manage legislation for the EU. These powers are often not widely appreciated or even known by citizens across Europe, who are at times unaware that we are slowly (and some would say inexorably) moving to a system of European government that could eventually replace our national ones. Other responsibilities of the EC include the development of medium term strategies, representing the EU in trade negotiations, drawing up the budget of the EU and scrutinising the implementation of treaties and legislations.

The EC is composed of 27 Commissioners including the President and operates as a cabinet government. All 27 are appointed by their respective national governments, but are not supposed to represent their countries' national interests, though inevitably this still happens sometimes. The EC is therefore the only body that is expected to solely represent the interests of Europe, rather than national ambitions.

The President is nominated by the Council and elected by the EP, while the group, or College, of Commissioners is subsequently proposed by the President in agreement with Member States and each one of them has to undergo a parliamentary hearing by the relevant Committee. The EP will then either approve the whole group as a body or reject it altogether.

The power of each Commissioner is dependent on the portfolio allocated to him, which in the run up to a new Commission (renewal happens every five years) is hotly debated and negotiated between Member States behind closed doors. Each member of the College is supported by a personal cabinet for the purpose of political guidance and all are served by the famous Civil Service, a good 25,000 civil servants, divided into Directorates General (DG) and services departments, who are there to advise on technical matters as well as being in charge of drafting legislative proposals. Whether or not you subscribe to the view held in some quarters that the powers of the EC are perhaps excessive, a certain democratic deficit could be perceived in the fact that the EC President is not directly elected by the citizens of Europe.

Legislation triggered by the EC is not only of a concern to markets, but in most cases also has a real impact on people's day-to-day lives (even regarding a matter as apparently arcane as payment services).

Therefore awareness and understanding by citizens is key to enable their action and reaction (albeit more indirect) to the EC's proposals and legislative acts.

Next to these three key institutions there are also two consultative bodies, both suffering from ever-diminishing powers: the Economic and Social Committee (ECOSOC), a representation of the European employers, employees and various interest groups (in other words the organised civil society) and the Committee of Regions (CoR), which strongly supports the principles of subsidiarity and proximity to ensure Member States' national interests.

To ensure the overall legal order in Europe we have the European Court of Justice and the Court of First Instance.

And finally, European finances are controlled by the European Court of Auditors, which is appointed by the EP.

EU legal basics: sources and legislative instruments

As this book explores the European payments market evolution, our focus will be mainly on the types of legislation that are encountered in the context of the Internal Market for Financial Services.

Let us start with a general overview of the different sources of EU law, before going into more detail on some of the specific types of legislation issued by Brussels.

As already mentioned the Treaties – so-called primary legislation – constitute the basis of the EU itself. The main treaties of the EU are the Treaty of Rome (1957), the Merger Treaty (1965), the Single European Act (1986), the Maastricht Treaty (1992), the Amsterdam Treaty (1997), the Nice Treaty (2001) and finally the Lisbon Treaty (2007, in force since 1st of December 2009). The Treaty of Lisbon has at last given a consolidated legal personality to the EU.

Secondary legislation (for example, Directives, Regulations, and Recommendations) covers everything that we see issued by the EU in terms of legislative output.

The third source relates to International Agreements, with third countries/organisations or agreements between Member States (for example, WTO agreements).

The fourth and final source of EU legislation is made up by the Case Law that has emerged from decisions taken by the European Court of Justice and the Court of First Instance (for example, for anyone who has studied EU law, an all time favourite is the 'Cassis de Dijon' case).

To understand the legislative framework set by the EU in so many areas, we will focus next on the types of laws and guidelines the

European regulator actually has at his disposal in the context of secondary legislation.

The most important types of secondary legislation are binding measures such as Regulations, Directives and Decisions. In the area of non-binding legislation, the EU can use Recommendations, Resolutions or just express an official Opinion. Returning to binding legislation, the most straightforward type is the Regulation. As soon as adopted by the lawmakers a Regulation immediately becomes binding in its entirety for all Member States, which of course also means that no additional enabling legal action at national level is necessary. One could say that when a Regulation comes into force 'the law is the law' – nothing more to add.

But, as you can imagine, a legislative text that will be directly and totally applicable once in force is not easy to agree at EU level. Very often, and all too easily understandable, Member State representatives in the Council and the EP are not prepared to agree on a single fully applicable text. Too many voices are raised claiming the need for specific national variants to protect the continued existence of certain business types or services and thus a Regulation, for lack of compromise, is considered simply 'too much to handle'. In those circumstances we luckily have the alternative approach of a Directive, which is, if you like, a watered-down version of a Regulation. To start off with, a Directive is written in a more open way – and is thus open to more interpretation! The next advantage (from the point of view of a Member State) is that it permits them to choose how – and into what – they want to implement the measures. Once adopted by the EU decision-making bodies, a Directive has to go through the so-called transposition process where these EU wide provisions have to be woven into Member State law. This means two things. Firstly, from a practical perspective the legal rules of the Directive can end up in various existing national legal texts in the form of revisions, or alternatively all provisions could be bundled into a new national law (the so-called 'copy-out' approach). Secondly, Member States are often tempted to think about slightly changing the Directive's provisions to make them work more seamlessly in the context of their national body of law, as well as to add on to them to reflect national political ambitions – the practice known as 'gold-plating'. Both permutations do not necessarily assist the goal of a harmonised outcome.

The third type of binding instrument, a Decision, has little relevance in the context of the evolution of Single Market legislation. However, for completeness, it is worth noting that a Decision is different from a Regulation in that it is addressed directly to an individual and not a Member State, which is why Decisions are often used in the context of EU competition policy for the purpose of enforcing a ruling against a particular person or company.

Turning to the field of non-binding (and therefore rather less exciting) legal instruments, a key one often seen in financial markets legislation as a precursor to a binding text, is the Recommendation. In a Recommendation, the issuing EU institution makes its views and opinions on a specific topic known and proposes its ideas around possible actions in order to remedy/improve the situation. There are no legal obligations on the addressee, which can be a Member State, a citizen or even another EU institution.

The other, very similar, instrument used to share views and possible approaches to an issue would be a Resolution – this is very often used by the EP. Finally, there is the Opinion, which is a means to make a statement on a particular question asked. It is again non-binding and can be used by all EU institutions.

Reflecting the nature of the legislation, as well as the area being legislated and the degree of difficulty in achieving a political compromise, there are also different approaches to the degree of harmonisation that is envisaged. Terms we will encounter again in this book are Maximum Harmonisation and Minimum Harmonisation. EU Directives, and occasionally EU Regulations, are normally classified into one of these two categories. To achieve a fully integrated Single Market in Europe, Maximum Harmonisation is the key mantra that should be followed. Under Maximum Harmonisation, Member States are explicitly prohibited from producing further add-ons to (typically) a Directive. This, in essence, is a protection mechanism against the 'gold-plating' phenomenon. The effects of this approach can in practice go as far as requiring either changing or abolishing certain existing national laws. The use of Maximum Harmonisation provisions in EU legislation became more and more attractive to EU regulators once it was clear that Member States did not always refrain from implementing laws at local level in ways that were designed to protect local markets.

The opposite legislative approach is Minimum Harmonisation, under which Member States are forced to attain a defined threshold of legislation at a national level, and it is permissible to exceed terms of the stipulated legislation in the context of national laws. Of course, it is easier to reach political agreement on the basis of minima, as national laws are permitted to stay in place with potentially higher levels of requirements, for example, in the context of consumer protection. Not surprisingly, most EU Directives include features of Minimum Harmonisation (you can even find this term in the title of some Directives). In practice, the degree of harmonisation can vary across a single legal text with certain provisions being explicitly highlighted as Minimum or Maximum Harmonisation.

For obvious reasons, there has been a trend towards greater use of Maximum Harmonisation, however to achieve the required level of agreement, concessions often have to be made in the form of derogations (generally domestic or national in application) leading to imperfections in the resulting 'full harmonisation' measure.

From drafting to decision-making: the law-making process

The process of decision-making in the EU can be a very complex and tiring one, reflecting in practice a sort of ping-pong dynamics, which in extreme cases, such as the PSD, can result in a double re-writing of the initial proposal.

The whole creative process around EU legislation can be broadly explained in three phases:

1 proposal drafting
2 decision-making
3 application/transposition of the law.

In phase 1 the EC begins by defining a political objective at European level such as, for example, the harmonisation of payment services across Europe. Such a political objective, which has to pass the Single Market Test, is then taken on board by the relevant EC Services in this example the Directorate General for the Internal Market (DG Markt). DG Markt will go ahead and prepare a public consultation that sets out the high level objectives and the different elements considered to be able to achieve the objectives in question. They will ask for feedback from all possible stakeholders, ranging from market practitioners and consumers to business and public sector stakeholders and users of a particular service that is being examined. The EC then publishes the responses received on their website at the same time as taking the next steps to formalise their understanding and approach around the given topic.

The next formal step following a consultation and publication of responses is the creation of a so-called Green Paper, which will contain the first and usually still quite high level attempt to specify the legislative action envisaged. This can then be followed by a White Paper, naturally going into more detail on the practical ways considered to solve the issue addressed – for example a perceived market failure in payment services provision in Europe. Again for both steps the EC usually invites public feedback, though in practice this only tends to come from trade bodies and national governmental agencies that are more closely involved in the specific topic. The time that can pass between the first consultation and the White Paper can range from months to years (or sometimes be skipped altogether). Throughout this process – from the first thoughts to a set of recommendations for action – the EC also in some areas utilises so-called Expert Groups that have an advisory function and are usually composed of market practitioners, academics and other individuals that are expert in a certain field. These groups are official bodies institutionalised by an official EC Decision, of relevance in this example the Payment Systems Market Expert Group, which was established via EC Decision 2009/72/EC.

Following the completion of the processes around consultation and Green and White Papers (not required in all cases) there are then a number of legislative options at the disposal of the EC, as already explained above.

From personal experience, it has to be said that the most important time to try to influence the future direction of an EU law is during the time that the initial policy discussions are taking place within the teams of the relevant DG. As soon as a proposal is formulated and shared at the level of the DG, the approach is already more formalised and therefore harder to change – and even more so once it has received the political rubberstamp to leave the EC as an official proposal to the EP and Council.

Once a proposal has started down its legislative path with the EP and Council, amendments have to be proposed in order to achieve alterations. Therefore, before the first reading of a law in the EP, lobbyists and other stakeholders need to target MEPs to negotiate key changes to the text. This is a time where the level of influence can relate strongly to the quality and persuasiveness of individual stakeholders or lobbyists, as well as to the strength and size of the industry or interest group that is being represented. During the First Reading phase, but before actual decisions are taken in the EP, there is also a further lobby opportunity with the Council, which has to evaluate the proposal once the EP's amendments have been decided by the relevant EP Committee. While this is a very difficult and fast moving period in practical terms, not least as often it is rather ambiguous as to what is the current 'master version' of the text at any given point in time, it still allows further changes to be made to the text – prior to the final countersigning by the EP. If a proposal fails to be adopted in First Reading, the text is once again open for discussion. Arguably, this second round is much more challenging in terms of representing external stakeholder interests as new angles or argumentation may need to be found to ensure ideas are considered this time around.

If the Second Reading also fails, the Conciliation process, which is done behind closed doors assisted by the Conciliation Committee – composed of EP and Council representatives with the EC as observer – is a stage when no further external changes and ideas are able to reach the decision makers.

The below figure (see Figure 2.2) illustrates the different time periods in the lobbying process, giving a clear indication as to when the best opportunities arise for influencing a legislative proposal before, during and after co-decision.

As a general observation, the nature of the lobbying approach adopted is a crucial element of the likely success or failure to achieve changes in

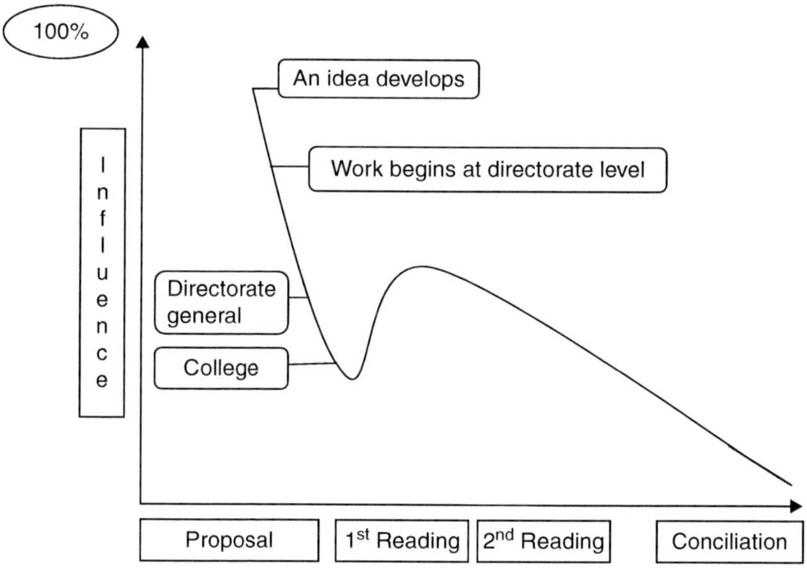

Figure 2.2 The curve of legislative influence

legislative proposals. From experience as well as historical evidence the so-called top-down lobbying approach, hierarchically structured with a key focus on influencing policy makers at a very high level (for example, Commissioners themselves or even their President) does not work terribly well in practice as these levels of the organisation perceive such a method as rather aggressive and not in line with the 'greater good' that is aspired to. Interestingly, the US and French classical lobbying approach traditionally follows this path. The alternative, a lobbying style that focuses on sharing technical and legal knowledge on a legislative proposal with the relevant Commission Services, thus representing a bottom-up approach, is more likely to be successful. As will be explained later in this book, the sharing of specific industry knowledge with Commission Services forms a key part of assisting them to acquire an understanding of the subject matter that is being regulated and thus facilitating more efficient and targeted legislation that can actually be put into practice and serve its purpose over time.

Co-decision

We now move into phase 2 of the EU legislative creation process – the decision-making. In terms of decision-making, EU institutions have three methods at their disposal depending on the type of legislation that is being decided upon: (1) co-decision; (2) consent (formally assent); and (3) consultation.

The procedures of consent and consultation are not used in the context of Single Market legislation, but it is worthwhile briefly highlighting what they entail. Consent is when the Council has proposed a decision which needs to be supported by the EP giving its consent with an absolute majority of votes cast. The only alternative open to the EP in these cases is to reject the proposal altogether, as no amendments are possible under this decision-making method. The consent procedure mainly comes into play in the context of agreements with other countries, for example, the adherence of new countries to the EU.

Consultation is the procedure by which, upon receiving a proposal from the EC (in certain areas such as taxation, competition or agriculture), the Council is obliged to consult the EP as well as the two committees – the ECOSOC and the CoR. The EP has the option to accept, or reject, or require the EC to make amendments to the proposal. Any amendments accepted by the latter will then be forwarded to the Council, which in turn also either has to accept the changed version amend it further. Anything amended by the Council must be done so unanimously.

The key procedure used by the EU for all matters concerning Internal Market legislation is the so-called co-decision procedure,[4] defined by Article 95 of the Treaty of Nice and today termed as the 'ordinary legislative procedure'. Only a few areas still operate under the 'special legislative procedure', including justice and home affairs, budget and taxation and fiscal aspects of environmental policy.

As explained earlier, all legislative proposals can only come from the EC and for topics proposed under the co-decision procedure the EC also has the right to alter its proposal subsequently (according to Article 250(2) EC Treaty). In the context of financial markets, legislation is always passed under the co-decision procedure, which is therefore worth explaining in more detail to give further background to some of the intricate debates that took place in the context of the negotiation of the PSD.

In the best-case scenario – where all bodies agree with a Commission proposal – the steps of co-decision are as follows:

1 The EC issues its legislative proposal.
2 The ECOSOC and the CoR are invited to comment (Expert reports, constituting the opinion of each body, are drafted and issued to the EC).
3 The EP goes through a first reading of the proposal. The reading is performed by the Parliamentary committee(s) in charge of the particular topic of the legislation proposed (for example, payments legislation would go to the Economic and Monetary Committee with an additional shadow committee, for example, the Legal Committee). The committee Rapporteur in charge prepares a full analysis report and collects amendments proposed by members. The amended report is then issued back to the EC.
4 The EC receives and incorporates where agreeable the amendments of the EP.
5 The Council performs its first reading on the amended text and, if everything goes well, adopts the text without amendments.
6 This adopted text is then confirmed by the EP, which gives its official approval and the law is adopted.

Unfortunately it is very rare that EC proposals get voted through without any amendments that would require further discussion in the Council. This is why most legislative proposals, even though decided in First Reading, go through much more negotiation *à huis clos*, with the EC often acting as a mediator between EP and Council, while at the same time trying to ensure that its key proposals are not too watered down by either of these bodies.

An illustration of how complicated a co-decision procedure can get, see the pictorial procedure flow in the figure below (see Figure 2.3):

If a legislative proposal fails to go through the First Reading, the Council's Common Position is sent back to the EP for further examination and within three months the EP will have to provide its opinion, with the option of a further month's extension. If the EP unanimously agrees to the Council's Common Position, or abstains from a position to the contrary within this time period, the act is adopted in Second Reading. Alternative possible outcomes are where the absolute majority of MEPs reject the proposal, resulting in non-adoption of the text, or where a proposal for a set of amendments to the Council text is agreed by absolute majority, which is then subject to the EC accepting or rejecting this proposal before the text returns to the Council. If the Council is not able to agree on the EP's amendments in the following three to four months, the EP/Council Conciliation Committee is called upon to resolve this issue during a six-week timeframe reserved for the elaboration of a joint text. If a joint text emerges from the work of the Conciliation Committee, the Council and EP are given another six weeks (with the option of extension by two months) for providing their

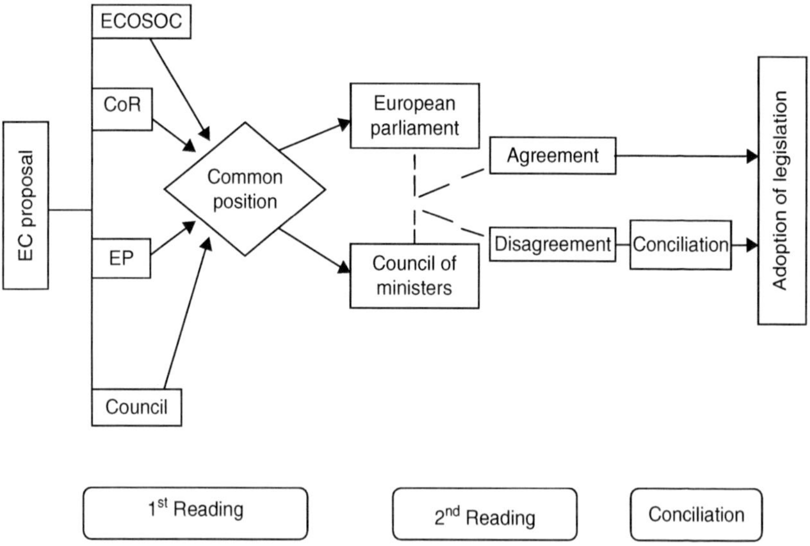

Figure 2.3 The Co-decision process

formal approval and, once signed by the Presidents of both institutions, the act is adopted.

This was rather more than I ever intended to say about the co-decision procedure, but at least it gives an overview of how complex and time-consuming the EU legislative process can be and, as we shall examine later on, how desirable it is (at least at face value) to get key legislation adopted in the First Reading.

The Lamfalussy Process: a new approach to EU lawmaking

When Member States had collectively agreed in 2000 that the Single Market for Financial Services was nowhere near completion, and once 42 measures supporting the creation of such a market in the areas of wholesale financial services, retail markets and supporting prudential supervision had been drawn up in the EC's Financial Services Action Plan (FSAP), there was a clear realisation that without a more efficient and speedy rule setting and decision-making mechanism Europe would never be able to fulfil its objectives.

This realisation was to trigger the creation of the famous 'Lamfalussy Process' in 2001, which started off as a set of recommendations by a Committee of Wise Men led by Baron Lamfalussy on the regulation of European securities markets. The Lamfalussy Process primarily aims at speeding up the creation and enforcement of financial services legislation while at the same time ensuring a higher degree of output legitimacy due to close consultation and co-operation with industry bodies at technical level. To that effect the Lamfalussy Process builds on four key levels.

Level 1 is the adoption by the EP and Council of a high level legislative instrument. In Level 2, the EC works with the specific regulator committee in charge. For example, in the context of a securities related legislation the EC will join forces with the Committee of European Securities Regulators (CESR), a body especially created for this procedure in the field of securities markets, which results in the EC adopting specific implementing measures that are more technical and detailed, but which should still reflect the principles set out in Level 1. The EP is rather left out of this process and, while kept informed about what is going on during the process of establishing Level 2 measures, it can only voice its concern (by adopting a Resolution) if it considers that the proposed measures are exceeding the implementing powers reserved under this process to the bodies involved. At Level 3, CESR (in this example) would have the task of preparing common interpretations and recommendations to ensure that all market participants implement the rules in a harmonised and correct way. Finally, at Level 4 the EC comes into play again, tasked with checking Member State compliance with EU legislation – including the usual possibility of EC legal action if any Member States are found to be in breach.

Even today, this process is a source of inter-institutional power struggles (as noted the EP is rather left out of much of the process) and despite its application to key legislation in the field of securities since 2001, and banking since 2004, there are still negative sentiments, ranging from confusion to suspicion, that have yet to be fully overcome. Additionally, stakeholder engagement works slightly differently under this process compared to the classical co-decision procedure, as external influence can be exerted at more than just the level of the creation of secondary law (Directive or Regulation). Stakeholders here have the opportunity to lobby at various additional levels – Levels 2 and 3 – to ensure that after the adoption of legislation at Level 1 there is still scope to define the detailed rules and interpretations in a more technical context, which should overall help to make Lamfalussy Process legislation more effective. Unfortunately the process currently suffers from its intrinsic complexity, which therefore has the potential of creating a significant gap between theory and practice.

(3) EU legislation in action and the Heisenberg principle

The second largest challenge following the creation of EU legislation is to ensure that it is properly applied across Member States. Just like Heisenberg's uncertainty principle, which determines that 'the more precisely one property is known, the less precisely the other can be known',[5] a straightforward legal act adopted by the EU can look wildly different when implemented at national level.

To shed some light on the practical challenges and uncertainties surrounding the process of embedding EU laws and principles into the domestic environment this section will focus on phase 3 of the EU legislative process – the implementation. Besides the overview of the 'should-be-process' I will highlight the challenges which are often faced in practice.

Looking at the three main legal instruments that need to be in some shape or form implemented by Member States – Recommendations, Directives and Regulations – let us begin with the Regulation.

A Regulation is, by definition, immediately applicable to and binding on all Member States. This in theory ought to make it the easiest type of legislation to implement in a harmonised way once adopted by the EU. However, there has been a notable struggle to achieve this in the case of various Regulations due to the fact that provisions were not consistently understood by Member States in the first place, and thus domestic legal application has in the event been inconsistent. Essentially, every country sees EU provisions through the lens of their existing domestic practices and traditions. For example, in the field of payments harmonisation, EU legal provisions are still understood in the context of the nature of the local payments market, including its maturity and complexity (or lack thereof) and the services, including their specific features, currently offered there. This makes it often very hard to conclusively say that a Regulation has been properly applied in practice; hence the EC runs implementation studies to follow this up.

A Directive, on the other hand, is a tool that makes decision-making at EU level easier due to the much larger room for compromise, interpretation and national add-ons. The flip side is that this can of course lead to serious practical problems when it comes to transposition. The more that Directives are used, the more there is a need to ensure Member States implement them in a maximum harmonised way, avoiding national gold-plating. Also, it is important that all Member States should be on time, requiring an appropriate sanctions regime for late implementation. All these potential issues with implementing a Directive can be observed in the implementation of the PSD, as I will explore in detail later in Titles IV and V.

Recommendations, while the weakest of these three types of acts, are, however, not to be underestimated. They come with a clear demand on Member States to be followed and implemented, but do not constitute binding law. However, once adopted there can still be a proactive real-life follow up, as was seen in the case of Recommendation 97/489/EC for payment instruments, which will be discussed in more detail in the next Title. Suffice to say that if something is big enough on the EC's radar it will get dealt with seriously, which means that, for example, in-depth studies on Member State implementation of a Recommendation may be prepared, which depending on the result can lead the EC to take more radical steps by preparing a Directive or Regulation.

Better Regulation: or how to improve laws in the first place

To close this introductory tour of the labyrinth of rules and procedures that constitute EU law-making, I would like to ask a fairly obvious question: is there no way regulations can be made better, easier to understand, more practical to implement and thus overall more successful in terms of achieving their objectives? It is not surprising that this question has been asked many times in the past, often by those that have at least once lived through the law-making process first hand. Equally unsurprising the EC took such questions and related complaints by Member States and the vast stakeholder community seriously and in response issued ... another policy. The EC's Better Regulation policy![6]

What started with an EC report in 2001 developed into an action plan for simplifying the regulatory environment in 2002. By January 2009 we had already arrived at the third strategic review of Better Regulation in the EU. To cut short a long story – one underpinned by many documents since this train of thought left the station – this policy is a laudable attempt to cut through the forest of procedures and papers with the intent of arriving at a more straightforward and understandable law making process for Europe. Built on the four pillars of simplification, dialogue, impact assessment (IA) and ex-post evaluation it can be described as 'a hybrid, combining the American tool of regulatory impact assessment (RIA) with European strands such as simplification and a standardized approach to measuring administrative costs.'[7]

As part of the Lisbon programme the EC started a process of simplifying and reducing the volume of existing EU legislation in 2003. The simplification is intended to benefit market operators and citizens. Similar to the objectives of many EU laws themselves, this simplification strives to promote innovation and competition, while also focusing on reducing the administrative burden of regulatory requirements and promoting a transition to more flexible regulatory approaches. In detail, the EC's simplification strategy[8] focuses on repealing existing obsolete legislation, codifying law to enhance transparency, recasting (amending and codifying acts simultaneously), co-regulating (involving standardisation bodies) and increasing the use of Regulations as opposed to Directives to ensure direct applicability and consistency of rules. This is all of course easier said than done, and in practice EU legislation often still surprises by its degree of complexity and detail. At the same time we continue to see an inflationary use of Directives versus Regulations. Hand in hand with this goes a rather significant degree of administrative burden that does not help when trying to keep track of new legal requirements versus old, obsolete ones. In addition, repealing obsolete legislation, crucial to avoiding administrative inconsistencies, can still sometimes be an issue.

Turning to the second pillar, the formalisation of dialogue in the EC regulatory process began in 2002 when the EC issued minimum standards for consulting external parties.[9] EC dialogue and consultation of stakeholders is generally quite extensive and, as previously mentioned, specialised EC Expert Groups tend to assist in the process. However, all too often legislative drafts in a pre-publication stage are treated as confidential information and very little transparent public consultation is carried out.

The definition of IAs as part of the Better Regulation policy in the EU 'is perceived as a response to the problem of legitimacy deficit of the Community's regulatory system'.[10] As such it is even more important that IAs deliver the methodological soundness and analysis of potential impacts including overall cost-effectiveness. However, in practice there are many cases where IAs have demonstrated shortcomings in that respect – pointing to the need for the EC to establish clear guidelines for cost-benefit and effectiveness analysis in order to improve the IA process.[11] In realisation of the fact that many IAs had been badly prepared in various legislative areas in the past, the EC decided to strengthen the quality control of IAs by creating the so-called Impact Assessment Board[12] (IAB) in November 2006. The IAB is an independent body composed of high-level EC officials working under the direct authority of the EC President. The Board's task is to examine the draft IAs carried out by individual EC departments, give opinions on the quality, and advise on any further work that may be required. The IAB's opinions are published on their website[13] once the relevant legislative initiative has been adopted by the EC.

Despite these very welcome developments, the total impartiality of IAB members cannot arguably be guaranteed in all cases since the members are all EC officials. This points to the need to enhance the process still further by incorporating external expert involvement, as well as 'external checks on the EC because of the EC's monopoly on initiating legislation'.[14] In line with Wiener's (2006) recommendations, expert oversight regarding this process should be centralised 'so that impact assessments actually influence decisions, both to say 'no' to bad ideas and 'yes' to good ideas'.[15] Additionally, the role of the other European institutions in the IA process should arguably be enhanced, in the sense that (as proposed by the UK Better Regulation Task Force) 'Parliament and Council should review the impact assessment and in particular the extent to which alternatives have been considered'.[16]

Finally, Better Regulation procedures on paper need to be compared more strictly and consistently against the actual results of legislation, in form of a thorough ex-post evaluation designed to see whether the law has indeed delivered all its intended benefits. Impacts in areas ranging from gold-plating, administrative burden and market integration to competition and effectiveness of consumer protection should be considered in a transparent and objective way and might sometimes lead to a review of the law in question.

So much for European law making theory; let's now look at the payments space in Europe, which has recently been given its fair share of EU legislation.

Title III
SEPA: 'A New Hope'

Introduction

One of the notable characteristics of Europe is its penchant for legislation. As we have established already, this book examines this feature, with a particular focus on the area of payments legislation. In the spirit of this objective, the following Title examines the early patchwork quilt of legislation that the EC started to create to cover the broad landscape of payments and how the markets in Europe reacted to these developments.

We start by taking a brief look at the myriad of laws and recommendations that started popping up in the 1980s and the early 1990s and their significance in laying the foundations for the Single Euro Payments Area (SEPA) as well as the associated major overhaul of payment legislation in the form of the Payment Services Directive (PSD).

With this foundation in place we will then look at industry's parallel journey, examining how the payments business in Europe responded to these developments, initially via a body which became known as the Heathrow Group (no prizes for guessing where they used to meet!) and then via the creation of the European Payments Council (EPC) and the development of its ambitious programme.

(1) The growing web of payments legislation

In the build up to the launch of a common currency for Europe, legislation was urgently needed to keep pace with the ongoing evolution and to ensure the appropriate degree of consumer protection – a key mantra of the EU as we have already learnt. Particularly in the context of the creation of the Single Market (Article 14 EC Treaty) not only are people, goods, services and capital supposed to move freely, but in particular payments get their own special mention – in Article 56 – where we find a provision that requires all restrictions applied on payments between EU Member States shall be removed.

With this in mind, we will take a brief tour of the range of legal measures adopted by the EU between the late 1980s and early 2000. This period was characterised by exponentially increasing regulatory attention and activism and it merits analysing how far this period helped to spark the integration of the payments market and the improvement of efficiencies in this space.

Before we dive into a few of the more important examples, the following two figures (see Figures 3.1 and 3.2) give a sense of the overall picture by 2002 and indeed the sheer number of diverse components that had already been seen by then.

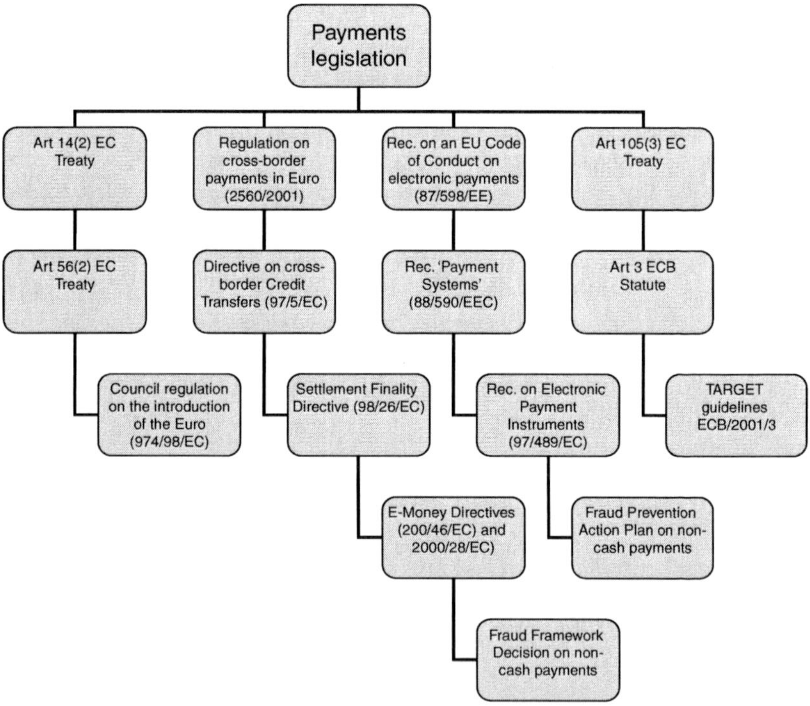

Figure 3.1 An overview of EU payments legislation in 2001

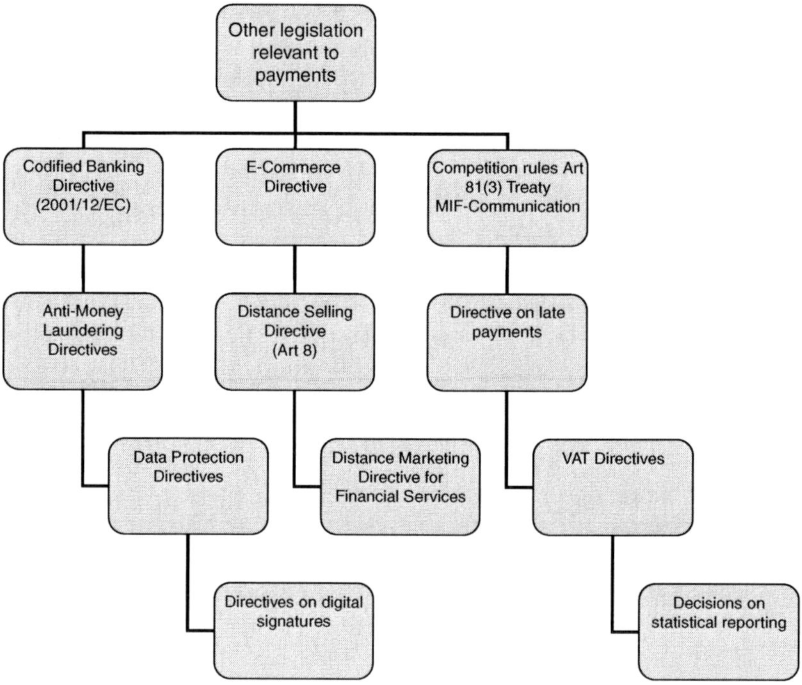

Figure 3.2 Other EU legislation relevant for payments in 2001

This early web of payments-related legislation can be roughly spit into five categories as follows:

1 Legislation to protect and sustain payment systems
2 Legislation of actors in a payment system (payment service providers)
3 EU Competition principles and rules
4 Consumer/User protection legislation
5 Ancillary legislation around anti money laundering and prevention of terrorist financing.

In the following section, we briefly explore some of the key examples relating to each of these aspects.

Legislation to protect and sustain payment systems

The key example to highlight here is the Settlement Finality Directive of 1998 (98/26/EC), a legislation that was instrumental in keeping systemic risk in a payment and securities settlement system at bay. This Directive was to undergo a subsequent revision to become Directive 2009/44/EC, with amendments to reflect the changing risk pattern around settlement in the context of the financial crisis that unfolded in 2008. As a consequence, key provisions covering the insolvency risk of system participants are now included. Another important legislation in the context of minimising risks from financial losses is the Financial Collateral Directive (2002/47/EC), which provides the EU-wide legal framework for collateral. It is probably one of the rarer types of legislations in the sense that the December 2006 Commission Evaluation Report has found that overall Member States have adequately implemented this Directive! That certainly cannot be said of most EU legislation ...

Legislation of the actors (Payment service providers)

This second category includes a range of prudential legislation for financial market actors such as credit institutions and e-money institutions.

The mother of all laws in this area is the Capital Adequacy Directive (CAD), which since 2006 has combined the Codified Banking Directive – also called the Credit Institution Directive (two versions of this law existed until that point: 93/6/EEC and 2000/12/EC) and the Capital Adequacy Directive of the early nineties (93/6/EEC). The CAD covers requirements for capital that have to be satisfied by investment firms and credit institutions with a view to limiting risks. This legislation is undergoing regular reviews and extensions and continues to embed the recommendations of the BIS Basel Committee (latest change applied 07/2010).

Another key example in this category was the Electronic Money Directive (EMD) adopted in 2000 (2000/46/EC). To stimulate new forms of electronic money services in the market a legislative framework was devised, establishing a regulatory regime for companies that issue e-money. The provisions were designed to enable appropriate prudential supervision and competition between these new e-money institutions and the traditional banking sector. E-money institutions were also added under the definition of credit institutions within the Credit Institution Directive, which was amended to Directive 2000/28/EC. We will see later in Title IV how the EMD later needed to be revised to align with the PSD.

EU competition Law

The main competition rules that apply across the EU are contained in Articles 101 and 102 of the Treaty on the Functioning of the EU (TFEU).

These are policed by the European Commission's competition directorate, DG Comp, with legal recourse to the General Court (formerly known as the Court of First Instance) and, ultimately, to the Court of Justice, the EU's top court. The two competition rules are integral to achieving the fundamental Treaty aim of establishing a single, harmonised European market by minimising barriers to cross-border trade. Importantly, the rules are directly applicable, meaning that persons or companies directly affected by anticompetitive behaviour can take enforcement action in their national courts, alongside possible action by the competition authorities.

Traditionally, the EC wasted considerable resources examining industry's requests for individual exemptions under Article 101 for agreements containing restrictions on competition. A significant change in approach, however, has taken place over the last ten years, not least with the introduction of Regulation 1/2003, which sought to modernise the EC's procedural rules. Amongst a raft of changes, the ability to notify agreements for individual exemptions was replaced by a system of self-assessment. Allied to this, the EC moved decisively away from its old approach of applying the competition rules in a formalistic manner, where little regard was had to the actual competitive impact of a particular agreement or conduct, to one where an assessment of the competitive effects is central to the analysis. To assist companies in applying the competition rules, the EC has also published a series of detailed guidance notes. While not legally binding, these guidance notes provide practical help to companies and cover most common forms of agreement.

Regulation 1/2003 also gave national competition authorities the right to apply EC competition rules in full, enabling them for the first time to determine whether agreements qualified for exemption. In addition, each EU country has its own competition rules, which are modelled closely on the European rules. National competition rules only apply where the agreement or conduct does not have any effect on trade between EU member states.

Given the vital importance of financial services to consumers across the EU, DG Comp has become increasingly pro-active in monitoring the effectiveness of competition over the last few years. This has manifested itself in a willingness to carry out a series of market-wide investigations, rather than just enforcing the competition rules in individual cases. As we shall see later on, the sphere of payments turns out to be one of the areas that often prompts attention from DG Comp.

Consumer/user protection

The EU's first attempt to respond to the evolution of electronic payments in the market can be traced back to 1987, when an official Recommendation 87/598/EEC concerning a European code of conduct relating to electronic payments was issued. With this measure the EC intended to provide a set of code of conduct principles to providers of those services with a particular focus on card issuers in the context of information security and data protection.

Ten years later this Recommendation was refreshed with the launch of Recommendation 97/489/EC on electronic payment instruments. This new version was intended to further increase consumer confidence in new electronic payment services. Already at the time a large list of transparency requirements had been set out, including details to be provided on electronic payment types, their functionalities, the liabilities of user and provider, the charges to be paid for use of a particular electronic payment instrument and the timelines during which customers could contest a specific transaction.

The EC did not limit its efforts at the time to non-binding Recommendations and went on to issue the (reasonably) famous Cross-border Credit Transfers Directive in 1997 (97/5/EC). This marked the first major attempt to define rules around the performance of payments, with a focus on cross-border. Under this Directive, all providers of cross-border credit transfers with a transaction value of up to 50,000 ECUs (European Currency Units – the Euro was not around yet) or the local currency equivalent, were required to set out their conditions and information for the execution and pricing of these payments in a transparent way to their clients. In terms of charging approach and options (a subject we will return to a number of times later on) the Directive expressed a preference for the OUR option (whereby the sender pays all charges), and made clear that in cases where the sender specified that the beneficiary will bear all charges, there was now a requirement for this to be clearly communicated to such a beneficiary by his/her own institution.

The Directive also introduced quite stringent rules on the maximum execution time for transfers and established a default maximum (in the absence of agreement to the contrary) of D+5[1] plus a clear requirement to credit beneficiary customers at the latest one day after receipt of funds, thus limiting a beneficiary institutions' ability to take float to one day.

The 'full amount rule' (later to become very famous indeed in the context of the PSD) was also institutionalised for the first time by this legislation. The text specifically mentions the following: 'If the originator's institution or an intermediary institution has made a deduction from the amount of the transfer, the originator's institution must, at his request, credit the amount deducted to the beneficiary free of all deductions and at its own cost, unless the originator instructs it to credit the amount to him' (so much for EU legal speak).

Finally, all institutions involved in a cross-border credit transfer were explicitly required to ensure that for any error, omission or non-agreed charging of customers, appropriate compensation would be provided by the institution that was at fault. Only in circumstances of *force majeure* could institutions be released of those obligations.

Another helpful attempt to support the use of electronic payments, particularly in the context of e-commerce as well as to encourage the move to a non-paper environment was the Digital Signatures Directive (1999/93/EC). This legislation introduced common criteria that allow for a harmonised basis on which electronic signatures could be recognised across Europe by focusing on certification services. The law describes an advanced electronic signature, a so-called qualified signature (without however actually precisely defining it – unfortunately not totally unheard of in the area of EU legislation), as something which should legally satisfy the requirements for signing electronic data. The idea was that such an electronic signature should be valid even in the context of legal proceedings, and should be allowed to be used instead of costly handwritten and paper-based procedures to authenticate oneself.

The most striking point, besides the lack of definition of the lynchpin of this law (the advanced electronic signature itself), is the fact that Member States were put under the obligation to ensure that all certification providers and national bodies that accredit or supervise them comply with a further, even more complicated and elusive law, the famous Directive 95/46/EC on the protection of personal data. As these topics merit a book on their own I shall conclude my brief excursion at this point.

Ancillary legislation (Anti-Money-Laundering and Prevention of Terrorist Financing)

Two important EU laws, both originating from the recommendations given by the international Financial Action Task Force (FATF), are also worth highlighting here to complete our high level picture of EU payments-related legislation.

The Anti-Money Laundering (AML) Directive came into existence in the early 1990s and was ensure that financial systems in Europe would be sufficiently focused on preventing money laundering and other illegal activities in this field. This law, which was subsequently revised in 2001 (2001/97/EC), 2005 (2005/60/EC) and yet again in 2008 (2008/20/EC) stipulates that all professions handling money as part of their business (banks, accountants, estate agents etc.) need to apply a set of defined due diligence measures in relation to their customers. Those range from the identification of customers to obtaining information on the nature of their business and possible identification of recipients of funds in that context.

Secondly, another FATF recommendation, Special Recommendation VII on alternative remittance, also had to be embedded into EU jurisprudence – a requirement to allow for appropriate regulatory capture of non-bank payment service providers. We shall deal with this topic in more detail later on.

(2) European banking and payments landscape

Before we turn back to our main story and to find out what happened next on the evolutionary path that was leading inexorably towards the creation of SEPA and the PSD, we should take a brief look at the nature and composition of the European banking industry, in other words the fabric of the retail banking and payments market in Europe itself. This is important in terms of being able to contextualise the nature and degree of challenges to come with the unfolding of market integration for payments in this region. Indeed, it is only by gaining an appreciation of just how diverse the starting point was (and to a large extent still is!) that it is possible to appreciate the scale of the regulatory and practical challenge of seeking to fashion a single payments area.

European banking industry: market structure and trends

The EU banking sector can best be described as complex – with nearly 8,500 credit institutions operating across 27 countries as of 2007. Historical, demographic and cultural differences are combined with equally different economic environments – so the usual story of Europe in fact! There are differences in retail financial services across Europe, reflected in banking practices, product design and availability as well as the approach to pricing. At the same time, the number, size and types of credit institutions as well as their respective structures and business models vary greatly across Europe.

To illustrate this point, the following table (see Table 3.1) summarises the number of credit institutions and branches for some of the key EU Member States as at 2007 (source ECB statistics).

Table 3.1 Summary of credit institutions and branches in key EU member states as at 2007

Country	Number of credit institutions	Number of branches
Belgium	110	4425
Germany	2026	39777
Spain	357	45500
France	808	39560
Italy	821	33227
Finland	360	1638
UK	390	12425
EU27	**8348**	**233581**

As well as the great variety in the concentration of credit institutions across European countries, there is also considerable variety in their type. In part, of course, this is a result of differences in country size and in the respective importance of the financial sector as an industry. For example, the largest country in Europe is up to 200 times the size of the smallest in terms of population. Nevertheless, structural differences play a role, too. In several countries the banking sector features a large number of smaller banks – often organised in networks and/or operating within a limited geographical radius. In other countries a small number of comparatively much larger credit institutions characterises the market.

The three main sectoral groupings of banks are the commercial banks, savings banks and co-operative banks – all represented at EU level by their respective trade body, known as the three European Credit Sector Associations (or ECSAs). It is worth spending a moment introducing these three key players, as their existence, as well as some fundamental differences in philosophy and approach between them, have played (and are still playing) a key role in shaping the SEPA initiative, including on occasion determining the pace at which the initiative has been able to move.

Set up in 1960, the European Banking Federation (EBF) is the voice of the European commercial banking sector. The EBF represents the national banking associations of the 31 EU and EFTA countries, totalling some 5000 European banks: large and small, wholesale and retail, local and multi-country financial institutions.

The European Savings Banks Group (ESBG) is the voice of savings and regionally oriented retail banks in Europe. Together, ESBG members represent about one third of the retail banking sector in Europe with total assets of €6,028 billion (as of 1 January 2008).

Founded in 1970, the European Association of Co-operative Banks (EACB) represents the interests of co-operative banks. In total EACB membership covers more than 4,000 local and regional banks, comprising approximately 60,000 branches.

The relative territorial presence of these three different groupings (which those of you with a mathematical eye will have noticed would seem to represent rather more banks than appear to exist, suggesting good marketing or a degree of double counting!) varies significantly from one Member State to the next, due to historical factors as well as local legislation. To use the co-operative banks as an example, the average market share of the sector is about 20 per cent (by weighted average of deposits). In some countries, the market share lies well above this figure, as is the case in Austria, Germany, Finland, France, Italy and the Netherlands, ranging from 30 per cent up to 50 per cent.

National trends in the use of payment instruments

The other key variable that is of relevance to our story is the significant difference in the usage of payment instruments within the countries which were destined to come together under the SEPA initiative. Again, it is essential to understand some of these trends and starting positions when exploring such questions as (for example) in what way the SEPA schemes were designed; which features were (or were not) included and why; what are the challenges that present themselves when persuading clients to use SEPA based services in replacement of their old and familiar national services.

It is worth reflecting on the fact that the vast majority of payments have actually, and rather naturally, always been made at domestic level. Indeed, most market analysts agree that at the beginning of the SEPA journey a maximum of only 2 per cent of all retail payment transactions in the EU were being transacted across borders in Europe. This was in spite of the fact that products and services for cross border credit transfers as well as payments by card had existed for decades. Still, when it came to the creation of a single domestic payment area for the EU and the huge infrastructural development costs that this would entail, the EC adopted a 'If we build it, they will come' visionary approach. We will later on examine the extent to which this approach has so far been crowned by success, but the point for now is that even today (in 2010) different patterns remain in the absolute volumes and the mix of payment types usage across EU Member States.

As an illustration, the following table (see Table 3.2) gives a brief overview of the relative usage of different payment types on a per capita

Table 3.2 Overview of average use of payment types per citizen across a number of individual EU member states plus the EU 27 as at 2007

Country	Credit transfers	Direct debits	Cheques (plus bills of exchange and other paper instruments)	Debit cards	Credit cards (and deferred debit cards)
Belgium	84.5	22.6	1.0	72	9.2
Germany	62.9	83.9	1.0	21.1	4.1
Spain	16.3	49.5	5.0	19.2	24.1
France	41.1	45.8	59.2	96.7	0
Italy	18.5	8.6	13.1	13.9	8.5
Finland	132.5	14.4	0.1	156.3	17.0
UK	51.3	48.8	26.3	83.7	34.8
EU27	**42.5**	**38.3**	**13.9**	**44.5**	**10.4**

basis across a number of key EU Member States based on 2007 data (source: ECB statistics).

Studying these figures a little, it becomes clear why certain countries going into the SEPA initiative were – and still are – so concerned about certain payment types, but much less so about others.

According to the ECB's figures, there is a 20 to 1 difference in the number of per capita non-cash payment transactions between the EU country using them most (Finland), and the country using them least (Romania). Countries with a high number of transactions per inhabitant include Finland and the Netherlands, which have both worked hard to drive adoption of electronic means of payment. Furthermore there are completely different usage patterns for non-cash instruments, with broad groupings between countries still using cheques, countries preferring credit transfers, and countries favouring direct debits. Finally, the usage of cards also differs greatly, between countries where cards are used effectively for point-of-sale payments and countries where cards are used mostly for cash withdrawals at ATMs (Automated Teller Machines).

In Europe, the three largest electronic payment markets are Germany, France and the UK, but the use of individual instruments again varies greatly between these. Germany leads in terms of usage of credit transfers at 43 per cent of their overall payment volumes, followed by the UK with around 18 per cent and France representing only around 12 per cent in 2003 (ECB Blue Book). For the usage of direct debits, levels are generally similar to those of credit transfers except for France, which shows a slightly higher usage with 17 per cent. The lowest usage of credit transfers is in Portugal and Spain, while the lowest adoption of direct debits is in Finland. Overall, cards are the preferred means of electronic payment throughout Europe (by volume). Cheques are being used less and less across the EU, but are still commonplace in some countries such as France and the UK, whereas they are largely a thing of the past in the Netherlands, Austria and Finland.

The diversity of the EU banking industry makes it easy to surmise that the level of effort required in each market to migrate to one common standard with one common set of core payment instruments under the SEPA initiative was going to be considerable.

So, while the EC's dream may have been a one-size-fits-all harmonised solution, the starting point could not have been much further away from this ideal. Hence the need for some action.

(3) The Euro as a trigger for further evolution

The necessary prerequisite to getting the European payments integration project off the ground was of course the introduction of the Euro itself. Let's therefore take a brief look at the history of the Euro project.

As is widely known, this currency, especially designed for Europe physically entered our pockets in 2002. The history of the Euro starts with the economic and monetary union, which was already being discussed in a 1962 Memorandum of the EC (Marjolin Memorandum), followed by the creation of the European Monetary System in 1979, the Delors Report of 1989 which triggered the three stages of European Monetary Union and the definition of the European Monetary Union in the Treaty of Maastricht in 1991 alongside the official timetable to its introduction.

Before European citizens were able to benefit from a common currency, many years had to pass during which the required institutional set up was developed and the necessary principles and tasks in the context of monetary union were laid down in the European Community Treaty. Three major stages of European monetary integration, as defined by the European Council in 1989, had to be completed, leading to the creation of European Central Bank (ECB). The ECB was from then on responsible for monetary policy as well as the irrevocable fixing of exchange rates between the first group of countries that satisfied the convergence criteria and thus were allowed to participate in the monetary union (11 EU Member States). The Euro was officially introduced in January 1999 for electronic payments. Only in 2002 were domestic currencies physically changed to the new money.

Formally, the legal basis of the ECB and the European System of Central Banks is laid down in the Protocol to the Treaty establishing the European Community with key tasks of the ESCB listed in Article 3 of this Protocol. These cover the definition and implementation of monetary policy in the EU, the conduct of foreign-exchange operations according to the Treaty, and the holding and management of the official foreign reserves of Member States. However, most importantly for our story, the ECSB is also responsible for promoting the smooth operation of payment systems.

Continuing even today, the construct of the ESCB reflects a dual nature. While the Eurozone is bound by ECB monetary policy, the non-Euro countries are able to pursue their own monetary policy decisions. In addition, the role of an NCB varies across Europe with some institutions including and others excluding supervisory functions at the domestic level and some acting as a domestic clearing provider while others do not.

One of the key joint efforts made by the ESCB has been the development of the high value payment system for the Euro, the TARGET system (replaced by its successor version TARGET2 in 2007). TARGET, the first Euro real-time-gross-settlement-system (RTGS), was launched by the Eurosystem in 1999 to coincide with the introduction of the Euro. The system permitted banks across the EU to benefit from real-time payment processing with intraday settlement finality and most importantly facilitated the rapid integration of the EU money market and associated business practices (until then rather fragmented). The key focus of the TARGET system was to enable high value inter-bank operations and thus in itself became instrumental in reducing systemic risk.

Around the same time, the banking industry's Association Bancaire pour l'Ecu (ABE), which had already provided the settlement system for the ECU since the mid-1980s, changed its name to Euro Banking Association (EBA) and launched a same-day deferred net settlement system for single Euro currency payments – Euro1 – providing 'an efficient, secure and cost-effective infrastructure for large-value payments in the new single currency environment'.[2]

(4) Coping with the Euro introduction: the Heathrow Group

With all the market agitation in the run up to the Euro launch some individuals in the banking industry had realised that there would be a need for close coordination and cooperation on a range of operational issues to ensure that practical problems would be kept to a minimum as soon as the settlement in Euro began. The key question was: how to manage the three-year adaptation period during which settlement in Euro and non-Euro (for the future Euro Member States) was to be maintained in parallel?

In early 1998 a group of banks started to meet regularly to address the common interbank problems that were expected to arise as a consequence of the Euro introduction. The group, which operated as an informal gathering of the largest multinational banking institutions in Europe, started off with 14 banks, increased to 31 in May of 1999 and by the end of that year had 50 member banks. It became initially known as the Heathrow Group (because they met at Heathrow airport) though eventually they started convening in Brussels and changed their name to the European Payments Group (EPG) which had a more appropriately international feel (though surely Heathrow can claim to be international, too!). The move to Brussels was in fact partly motivated by the European Monetary Institute (the future ECB), which wanted to join the work of the group, but was not too keen on London as a meeting place.

Initial discussions and work were focused on the potential risk of Euro payments going wrong, such as ending up being settled in a payment system that the beneficiary bank was not expecting, arriving in the wrong accounts in the wrong country or simply arriving late. Under the no-compulsion-no-prohibition principle, national currency denominations (NCDs) were permitted to circulate alongside the Euro between the January 1999 launch of the currency and the January 2002 conversion date for notes and coins. This meant a potential three-year chaos period during which there would be a significant risk of routing a payment to the wrong destination. With 19 different Euro payment systems – 15 national RTGS payment systems of both in and out countries, 3 national non-RTGS systems (EAF in Germany, SNP in France and CAMARA in Spain) and 1 cross-border system, the EBA's Euro1 clearing system – the existing conventions used by banks to direct payments would disappear overnight. This was down to the fact that those conventions in a pre-Euro environment had uniquely linked a currency to a country and by default the payment would thus be paid and settled in NCD using that country's national payment system. With the introduction of the Euro this unique country-currency link would be removed as the Euro was going to be linked to 15 financial centres in the – at the time – 15 EU Member States. From that moment onwards there was a choice as to which Euro payment system to use and with it came the risk that default procedures of the past would risk payments turning up at the wrong destination.

To cope with this situation, a bank's internal systems needed to be changed in order to allow payments to travel to where the beneficiary bank intended to receive its funds, thus ensuring correct routing. The industry needed to lay some ground rules to make this work in practice, while at the same time noting that it wasn't really desirable for any single country to become the dominant payment system provider – Germany was big in the running at that time to do so with its EAF system.

For the banks, this was a time of nightmare revelations as few of them had any idea of how many internal systems needed changing. As an example, one of the large multinational banks apparently had to change 700 internal IT systems to cope with the arrival of the Euro, while more domestically oriented banks with plenty of manual processes had a much smaller challenge.

Although the rules of a domestic clearing system had clearly defined the obligation of banks, the EU RTGS TARGET system had no 'scheme rules' as such, and as a consequence the management of intraday liquidity between the different RTGS and non-RTGS systems across Europe was going to be a problem. Settlement banks needed to agree on how to use the payment systems in order to be able to manage intraday and end of day liquidity. The Heathrow Group therefore developed and agreed standard Interbank Compensation Guidelines and Guidelines on Liquidity Management (which must have been reasonably robust given that they were to stay in place more or less unaltered until a revised version was issued in 2010).

Furthermore, the global banking community needed to be made aware of what was happening in Europe in terms of the impact this would have on the issuance of Standard Settlement Instructions (SSIs) and any other standing instruction for clearing payments in Euro. To that effect the Heathrow Group concluded that standard settlement advices should remain as they were unless specific cases were to require settlement in RTGS funds.

Despite these preparations, during the first three days of the Euro launch around 1 million inter-bank claims were triggered by one little thing that banks had not considered; and in fact one of the larger banks apparently processed its last claims of this wave a good six years after the Euro introduction!

For any bank that did use correspondent banks in Europe and thus was not directly connected to the multitude of different payment systems across this market – this was the majority – many payments effectively arrived at the wrong place. This happened even though the SSI clearly specified the destination country. So, what went wrong? While industry had spent a lot of time in ensuring that the SSI clearly specified the destination country for funds under the common currency, everyone had forgotten about the SWIFT message. Here is a practical example of what this meant: a French bank in Paris wanted to pay Euro to a German bank in Frankfurt. Because the SWIFT message currency had not been changed to the Euro, the payment that was actually executed was a French Francs payment, not a Euro one. Another challenge was that the SWIFT automation rule would check if the German beneficiary bank had a nostro account with the French bank in Paris. Due to the fact that most banks were using correspondent banking, as previously explained, the likelihood of this being the case was high. So, here it was, the German bank had a nostro account with the French bank which triggered the SWIFT message to automatically follow the logic of crediting this nostro account in order to limit complexity and cost. Instead of receiving Euro in Frankfurt, where these were urgently needed, the German bank now had a credit on its nostro in Paris in French Francs far away from the expected destination! The fact that payments ended up in the wrong destinations created a serious liquidity gap that even meant that national central banks had to start ad hoc lending to banks during the first few days of the Euro.

Specific SWIFT routing guidelines for Euro payments were therefore agreed by March 1999, stressing the importance of routing payments directly where possible rather than using the alternative 'cover' method where the payment instruction and the value travel by separate routes. This instruction came at a time when the first wave of disaster had already swept over the markets. For those not too familiar with the term 'cover payment' a short explanation of the key difference here is that with the 'direct' method the payment instruction and the funds travel together (such as when a bank sends a SWIFT MT103 payment to the beneficiary bank via a payment system, for example, TARGET2) whereas in the 'cover' case, the sending bank sends information on the payment to the beneficiary bank through SWIFT, but arranges for the actual settlement of the value to take place by sending a separate request (a SWIFT MT202 message) to an intermediary bank asking them to transfer the funds to the beneficiary bank. As a small footnote to this point, the subject of cover payments became a hot topic between regulators and the industry much more recently due to the fact that intermediary banks handling these MT202 requests did not get to see all the information related to the underlying payment. Regulatory concern at this situation led to the introduction of a new form of MT202 – the excitingly named MT202COV – in November 2009, which now has to be used for these types of payments and allows for inclusion of all relevant information.

Returning to our story, the Heathrow Group was mission critical in ensuring damage control by helping to resolve the significant problems that were experienced by all banks over this period and in doing so established a high profile with the ECB, who had found their activities very helpful. In fact, the Heathrow Group was highly instrumental in getting the practical Euro adoption right.

Overall, the success of the group was mainly due to a number of key factors: the hard deadline for the Euro launch, the fact that the group was small in size and composed of like minded international bankers and the consequent ability for ad hoc – and speedy – action. The group operated a war room during the launch period and due to the close network of players many payments that ended up in wrong destinations were effectively netted off between them over the phone. Everyone shared the same problems and the solutions were found together – legitimacy by action.

Once these issues had been resolved, and once the subsequent arrival of Y2K and the hotly anticipated doomsday millennium bug had also been safely dealt with (or squashed perhaps), the Heathrow Group looked for something else to move on to. And indeed a new topic was readily available. Banks had to find a way of responding to the seven requirements defined by the EC and the ECB that were included in a specific EC Communication of February 2000. This Communication will be examined in more detail in the next section, however, in the context of the Heathrow Group the following needs mentioning here.

One of the seven objectives set out by the EC was the requirement to deliver cheaper pricing for cross-border payments. To achieve this, the Heathrow Group looked to increase the level of automation of these transactions by defining a tighter form of inter-bank payment message, which would include key elements such as the International Bank Account Number (IBAN) of the payee, to minimise the risk of a payment needing to be manually repaired by an operator. In collaboration with SWIFT, and with the close involvement of the ECB, the result was the definition and launch in November 2000 of a special SWIFT 'straight through processing' (STP) transaction message, which became known as the SWIFT MT 103+ message.[3] In his speech at the Commission's Round Table in November 2000 (which we will also return to later in more detail), the ECB's Tommaso Padoa-Schioppa promoted the dialogue that the ECB had participated in with the Heathrow Group members and underlined the importance of the use of the IBAN and the MT 103+ message.

So far, so good. The necessary technical standard was now in existence, and to support it the Heathrow Group defined a certain number of associated business requirements and rules (which would turn out to form the basis for what would later be launched by the EPC as the Convention on Credit Transfers in Euro) as follows:

- All costs to be charged to the ordering customer (in line with the EC's Communication Objective no. 4) with the beneficiary being credited with the full amount (remember the 97/5/EC Directive?).
- Amount of the payment to be in Euro and of a value up to €12,500.
- The payment to be intra-EU.
- Mandatory use of the IBAN to identify the beneficiary.

From an infrastructure perspective, the EBA – note that many Heathrow Group members were also EBA members – launched their STEP1 clearing system in November 2000. This was based on the Euro1 system, but with membership opened up to a much wider range of smaller financial institutions, with a sponsoring Direct Participant in Euro 1 for settlement purposes. Overall, this increased the number of banks able to transact with each other across Europe by opening this second tier of STEP1 participants that would have been unable to fulfil the Euro1 admission criteria. It also allowed a more efficient solution compared to the more costly TARGET system. And so the use of the MT 103+ message was spreading.

However, things were to become a lot trickier for the Heathrow Group when they were asked by a number of banks in Europe to develop a standard mechanism to cover the costs of processing for beneficiary banks in the envisaged environment where only the sending bank would charge a payment fee (we will encounter this phenomenon again later on). This was to lead to the proposal to formulate and agree a standard charge (to be known as the 'STP-MIF' or straight-through-processing multilateral-interchange-fee) to be paid by the sending bank to the beneficiary bank in these circumstances.

The ECB was cautiously supportive at first – Padoa-Schioppa's speech at a Commission Round Table event in November 2000 stated that the ECB's conclusion was that the MIF represented a solution '... at least in the short run, provided the fee is low.' However, and not for the last time in the history of EU payments integration, DG Comp found that while they understood the desire of their colleagues in DG Markt to create a single payment area, they were not minded to let the banking industry put a new form of MIF in place without a major investigation into the competition implications.

Suddenly the Heathrow Group was faced with requests for detailed cost-based calculations and justifications for the MIF proposal, a tactic that was to work all too well, as eventually after various rounds of cost calculations and discussions the Heathrow Group decided to abandon its proposal.

(5) Rattling sabres and a pricing regulation

Following the arrival of the Euro on the scene, it was clear to the EC and Member States that the banking industry had risen more-or-less acceptably to the challenge of introducing secure and efficient mechanisms to make high-value systemically important payments in Euro – having created the private sector driven Euro1 high value payments system in response to the ECB's TARGET initiative. The creations of these two systems ensured that the motorways that the EC regarded as essential for making high-value cross-border Euro payments in a safe, secure and efficient way were in place. An analogy can be made here with the US system, where the Fed-owned Fedwire RTGS system runs along side the industry-owned CHIPS alternative to provide for the settlement of high-value and urgent payments in the US market.

However, to the EC's mounting dismay, there was no sign of the banking industry similarly stepping up to the plate when it came to the development of a harmonised cross-border retail Euro payments system, which they believed was essential to complete the Euro project. Despite dropping a series of increasingly unsubtle hints to the banking industry that 'something needed to be done' in this space, the industry's collective antenna were – not for the first time – insufficiently attuned to what would come next if they failed to act.

Pressure from the EC developed as early as the 5th of February 1999 when a press release signalled their intention to focus on the level of bank charges following the introduction of the Euro. This included the slightly ominous (if you were a bank!) statement:

> The introduction of the Euro represents a golden opportunity for adopting common standards in order to achieve a common payment area. While there are legitimate technical reasons (administrative reporting requirements and absence of linkages between Automated Clearing Houses) for cross border retail payments to cost more than domestic payments, there will be increasing pressure to remove these differences within a single currency area. This situation will be even more unacceptable once Euro notes and coins are in circulation in the Euro area.

On the 31st January 2000, the EC were to significantly turn up the heat, when they issued an official Communication (Communication 2000/36, previously mentioned in the context of the Heathrow Group) called 'Retail payments in the internal market'. Now, it is worth remembering (though clearly many did not do so at the time!) that a Communication from the EC is not something to be taken lightly. As explained in Title II, it is essentially a warning of legislation to come if whoever is being addressed doesn't sort out whatever it is the EC is concerned about pretty quickly.

All students of the history of SEPA (and payments legislation in Europe) will be excited to find out that the content and wording of this Communication were to prove to be of particular significance for the future. The Communication observed that 'The European Union has an internal market and the Euro. It does not yet have a "single payments area". Large value (wholesale) payments can now be made across borders nearly as quickly and cheaply as they can domestically, yet small value (retail) cross-border payments are less reliable, usually take longer and cost significantly more than domestic payments'. After expressing this concern, the Communication went on to demand a 'significant improvement in the efficiency of small value cross-border payments, and substantial reductions in cross-border charges to customers, by 1 January 2002'.

In an attempt to spell out what these improvements would look like, the Communication included seven specific objectives – pre-agreed with the ECB – which they wanted to see achieved within a certain timescale. These objectives deserve repeating in the following table (see Table 3.3):

Table 3.3 EC Communication 2000/36: Objectives

	Objective	**Comment**
1	The efficiency and cost-effectiveness of payments, notably credit transfers, must be improved. Ameliorating the basic infrastructure for credit transfers may also be of central importance in improving other areas such as direct and other debit transfer based payments.	Shows that the priority area was at that point still seen to be credit transfers.
2	The charges for cross-border credit transfers should be cut substantially towards the levels charged for equivalent domestic credit transfers.	This was to herald Regulation 2560/2001.

Table 3.3 Continued

3	Settlement times for cross-border payments should, where possible, not exceed the time taken for domestic payments. The end-to-end execution of a cross-border payment should not exceed the time taken for a domestic payment by more than one day.	Clearly an early signal of the Commission's concern to see shorter execution times – but note that at that stage execution times for cross-border payments would still be considered as taking slightly longer than domestic ones.
4	The fees for a cross-border transfer in a system should normally be borne entirely by the originator and not charged to the beneficiary, in line with domestic practice in most EU credit transfer systems.	Showing that at that stage the Commission was totally convinced that the OUR payment option was the right one for the EU. We will see that this approach was going to change significantly later on.
5	There should be no proliferation of standards. Existing standards should be implemented as soon as possible.	Here the Commission was thinking of the IBAN and also the IPI (International Payment Instruction – a proposal for a harmonised paper instruction form for initiating payments which was never really to take off).
6	Cross-border payment systems should have open access.	An objective which was to find its way into the PSD as Article 28.
7	These improvements leading to efficient systems should be in place by 1 January 2002.	A rather ambitious deadline.

As a slight aside, it should be noted that another sentence in the Communication gave a clear insight to the push-pull relationship between the regulatory community and the payment industry. It shows that the EU regulator was already having a more or less clear vision of the single payments area to come as the text declares that 'In this context the Commission builds largely on a market-led approach requiring voluntary co-operation by the banking sector and investments which should become a business case in the long run'. The phrases 'requiring voluntary co-operation' and 'should become a business case in the long run' are rather telling, and serve to highlight the arguably slightly schizophrenic approach which the EC was to take in later years to the question of whether SEPA was a private or public sector driven initiative.

The Communication also included a series of required action points against the various topics covered, which as well as those already mentioned spanned subjects as diverse as the need for a common minimum exemption threshold for balance of payments reporting (of 'an appropriate high fixed amount' – never high enough however!), electronic purses and e-money, cheques, cash and fraud prevention.

One of the key action points was for banks to come up with remedial proposals to fix the issue of high charges in the retail payment space for the transitional period leading up to the introduction of Euro notes and coins in 2002. Additionally, the EC announced that it would convene a major Round Table in Autumn 2000 'to consider various options set out in this Communication or proposed in the meantime by industry' – an event which was to turn out to be of major significance (and which we shall return to shortly).

With 'hints' like those in the Communication, it should have been abundantly clear to the market that the EC was rather seriously considering additional legislative intervention if its wake-up call was not listened to pretty rapidly. Just to make sure that there was no doubt on this point, on 23rd May 2000 the EC released the results of an independent survey carried out on their behalf into the costs of making cross-border payments between the (then) 11 Euro-zone countries, which showed that on average consumers were being charged a fee of €17.10 for electronically transferring €100 between Member States. Their accompanying press release again reinforced with great clarity the EC's growing agitation at the time concerning whether the 1997 cross-border payments Directive had been enough and was proving effective:

> Consumers who encounter problems such as double-charging when making cross-frontier transfers should contact the national ombudsmen which exist in each Member State. For its part, the Commission will be closely monitoring the application of the Directive, and in particular problems of the type highlighted by this latest survey, such as unauthorised double charging and excessive delays (5% exceeded the 6 day limit).

By this stage there should have been no doubt that the EC was deadly serious about requiring further change, and that while legislation was not necessarily the preferred route, the political capital tied up in demonstrating to all the success of the Euro project was such that legislative action would undoubtedly be taken if that was what it would take to force improvements in the average speed and cost of cross-border payments in the Euro zone.

The next significant event in the tale came on November 9th 2000 (previously mentioned in the context of the Heathrow Group discussion), when the EC convened its promised Round Table event in Brussels on the topic of 'Establishing a Single Payment Area: State of Play and Next Steps'. The event commenced with a set of scene-setting speeches by the EU authorities (though not including a representative from the European Council) in a coordinated display of political unity – commencing with Commissioner Frits Bolkestein, then Tommaso Padoa-Schioppa, Executive Board Member of the ECB and finally Karla Peijs, MEP, on behalf of the EP. The remainder of the packed program consisted of a presentations by academics, representatives from the payments industry (such as SWIFT, the European Committee for Banking Standards ECBS, Visa and the EBA) and representatives from users of payment services (such as the Bureau Européen des Unions de Consommateurs (BEUC) and Eurocommerce).

In his opening address, EC Commissioner Frits Bolkenstein made this very clear statement:

> The Commission's political objective remains a modern Single Payment Area for the entire EU where there is no frontier effect for cross-border payments. The execution time and price for cross-border retail transfers will and must be considerably reduced and I am convinced that technological progress will allow such development and competition will press strongly in this direction.

Interestingly, in case anyone was under the false impression that the EP were somehow less involved in the debate or less interested in the outcome than the other EU Institutions at this time, Karla Peijs was very clear in her speech that there should be a rigid deadline of 1 January 2002 for the implementation of concrete changes, including the greater automation of cross-border payments using the IBAN as the common standard. Her speech included references to the EP's view that the time limit for cross-border payments should be reduced to 3 days and an interesting comment (given what would follow) that 'It is not reasonable to expect cross-border transfers are carried out for exactly the same price as national payments'.

The wrap-up conclusion given by the EC at the end of the Roundtable made clear that they were determined to use their full powers to keep up the pressure and with a view to checking progress they would be going to publish a report on the progress of implementation of the Cross Border Credit Transfer Directive (97/5/EC) in autumn 2001.

Accordingly, they undertook yet another market study into the cost and execution times concerning retail cross-border payments – something received uneasily by the banking industry. This was released to the market accompanied by yet another press release on September 2001, including the following telling statement:

> 'The results of this new survey are very disappointing' commented Frits Bolkestein. '... in far too many cases customers are not receiving the information on charges to which they are entitled under the Directive and that there is still too much unauthorised double charging ... the fact that the level of charges has hardly changed since the Commission's directly comparable survey in 1993, despite repeated claims from the banking sector that they would act decisively to reduce these costs, clearly demonstrates that the Commission has no alternative to proposing legislation to require banks to levy the same charges for cross-border and domestic payments'.

Insiders, such as the original convener of the Heathrow Group had already picked up the vibes around a potential law to come during an EBA conference in 2000 where Karla Peijs had very clearly stated that the industry should either 'change or will be changed'! While this effectively was to lead to the drafting of the SEPA blueprint document, asking the industry to get its act together before the legislator would intervene ... it was unfortunately too late.

Regulation 2560 – a pricing regulation is born

The explanatory memorandum accompanying the EC's legislative proposal included the following key statements:

> The creation of the single currency has not been accompanied by the establishment of a single-payment area. The purpose of this Regulation is to reduce bank charges for cross-border payments in Euro to a level in line with those applying at national level. ... it will at last enable individual European consumers to become active participants in the Internal Market, ensuring that individual consumers are able to benefit from increased price transparency and choice.

Essentially, the drastic logic underpinning Regulation 2560 was that if the EC forced banks by law to cap their charges for cross-border Euro payments at the level of equivalent domestic services, this would eventually have the effect of provoking the industry into developing more efficient cross-border payment systems if they did not want to make an ongoing loss on such payments. Based on this blunt – but undoubtedly effective – psychology, Regulation 2560 introduced a requirement that all cross-border payments in Euro made up to a ceiling of €50,000 (after a short introductory period where this was limited to €12,500) would in future have to be priced the same as the 'corresponding' domestic product or service. Additionally, the EC took the opportunity to adopt the same approach for cross-border cash withdrawals in Euro, ensuring that Euro cash withdrawals made outside the home country would be no more expensive than at home. In addition the EC promoted the adoption and usage of the IBAN in conjunction with the appropriate Bank Identifier Code, or BIC, when initiating cross-border payments in Euro to support a more harmonised approach. Accordingly, the Regulation included provisions which required banks to ensure that they made all clients aware of their IBANs – typically by printing these on their bank statements; required corporates throughout the EU to quote their IBAN on their invoices; and incentivised payment service users to use IBANs in their payment instructions by allowing banks – by law – to charge their customers more for a transaction where the IBAN was not provided.

After a speedy passage through EP and Council, the final text of Regulation 2560/2001 was published in the Official Journal on 19th December 2001, and came into effect on 31st December of that year.

Of course, it was not necessarily in the interest of banks to actually inform their customers about the IBAN and the BIC because that meant the payments could not be charged for as much as in the past. The other issue with the Regulation was that it picked up on the industry's definition of STP that had been elaborated by the Heathrow Group. Using an inter-bank guideline which was itself designed at a particular moment in time – in response in fact to the earlier 1997 Cross-Border Credit Transfers Directive – as the ingredient for a law was not necessarily the most future proof approach due to the fact that any necessary change of rules and technical definitions in the inter-bank space would require a change of legislation.

To accommodate the Regulation's requirements in a more structured and harmonised way, what was really needed was one payment system standard for retail payments in Euro. This realisation ultimately led to the birth of the SEPA initiative, and it was SEPA – as well as the need for a series of conceptual alignments with the PSD – that the EC had in mind a few years later when they realised the need to upgrade the Regulation in 2008/2009, which will be examined later on in this book.

(6) The birth and early years of the EPC

In light of the success of the Heathrow Group, but with the realisation that a more formalised and representative set up was required to maintain the dialogue with regulators at EU level, the banking industry was now poised to create a new body, with a broader membership and a more formal governance.

A workshop and a white paper

As mentioned already, it took a substantial number of signals from the EC before the banking industry truly woke up to the fact that a single payment area had to be brought about and that the various regulatory communications and market statements had been much more than mere rhetoric. As we know, the Heathrow Group was the banking industry's first attempt to create a forum to debate a response, but the qualities which had made that group so successful in being able to tackle the practical issues surrounding the creation of the Euro – namely being a small ad hoc group of large players with a large market share able to operate with minimum governance and formality – were not the same ones as those needed to galvanise the whole of the banking sector in Europe into common action to review and replace national infrastructures and standards.

So, it is hardly surprising that despite having established credibility thanks to its original activities, the Heathrow Group was not able to fend off further legislation from the EC. As a consequence Regulation 2560/2001 had come about and indeed had its desired effect as a stimulus to the banking industry to at last – and rather belatedly – reach the common view that putting aside the fundamental differences between the various segments of the industry would be essential if there was to be any chance of managing the very real threat of further extensive regulatory intervention across all aspects of the bank-to-bank as well as customer-to-bank space. Perhaps then a classic case of 'the enemy of my enemy is my friend'?

As an interesting footnote, while the Heathrow Group had not been able to agree on the objective laid out in the SEPA blueprint – a document in which its author had highlighted the need for convergence of domestic and cross-border payment systems for Euro in order to reach a significant increase in efficiency and in consequence a reduction in cross-border pricing for Euro transactions on a voluntary basis – this document was now going to form the basis for the next step the industry was to take collectively.

This next step started with the organisation of a SEPA Workshop in March 2002 in Brussels in the Royal Windsor Hotel (again English inspired, however this time outside the UK), attended by 42 banks, the EBA and the three European Credit Sectors Associations (ECSAs), representing all geographic areas and all relevant types of institutions. The ambitious agenda of the workshop was to consider how the EU could potentially be transformed into a Single Euro Payments Area by self-regulation and market best practice. The starting points for discussion, already spelled out in the SEPA blueprint, were now further refined, with a high degree of consensus reached on a number of issues (perhaps rather due to the fact that the same large symbolic gun was pointed at all participants' heads by the EU regulator).

Recommendations from the workshop were consolidated into a White Paper titled, 'Euroland: Our Single Payments Area!' issued to workshop participants in May 2002. The White Paper articulated the rationale and commitment to industry action (in very cautious and careful language) and pointed out the need for convergence between domestic and cross border payments in Euro, a first attempt to describe a common vision of SEPA. It made recommendations in relation to Customer & Business Requirements, STP, Infrastructure, Cards and Cash and identified the payment instruments required to support SEPA and the need for a Pan-European Automated Clearing House (PE-ACH) framework. The White Paper also proposed an over-arching governance structure – recognising the need for a more formal and representative approach than the Heathrow Group had adopted if the conclusions and best practices were to have any chance of receiving a buy-in within the broader banking community, let alone outside of it.

The creation of the EPC

The result of the White Paper was the creation of the European Payments Council (EPC), formally established in June 2002 to facilitate the development and implementation of SEPA in line with the industry vision and the associated Roadmap as laid out in the White Paper. The EPC was to be the decision-making and coordination body of the European banking industry in relation to payments, with a declared purpose to support and promote the creation of SEPA.

Even from the outset, the EPC's objectives and scope were highly ambitious, and indeed rather unprecedented as a private sector initiative. The high level objective was clearly stated as being the creation of the architecture, instruments and processes for the realisation of SEPA with an initial scope of 'basic payment services in Euro in Europe: retail and commercial payments, and their settlement'. The payment instruments that were seen as falling within this mandate included Credit Transfers, Direct Debits, Cards, Cash, and even e- and m- payments. This wide scope and ambition was reflected in the

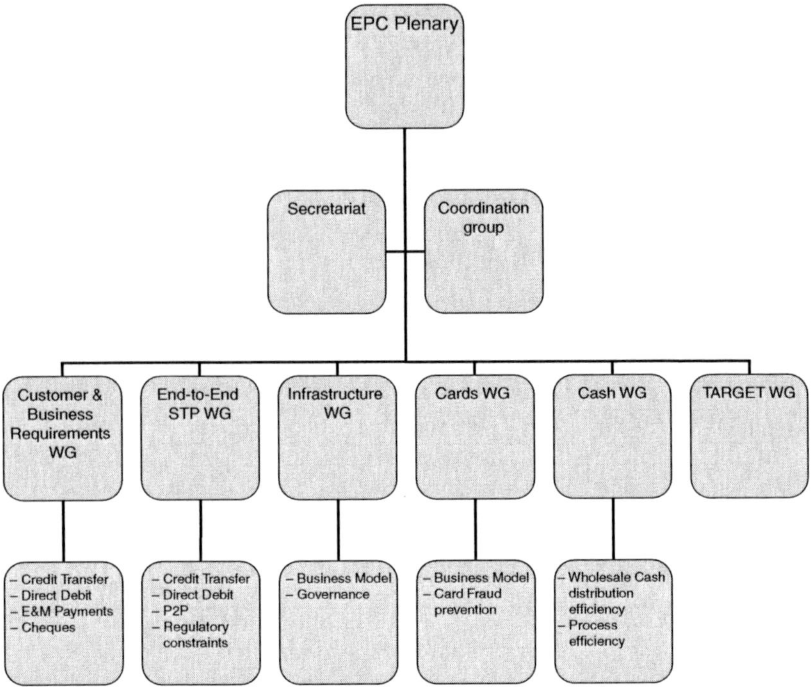

Figure 3.3 The original EPC governance structure

first EPC governance structure as shown in the figure above (see Figure 3.3).

The core principle was to have a 'Plenary' as the governing and decision-making body, supported by a 'co-ordination group', essentially a smaller management committee consisting of the various 'office holders', nominated country representatives and representatives from the 3 ECSAs, supported by a Secretariat. Underpinning this structure was to be a series of working groups, focussed on developing key aspects of the EPC's agenda. Initially, the working groups – all of which consisted of banking and banking association representatives from around the EPC community – covered 'Customer and Business Requirements', 'End-to-End STP', 'Cards', 'Infrastructure' and 'Cash'.

As an aside, given the size of the EPC's scope and ambition, you might have assumed that the resources of the Secretariat would have been very substantial from the outset. However, to the contrary, the decision taken was to keep the EPC Secretariat as lean as possible, supported by additional resources provided by the ECSAs. While the EPC would evolve reasonably quickly into acquiring its own Secretary General and a small support team, it is true to say that the EPC to this day is rather lightly staffed for such a huge strategic initiative.

Early activities and some forming and storming

Right from the outset, the roles and scope of the Cards, Cash and Infrastructure Working Groups were pretty self-evident, and later in this Title we will cover some of the highlights of these early activities. Rather less clear were the boundaries that separated the work of the snappily-titled End-to-End Straight-Through-Processing Working Group (or E-2-E STP WG for short) from that of the Business and Customer Requirements Working Group (or B&CR WG). The split of activities seemed logical on paper – separating the role of defining customer requirements (though at that stage of the EPC's evolutionary journey this was not to include much direct involvement of actual users!) from that of determining what inter-bank rules and procedures were needed to improve processing efficiency. The problem though was that 'End-to-End' by definition meant starting and finishing with customers and their requirements and would inevitably lead to some overlaps.

In its first few months, while the B&CR WG was busy forging ahead trying to figure out customer requirements across the various non-card, non-cash dimensions of the SEPA landscape, the E-2-E STP WG was to spend much of its time in somewhat philosophical contemplation of its purpose and objectives and drawing complex diagrams showing the interdependencies it had on the activities of other working groups and with the European Committee for Banking Standards (ECBS), which at that stage still existed separately from the EPC governance structure.

In the end, it was to decide that the work of the E-2-E STP WG should be split into four work streams focussed on credit transfers and direct debits as the first two, but also one on regulatory and legal barriers as the third, and the exciting new world of e-Payments and Person-to-Person (P2P) payments as the fourth and final topic. In the event, the two major achievements of the WG, before it was to disappear in the first of many EPC Governance transformations were to develop a set of 'Format Rules for Basic Cross-Border Credit Transfers denominated in Euro' as approved by the EPC Plenary in November 2002, and also to develop business practices in an attempt to ensure that the global Financial Action Task Force Recommendation VII could be interpreted in the same way by all sending/receiving banks within the SEPA area.

The Convention on Credit Transfers in Euro and the ICP convention

The key characteristics of the Convention on Credit Transfers in Euro, one of the EPC's first major achievements, are outlined in the table below (see Table 3.4). Interestingly, they have more than a passing resemblance to the idea proposed by the Heathrow Group for tackling the seven objectives in the EC's 2000 Communication:

Table 3.4 Convention on Credit Transfers in Euro: Key features

- To provide the standard for 'low-cost' processing of basic cross-border credit transfers within the EU.
- Execution time of three banking business days following date of acceptance by the originating bank to credit the beneficiary's account.
- Prerequisite: strict application of STP criteria (IBAN, BIC, amount < 12,500 €, no specific instructions, charge code 'SHA').
- Originator's and beneficiary's customer accounts to be maintained in the EU.
- Originator's bank is responsible to ensure that transfer amount is credited to account of beneficiary's bank at the latest two banking business days following the date of acceptance.
- Beneficiary's bank to credit funds to beneficiary's account not later than one banking business day following receipt.

To supplement the Convention on Credit Transfers in Euro, the EPC also adopted the Interbank Convention on Payments (ICP) – which went live in July 2003 – with a view to harmonising the interbank charging practices for cross-border credit transfers. The convention was intended to apply to basic STP processed cross-border payments falling under Regulation 2560 and it had a number of key characteristics as shown in the following table (see Table 3.5):

Table 3.5 ICP Convention: Key features

- Objective to agree and implement an EU banking industry wide set-up of interbank charging practices.
- To avoid bilateral negotiation between banks, enable standardised rules and procedures.
- Level of interbank charges still subject to bilateral agreements between banks.
- To apply to basic cross-border transfer in Euro, compliant with EU Regulation 2560/2001, up to 12,500 €, containing IBAN of beneficiary and BIC of beneficiary's bank, and no special instructions (e.g., in SWIFT field 23E and 73) with charge code 'SHA'.

It is important to underline that the default charging option under the ICP convention was 'SHA', meaning that the payer pays the sending bank's fees and the payee pays the receiving bank's fees. As previously mentioned, Regulation 2560 required the charges for both the originator (payer) and the beneficiary (payee) to be the same as for corresponding national credit transfers. The convention also stated that the practice of deducting charges by intermediary banks was no longer acceptable and should be replaced by interbank charges (something we will later on encounter in the PSD ...).

One other issue was to arise from the introduction of ICP and the Convention on Credit Transfers in Euro, due to the principle that payment messages that were not formatted in exactly the way that these conventions demanded would be able to trigger so-called non-STP charges. According to the ICP, the intermediary bank or the beneficiary bank receiving the payment is entitled to charge for the additional work resulting from transactions that do not meet the ICP's prescribed STP standards, for example in case a message contains information in field 23E or 73. This meant that many receiving banks felt entitled to levy 'repair charges' to be sent back to the originating bank and (potentially) passed back to the originating client. In this context, the ICP could of course not include the definition of an amount or upper limit for a repair since the area of pricing is fully off bounds under EU competition law principles. Neither was the timeframe within which a repair charge can be sent specified, or a maximum time limit defined. To make matters more complicated, there was also no definition around the reasons a beneficiary bank must give, or the format in which these must be provided, when it sent back a repair charge. (Note: Whilst the legal basis for sustaining this concept of a market definition of an 'STP payment' was going to be swept away by the repeal of the 1997 Cross-Border Credit Transfers Directive and Regulation 2560 as part of the implementation of the PSD and Regulation 924 in 2009, this was not going to be immediately appreciated by all parts of the payment industry, as we will explore later in Title VII.)

Just as a little historical anecdote before moving on, it is interesting to note that the initials 'ICP' in the title of the convention did not always stand for 'Interbank Convention on Payments'. Its original working title was the rather more descriptive 'Interbank Charging Principles'. This title was used right through the drafting stage until someone pointed out that it ran the risk of sounding anti-competitive (despite the innocent nature of the contents), but by then the ICP initials had widespread brand recognition, hence the need for a swift change to the slightly clunky final wording!

Pursuing 'the Ultimate Scenario'

With the Convention on Credit Transfers in Euro and the ICP in place and supported by the 'format rules' defined by the E-2-E STP WG, the B&CR WG started considering the next steps which would be necessary for credit transfers. This was to lead during the course of H2 2003 to the definition of the necessary steps to achieve what was at the time referred to rather dramatically as the 'Ultimate Scenario' for cross-border payments in Euro. Essentially, all this really meant was a process of self-regulatory migration to a state where for all cross-border payments up to €50,000 the use of the IBAN and BIC became the only possibility for a client wanting a 'basic transfer' – with an aspirational target date of 1st January 2006 for achieving this. Interestingly, at this point, domestic payments were still seen as out of scope of the EPC's proposals for credit transfers, as were payments over €50,000 (where Regulation 2560 did not have to apply); also excluded were payments that included 'value added services' (those involving special instructions or with same-day value).

The WG's proposals were to lead to the development of an EPC Resolution (of course!), this time known as the BIC and IBAN Resolution, to come into force at the beginning of 2006. The Resolution stated that for intra-EU/EEA Euro cross-border customer credit transfers, IBAN and BIC would be recognised as the only beneficiary customer account identifier and bank routing designation. If there was no valid BIC or IBAN in the payments message, then regardless of the amount of the payment, a bank would be entitled to handle the transfer as a 'value added service'. The Resolution also stated that from the start of 2007, banks would be entitled to reject any such payment if it didn't contain a BIC or IBAN!

The introduction of SEPA indicators

In order to monitor the progress of industry, the Eurosystem asked the EPC to publish a quarterly list of banks in each country that had adopted the Convention on Credit Transfers in Euro. The Eurosystem also asked the EPC to provide information on the share of Convention on Credit Transfers in Euro-compliant credit transfers processed by the adhering banks as a percentage of total payment volumes.

The below table (see Table 3.6) illustrates the EPC's response in terms of the production of initial SEPA indicators. The plan was to

Table 3.6 Initial SEPA indicators

1.	List of EU-15 banks (or countries, for ICP) having registered for Convention on Credit Transfers in Euro & the ICP Convention for their cross-border credit transfers in Euro
2.	Number of EU-15 (later EU-25/27) countries with at least one bank having declared a receiver capability in line with EPC Resolution
3.	Active and regular distribution of IBAN & BIC by financial institutions
4.	Number of credit transfers instructions processed by PE-ACH operators
5.	Cards WG Recommendations # 2, 3 and 7 (Rec. 2 & 3 on the basis of self-assessment forms presented to schemes individually)
6.	Formulation of national cash plans by the end 2003

produce these with a quarterly frequency and initial results to be made available by 31.12.2003. From a production perspective, a two step consolidation process was implemented: country level first with collection via national/sector associations, followed by European level via the ECSAs and the EPC.

The ECB, an early SEPA road map and the coining of the PEDD concept

On 30th–31st October 2003, the ECB convened a Workshop on SEPA in Frankfurt with high level payment industry participation from the EPC Community, designed to examine a number of topics that the ECB felt to be important, including the basis on which the ECB and EPC should work together in a way which would allow the ECB to carry out their oversight role, but still in such a way that preserved the ability for the banking industry to have sufficient privacy to be able to co-ordinate its position on key issues before discussing them with the ECB and other market stakeholders. From a governance perspective, agreement was reached to the ECB's request that going forward they should have observer status within the EPC Plenary and on all EPC WGs (with the initial exception of the working group on customer requirements), as well as to meet formally at a high level through the high level Contact Group on Euro Payments Strategy (COGEPS for short).

It is informative to take a quick look at the 'Roadmap' which the EPC presented to the ECB during this conference, summarised in the following table (see Table 3.7), as this gives a good flavour of the scope and focus of the EPC's ambitions for SEPA at the time.

Table 3.7 Key SEPA milestones presented during the October 2003 SEPA workshop

Milestone	Deliverables
31/12/2002	Substantiated, syndicated and detailed roadmap (e.g., working groups launched, choice for pan European infrastructure substantiated, systematic analysis of standards, rules, conventions for STP done)
01/07/2003	Achieve first tangible results (e.g., up-and running pan-European infrastructure, Direct Debit scheme defined, basic standards and rules agreed)
31/12/2004	Ramp-up Activity (e.g., 50% of cross-border volume on pan-European ACH standards for value added services defined)
01/07/2005	Next wave of innovations (e.g., first pan-European direct debit infrastructure)
31/12/2007	Achieve targeted service levels for the pan-European Infrastructure
31/12/2010	Achieve full migration for banks and their customers to SEPA

It is particularly interesting to note the primary importance that was being placed on issues concerning infrastructure development – a topic that we will take a specific look at in a moment – together with the reference to the objective of having a pan-European Direct debit 'infrastructure' in place by mid 2005.

We will be covering the development process of what would become the SEPA Direct Debit scheme in Title VI of this book, but it is worth noting at this point that much preparatory work was done by the B&CRWG during this next period, leading in particular to two key Resolutions that were agreed at the EPC Plenary meeting of 17th June 2004. The first was titled 'Pan European Direct Debit: Overall Approach', and the second 'Pan European Direct Debit: PEDD Model'. The first of these is particularly noteworthy, as it marks the point at which the EPC formally endorsed 'the creation of a new electronic PEDD scheme that can be used for intra-EU (that is, both cross-border and national) transactions'. The Resolution also included a target date of June 2005 to finalise the scheme and for the launch of a pilot by end-2006. The second Resolution was in its own way also notable, as it for the first time introduced an official EPC definition of the concept of the Pan-European Direct Debit (PEDD) as 'the instrument governed by the rules of the PEDD scheme for making payments in Euro throughout SEPA from bank accounts allowed to support Direct Debits'.

We will return to this topic in much more detail later, but now it is time for a preliminary exploration of the exciting worlds of SEPA for cards and cash.

SEPA for cards – the first tentative steps

Unlike the position for credit transfers and direct debits, the problem in the cards space wasn't a lack of common inter-bank schemes which could be used as the basis for making cross-border as well as domestic payments. For example, cards bearing the MasterCard and Visa logos could already be used throughout most of the EU and actually the world!

In fact, the conclusions recorded in the May 2002 SEPA 'White Paper' on cards, while quite grand sounding, were actually a little vague as to what exactly the issue was here that needed addressing. 'For cards, the banking industry should further explore options and develop platforms to put forward European interests in the context of global card networks, as well as launch specific initiatives regarding debit cards, ATM withdrawals and cash.'

As the industry needed to start somewhere, the first EPC Cards Working Group meeting took place on 20th September 2002. During this meeting it was confirmed that the scope of the EPC's cards activities should be limited to debit and credit cards and not extend to potentially related topics such as the e-Purse. It was also decided that an inventory of existing national practices would be a good place to start – in this case to determine the structure and nature of the cards market in each participating SEPA country. Additionally, the prevailing view among participants was that, unlike the case for direct debits or a pan-European processing infrastructure, there wasn't the need to develop anything fundamentally new in the cards space. Rather, the sense was to set goals for a more SEPA-specific view of how the existing global cards systems might need re-organising or amending to cater better for specific EU needs. Accordingly, the EPC decided fairly early on that the strategy for cards would be one of adaptation rather than 'from-scratch creation'. European consumers should be enabled to use their general purpose cards to make and receive card payments and cash withdrawals in Euros throughout the SEPA area 'with the same ease and convenience as in their home markets' (yes – that phrase again!).

The initial set of Recommendations issued by the EPC on cards, as set out in the following table (see Table 3.8), was consistent with this overall approach (albeit a little vague):

Table 3.8 The initial EPC recommendations on cards

1. Fraud must be combated through effective co-operation between banks, card schemes, the EC, ECB, retailers, police authorities, and governments
2. Card schemes' tariffs for members must be presented in a transparent manner consistent with the reality of SEPA
3. Amendments underway to make rules SEPA-compliant must be completed speedily
4. Banks restate their preference for self-regulation but will work with legislators and regulators to remove obstacles and discrepancies
5. Banks will strive at achieving greater levels of standardisation, develop best practices for issuing and acquiring
6. Banks must exert their responsibilities as stakeholders in domestic and international card schemes to the fullest extent
7. The banking industry and the Eurosystem shall implement a statistical data collection and distribution process
8. The Cards Working Group shall be the body to:
   - Report, and make further propositions to the EPC
   - Organise debates on new issues

A number of points did become clear quite quickly, as essentially the requirements in this area started to boil down to two key challenges – firstly the need to adopt the same security standard for all general purpose cards in Europe, and secondly to encourage the principle of general interoperability whereby cards would have a much higher level of acceptance across the EU market.

Tackling the first of these issues was relatively straightforward, at least in terms of deciding which security standard to use, and indeed one of the EPC Cards WG's first actions was to recognise the EMV (originally Europay MasterCard Visa) standard to be used for this purpose.

In 2004, the ECB expressed the clear expectation that within SEPA, cardholders should be able to use any card at any terminal to pay for goods and services or withdraw cash under the same conditions as in their home country. To realise this vision, at least the development of SEPA-wide applicable standards both for cards and terminals was now going to be necessary to complement and bring alive the concept of the SEPA Cards Framework.

SEPA for cash – staunching the bleeding

Given the EPC's mandate to provide harmonised and future proof payment solutions across the EU, it is at first glance somewhat counterintuitive that the EPC decided to also invest considerable time to debate the topic of cash (a similar question perhaps could be asked of the EC in the context of the PSD). However, far from promoting cash, the EPC approach and goals here were to look to reduce the cost of cash processing and to 'reposition cash as a payment instrument' (given the long history of cash, not an easy task).

The situation here was that prior to the introduction of the physical Euro every country had its own, distinct organization (a set of laws, regulations, practices, infrastructures) for distributing and recycling cash, from the issuing NCB down to ATMs and retailers and back again. Apart from a handful of exceptions, such national organizations had in effect changed very little in response to the introduction of the Euro, retaining many country specific particularities regarding the distribution and recycling of cash, which meant that the single currency was still being distributed to banks throughout SEPA at very different costs.

Against this background, the EPC's Cash WG estimated in 2003 that the cost of cash to society as a whole was around €50 billion p.a. and established nine recommendations for action in this area, as summarised in the following table (see Table 3.9).

Table 3.9 SEPA for cash: the nine recommendations

1. Banks to develop joint cards and cash strategies (endorsed at national level)
2. Banks to promote electronic products, in liaison with other stakeholders (retailers)
3. Promote Europe-wide standardisation of requirements for equipment (hardware and software)
4. Cash Working Group to oversee implementation, consolidate information, act as catalyst for standardisation
5. Develop 'best practices' to guide banks in enhancing cash service operations
6. The banking industry & the Eurosystem to evaluate the pros and cons of a Europe-wide infrastructure for cash handling in SEPA
7. ESCB to implement a timely data collection and distribution process
8. ESCB to support legislative and regulatory changes to implement the above strategy
9. ESCB to harmonise NCB operating conditions

From 2004 onwards, a constructive dialogue between the Eurosystem (ESCB Banknote Committee – BANCO) and the EPC's Cash WG started to take place concerning how to achieve a greater harmonisation of Eurosystem NCB operational conditions. This was to result in the formulation of the Eurosystem Framework on cash recycling, adopted by the ECB Governing Council in December 2004.

SEPA and the evolving Infrastructure model

It was obvious to all concerned that if there was to be any chance of being able to process cross-border payments within SEPA with anything approaching the same low cost levels as that of existing domestic payments in many of the existing markets (essential now that the EC had helpfully already ensured pricing parity via Regulation 2560!), SEPA credit transfers and direct debits would have to be cleared and settled in an extremely efficient way.

This was in fact realised right from the very outset, as the original May 2002 'Euroland: Our Single Payment Area!' White Paper stated that

> The participating banks have expressed a clear preference for the development of a Pan European Clearing House with fair and open access. In the near term, multiple infrastructures will continue to exist. However, a vision is required for the long term architecture, and a smooth migration path from the current systems to this new infrastructure will be necessary.

A couple of interesting points to note here, in the context of what was to follow much later in our story, was the clear recognition that something big, new and exciting would have to be built, in payment processing infrastructure terms at least, to handle the new environment, and secondly that while multiple infrastructures were expected to coexist initially there was an assumption that some form of consolidation – and hence a reduction in the number of processors – was inevitable. The starting point here of course was that each country was coming from a position of having at least one national processor handling its domestic low value transactions, operating under a variety of ownership and governance structures including central bank ownership, banking industry not-for-profit ownership and fully commercial arrangements. Vested interests were going to make the logical consolidation process a rather more protracted experience than was initially expected by the brave pioneers who took part in the early EPC discussions on this complex topic.

Under the initial EPC governance model, the role of defining the infrastructural architecture model was to fall to the appropriately named 'Infrastructure Working Group' (IWG). By October 2002 it was clear to the members of this group that they essentially had three core objectives: to define a pan-European automated clearing house model and to facilitate discussion on business requirements and change processes; to foster development and convergence towards this model; and to monitor progress. As such the group started, reasonably enough, with a review of existing infrastructures (national and cross-border), leading onto a definition of the requirements, governance principles and key access principles for the new ideal pan-European model, with the rather ambitiously sounding goal that by mid-2004 some 50 per cent of current cross-border credit transfer volumes should be processed on the pan-European infrastructure and by mid-2005 the new infrastructures should be able to handle Euro direct debit transactions. Let's remember here that the rate of cross-border Euro payments at that time was only around 2–3 per cent of domestic Euro traffic.

Initial discussions identified what was destined to be called the 'concentric model approach'. This concept was discussed by those involved at the time in brilliantly cryptic language – lots of references to the need to 'recognise the market value of regional praxis to increase usage options' and that 're-modelling of the payments culture towards SEPA is a process not just a statement'. Stripped of the jargon though, the concept was actually a rather compelling one as it essentially meant building a common core of processing requirements, out from which could be built successive layers of additional functionality to support the needs of specific user communities. Though no one knew it at the time, this was perhaps the moment at which what would later be called the SEPA Additional Optional Service (AOS) concept – which we will cover in much more detail in Title VI – was born.

Eventually, and after many hugely technical discussions, the concept of a clearing and settlement framework involving the creation of a new type of animal called a pan-European automated clearing house (PE-ACH) was finally nailed down. In January 2003, EPC Plenary endorsed the definition of PE-ACH as: 'A business platform for the provision of Euro retail payment instruments and basic related services made up of governance rules and payments practices and supported by the necessary technical platform(s).'

This concept was later to expand into the five layer SEPA Clearing & Settlement Mechanism (CSM) model, where all five layers would need to operate in a SEPA scheme compliant fashion. These were as set out in the following table (see Table 3.10):

Table 3.10 The CSM Model

1) **PE-ACH:** an Automated Clearing House (ACH) that is itself or is part of a Pan-European ACH, a SEPA-wide, country-neutral clearing organisation, providing reach to all banks participating in the SEPA schemes, and which banks from anywhere within SEPA can select to use on the basis of price and service.
2) **SEPA Scheme-Compliant ACH:** an ACH capable of processing SEPA scheme transactions within a defined market and which may or may not (yet) be in transition to a PE-ACH.
3) **Multilateral CSM:** a decentralised form of multilateral clearing and settlement (not an ACH structure) capable of processing SEPA scheme transactions within a defined market.
4) **Bilateral clearing and settlement:** a decentralised form of bilateral clearing or settlement (for example, correspondent banking).
5) **Intra-Bank/Intra-Group** clearing and settlement: an intrabank and/or intragroup clearing and settlement arrangement, typically where both the originator/creditor and beneficiary/debtor have their accounts within the same bank or group.

Anyway, returning to the three goals the IWG had set for themselves, it will be recalled that the second of these was to foster development of – and convergence towards – this new model. What immediately became clear here was that there was a classic chicken and egg dilemma that first needed to be resolved. It was obvious that banks and their clients would only be interested in using these new infrastructures if all other parties were also connected to them, but how would that position ever be reached in the first place?

This issue – the need for universal reach – was to prove again and again to be one of the greatest problems for the SEPA project generally, and as we shall see later was to require some further direct legislative intervention. For now though, the IWG hit upon the idea of using the secret weapon of an EPC Resolution (becoming by now increasingly popular as the EPC 'weapon de jour' for pretty much any issue) to tackle the issue at hand. The 'Resolution on Receiver Capability' was approved by the EPC Plenary in June 2003 and essentially called for each national community in the EU to ensure that all of their financial institutions were reachable via a PE-ACH for credit transfers by 31 December 2003 at the latest.

The honour of being the very first PE-ACH was to fall to the EBA's STEP2 system, which was to start operation in April 2003, processing credit transfers that were compliant with the EPC's Convention on Credit Transfers in Euro – so retail payments of up to €12,500 per transaction, in accordance with the initial requirements of Regulation 2560. In order to assure the required high level of processing efficiency, each payment instruction had to include the IBAN of the beneficiary and the BIC of the beneficiary's bank in order to comply with STEP2's STP criteria. Accordingly, and again in line with the Convention on Credit Transfers in Euro, the payment messages for STEP2 were based on the MT103 + message structure (data set) which was defined by SWIFT in close conjunction with the former Heathrow Group. Interestingly, because at that stage there had been no decision by the EPC to adopt XML as the technical basis for what would become the SEPA CT and DD schemes, STEP2 was also able to support files formatted in XML using the SWIFT Bulk Payment standard. The STEP2 service was to achieve the necessary 'reach' through the registration of a number of Direct Participants (over 100 in the end), who in turn registered many more BICs of their customer banks as Indirect Participants, thus ultimately connecting thousands of institutions throughout Europe.

A number of other key EPC Resolutions – including one on 'PE-ACH Governance Guiding Principles' in September 2003 – were to mark the further progress of the IWG until it reached the end of its life span in mid-2004, when it migrated into the far more excitingly titled 'Operations, Infrastructure and Technology Standards Support Group' (or OITS for short) to support the work of the four 'Payment Instrument Working Groups' which were set up at that stage to progress the further design work on what would later become the SEPA schemes.

(7) A Roadmap emerges

The EPC underwent a further re-structuring and expansion in the second half of 2004. It was revised to consist of 64 members, still composed of banks and banking associations and at the time it was stated that over 250 professionals happened to be engaged in the work programme of the EPC from all across Europe. Following the Charter-signing in June 2004, the EPC's governance framework was now fully formalised. A 'Cooperation Model' was established between the ECB and the EC, with the EPC now formerly identified in their eyes as the leading interlocutor for the European payments industry on all Euro-related matters.

The biggest challenge that now lay ahead was to work out how to evolve the Convention on Credit Transfers in Euro into a more formal and comprehensive pan-European credit transfer service covering all domestic retail payments and at the same time how to define the basis of an acceptable model for a single Direct Debit scheme for SEPA. The latter being particularly delicate, given existing national models varied greatly in a number of core legal, contractual and practical aspects, including even such basic parameters as who should debtors give their completed mandates to once signed.

Realising that some encouragement might be needed to steel the EPC's resolve for tackling these genuinely thorny issues, in September 2004 Gertrude Tumpel-Gugerell, Member of the Executive Board of the ECB, delivered a landmark speech entitled, 'Time to act: clear objectives and a convincing roadmap for the Single Euro Payments Area' to the EPC Coordination Committee Members at the EPC's strategic offsite meeting. In this speech, she set out the ECB's expectations and vision of SEPA, views that were reiterated in the ECB's Third Progress Report on Retail Payments (essentially the ECB's annual school report on the progress of the EPC) issued just three months later. This report stated very clearly that 'a real SEPA will be achieved [for citizens in the Euro area] when they can make payments throughout the whole area from a single bank account, using a single set of payment instruments, as easily and safely as in the national context today'.

Among its wide ranging set of requirements, the ECB's report asked for a number of specific deliverables as summarised in the following table (see Table 3.11):

Table 3.11 Key Deliverables Requested in the ECB's Third Progress Report on Retail Payments

- Convention on Credit Transfers in Euro and the ICP Convention to 'become the compulsory minimum standard' for Regulation 2560-compliant retail payments.
- A PEDD (Pan-European Direct Debit) service to be made available as an option for national payments by 1 January 2008 and for Euro-area wide use by 2010.
- From a Cards perspective, interoperability was the key requirement to ensure customers could use their cards across the SEPA geography in a seamless way.
- Transformation of infrastructures should be fully underway by 2010, either by the conversion of national infrastructures into pan-European infrastructures or by their elimination as several PE-ACH operators gradually absorb payment volumes across Europe.

In response to this very clear set of challenges, the EPC reviewed its own plans (again) and came up with a response in the form of the well known 'EPC Roadmap 2004–2010'.

The result of the Roadmap review was a refocused set of 'primary' and 'complementary' deliverables. The key 'primary' deliverables were the SEPA payment schemes for credit transfers, direct debits and a framework for debit (and account-linked) cards. This was the key point at which it was announced that a new credit transfer scheme would be created – the SEPA Credit Transfer Scheme – which would address 'basic credit transfers' (a term which by the way remains a little unclear even today!), replacing the Convention on Credit Transfers in Euro and the ICP. Additionally, it was at this time that the cards deliverable was identified by the term 'SEPA framework', in recognition of the particular meaning of a 'scheme' in the cards industry.

As an additional element of the primary deliverables, it was announced that the PE-ACH framework was to be further enhanced, so as to separate the governance and management of the SEPA payment schemes/frameworks from their operation by service providers and infrastructures. In the 'secondary deliverables' camp, it was stated that the EPC would continue its work on cash and other card issues such as fraud prevention plus instigate 'workstreams examining opportunities for cooperation in both e-payments for web retailers and mobile payments'.

Additionally, the EPC drew up a revised timeline based upon three delivery phases; a scheme design and preparation stage (2004–5), followed by implementation and deployment (2006–7) and finally a transitional period during which there would be coexistence of national and pan-European schemes and gradual adoption of the latter (2008–10).

In order to accomplish these deliverables described above, the EPC made a decision to re-structure the detailed work (again!), this time under four Payment Instrument Working Groups (PIWGs) and two Support Groups, each of which was to be given responsibility for delivering the six workstreams which were now seen as underpinning the 'SEPA Programme' ... which is what indeed it now had at last become.

The stage was now set ...

At the EPC Plenary Meeting in December 2004, the SEPA vision was re-coined into the by now familiar language: 'SEPA will be the area where citizens, companies and other economic actors will be able to make and receive payments in Euro, within Europe, whether between or within national boundaries under the same basic conditions, rights and obligations, regardless of their location.'

Accordingly, with the launch of the SEPA Roadmap 2004–10 and the accompanying changes in governance and structure, the stage was now set for the EPC to move onto the next level of its ambitious work programme – as the 'scheme design and preparation' phase was to begin in earnest.

Maybe some kind of spontaneous declaration of commitment would be appropriate to mark this historic moment of renewal ...

Title IV
PSD – A Parallel Universe to SEPA: The Odyssey from the First Ideas to the Final Text

Introduction

The Payment Services Directive, commonly referred to as the PSD, was the result of a long process of legal drafting and political negotiation among the European Institutions as well as a plethora of market stakeholders. The story of this legislative text and the way it was created and finally implemented is one of the centrepieces of this book (though I hope this does not make you put it down now ...). This Title provides a detailed insight into the first stage of the PSD – its creation. The following analysis also serves as a case study of EU law making in practice and in doing so is intended to highlight how various steps and procedures leading up to the delivery of EU legislation could be enhanced to further improve regulatory output – and therefore implicitly Europe itself.

(1) A great idea ... or rather lots and lots of them

The prospect of further payments regulation in the EU in some shape or form was no longer a newsworthy item when in 2002 the EC published a consultative document entitled 'Working Document on a possible legal framework for the single payments area in the internal market'.[1] Various attempts to improve customer experience of cross-border payments, reduce costs, and generally make systems more efficient (even more relevant of course now that there was a common currency in Europe) had been made throughout the preceding two decades. Plus of course the almost forgotten EC Communication of January 2000[2] had already spelled out what was needed to integrate the missing piece of the puzzle – retail payments – at a European level, including the delivery of common technical standards, a European infrastructure, harmonisation of direct debits and the standardisation of transparency rules for banks.

Nevertheless, the banking industry got quite understandably nervous about this consultation and efforts were made at a national and European banking industry level to provide a coherent response to the many questions that were being raised by the EC. The stage, in the grander scheme of the EU regulatory process, was now set for the EC, having received comments on its consultation, to issue a Communication. With the banks by then in weary anticipation, this paper appeared a good year later (on the 2.12.2003 to be precise) and identified no fewer than 21 areas[3] that in the EC's mind constituted legal and technical barriers to payments harmonisation. While the payments industry, by this stage represented by the European Payments Council (EPC), had already had shared a small list of harmonisation requests to support the upcoming Single Euro Payments Area – or SEPA – project, the legislator's creativity produced this far broader list (see table 4.1) of areas for potential legislative intervention.

Table 4.1 An overview of the 21 Annexes

The 21 Annexes covered no fewer than the following subject areas:

1) The right to provide payment services *(subtly hinting at a potential supervisory regime for non-banks)*
2) Information requirements *(this was to become a long laundry list of T&C – type legal rules)*
3) Non-resident accounts *(the removal of Balance of Payments Reporting for intra-EU transactions should have been removed, but continues to be an issue today)*
4) Value dates *(a topic that will go down in history as having triggered significant market change in some geographies)*
5) Portability of bank account numbers *(more a dream than a practical requirement – though it nearly ended up in the PSD)*
6) Customer mobility *(covering measures that should facilitate change of provider; again, easy on paper but not so easy in practice)*
7) The evaluation of the security of payment instruments and components *(a measure that could risk an increase in costs without delivering future proof measures)*
8) Information on the originator of payments (SR VII of FATF) *(a global requirement that was later to be split out and handled via a separate Regulation)*

(continued)

Table 4.1 Continued

9)	Alternative dispute resolution *(very important with a view to reducing cost of disputes)*
10)	Revocability of a payment order *(it is still unclear why existing contractual provisions would not have been sufficient)*
11)	The role of the Payment Service Provider in the case of a customer/ merchant – dispute in distance commerce *(a key harmonisation rule needed for SEPA)*
12)	Non-execution or defective execution *(the idea of a substantial and harmonised shift in the burden of proof towards PSPs)*
13)	Obligations and liabilities of the contractual parties related to unauthorised transactions *(introducing new liabilities for PSPs)*
14)	The use of "OUR", "BEN", "SHARE" *(no clear strategy at this point, but was to lead to an ambiguous final text that would prove a serious headache for the payments industry in the years to come)*
15)	Execution times for credit transfers *(a harmonised effort to speed up service levels across the EU)*
16)	Direct debiting *(addressing the future development of SEPA Direct Debits)*
17)	Removing barriers to cash circulation *(taken up largely by industry self-regulation with ECB support)*
18)	Data protection issues *(a sensitive area, already underpinned by a plethora of existing EU and national legislation)*
19)	Digital Signatures *(a recurring topic that seems to find no solution)*
20)	Security of the networks *(not so far leading to any legislative action due to the sensitivity of this area and the need for individual provider solutions to be able to diversify risks in case of security network breaches)*
21)	Breakdown of a payment network *(years down the line this topic would lead to heated debates at EU level on the nature of 'force majeure')*

Despite the absence of any compelling evidence of market failure across the European payments markets, the proposed Communication already clearly indicated the EC's ambition to regulate all possible types of electronic payment services. However, from this substantial list of perceived issues, only a few areas were actually crucial measures in the context of building SEPA – annexes 3, 11, 16 and 17 as well as some of the principles found in annexes 13 and 15. All the rest bore no relation to the list of requests with which industry had approached the EC in connection with the SEPA project, which meant in practice that the SEPA aspects risked being drowned in the deep pool of broader ideas the Communication had delivered.

In fact, the overriding objectives were mainly related to the enhancement of consumer protection (not surprising given the EC's mandate for consumer protection) the increase in competition (hopefully accompanied by lower prices) and the modernisation of the payment infrastructure in Europe (that is, SEPA at an abstract level). In addition, the EC had in mind to take the opportunity to integrate into the same legislative vehicle a new prudential regime for non-bank payment service providers (PSPs) as their way of implementing FATF SRVI on Alternative Remittance[4] which states that: 'Jurisdictions should require licensing or registration of persons or legal entities providing money/value transmission services, including through informal systems or networks. ... [and] Jurisdictions should be able to impose sanctions on money/value transmission services, including informal systems or networks, that fail to obtain a license/register and that fail to comply with relevant FATF Recommendations.'

In line with European legislative procedure the EC consulted the ECB[5] and the ECOSOC[6] upon this Communication. The ECB provided a clear response in February 2004, recalling its Treaty obligations under article 105(2) and article 22 of the Statute of the ECB which 'entrusts the ECB/Eurosystem with promoting the smooth functioning of payment systems.'[7] Due to the fact that elements of the EC Communication clearly ventured into ECB territory, the ECB expressed its misgivings, in particular as regards the proposed creation of a prudential regime for non-bank PSPs. The ECOSOC provided its position in July 2004,[8] which expressed positive recognition of the banking industry's efforts to create a harmonised payment system for Euro payments in the form of the SEPA project and encouraged the EC to focus on addressing legal barriers to cross-border payments in Europe while avoiding over-regulation, which they saw as a potential threat to the competitive edge of the European payments market in the global context. The ECOSOC also stressed that in case regulatory intervention was deemed to be required the instrument employed should be a Regulation, as this would guarantee legal certainty and direct applicability in line with the EC's Better Regulation[9] principles. We should note this point and keep it at the back of our minds for now.

The first legislative draft appears

Despite the widespread criticism by the consulted EU institutions and the banking industry of the overambitious nature of this long shopping list of potential legislative measures, the EC stuck to its course and the future PSD began to take concrete shape during 2004, when the serious drafting process began for what was at the time given the working title of the 'New Legal Framework for Payments in the Internal Market', or NLF.

The proposal in annex 8 of the Communication, covering the regulatory requirement for information that should accompany funds transfers under FATF Recommendation VII was sensibly excluded from the NLF text at this early stage and spun off into a separate fast track Regulation as implementation was a matter of urgency. Adopted in November 2006, the final text was published in the Official Journal of the European Union (OJ L 345) a month later as Regulation 1781/2006, to go live in January 2007. As this all happened at 'light speed', at least from a European institutional perspective, a mistake was perhaps inevitably found in the text, leading to a corrigendum[10] issued end of 2007. From a supervisory perspective it was also agreed that bringing the Regulation into force from January 2007 would in fact be an unreasonably rapid compliance requirement for banks and other providers and so it was decided that in the spirit of market adaptation sanctions for non-compliance would not be enforced until end 2007, a date that also happened to coincide with the deadline for implementation of the Third EU Money Laundering Directive (2005/60/EC).

Returning to the NLF story, an equally logical move would have been to also exclude from the scope of the drafting the prudential legislation of non-bank PSPs (later to be called Payment Institutions) and instead to tackle the implementation of this 'other' FATF Special Recommendation – No. VI – by creating a separate supervisory law for those new PSPs, similar to the approach followed in the e-money Directive. The fact that this did not happen, and that the new supervisory regime was left within the scope of the NLF initiative, later nearly caused the whole proposal to be derailed during the intensely political debates and negotiations with European Parliament (EP) and Council that were to follow.

And so the drafting saga began.

In terms of the actual drafting process, the EC of course did not come up with the PSD (alias NLF) on its own on a Sunday afternoon. The development of the legal proposal was assisted by two standing advisory groups, the Payment Systems Market Group (PSMG),[11] composed of payment industry experts (banks, money remitters, telecom operators, corporate and consumer associations, central banks) and the Payment Systems Government Expert Group (PSGEG), composed of national administrations (finance ministries, financial attachés). The role of these groups was to provide technical advice in the legislative preparation of the PSD.

The first NLF-draft version was issued on 19 March 2004 with the second draft version following swiftly on the 16 April 2004. More versions were published to the PSMG and PSGEG that same year: NLF Draft version 3, (12 May 2004), NLF Draft version 4 (06 August 2004), NLF Draft version 5 (26 November 2004) and in 2005 the PSD (renamed) Draft version 6 (14 July 2005).

All those drafts papers were provided to the two advisory groups on a confidential basis and have never been published to the external world, which in itself perhaps raises a bit of a question around the nature of transparency of this aspect of the EC's law making process. In fact, these types of papers even have their own special name – they are called 'non-papers'.

Given the scale of the EC's ambitions for the PSD and their early policy determination that they wished to write a law that delved deeply into what might be described as the 'dark pools' of technical and procedural detail, it became essential that the officials responsible for the drafting developed a sufficient grasp of the subject matter. For example, an understanding of how the payment types in the market differed from each other was crucial to avoid a potential plethora of unintended consequences. It is a fact of life that credit transfers are very different from direct debits. Cards transactions are another thing altogether and cross-border payments are not the same as domestic ones (at least in a pre-SEPA world!). One clear danger at the outset, of course, was the fact that all citizens, including the politicians and civil servants of the EU, are users of payment services. As such, an easy trap was to assume that with familiarity of certain consumer payment types came automatic expertise on how things work in the payments engine room.

In terms of filling the educational gap, there was in part an expectation that the interaction with the PSMG and other payment bodies and associations should be a key way of ensuring the adequate level of technical know-how. Additionally, the EC services involved wisely took a number of opportunities to meet with industry bodies and individual PSPs to hear – and see – first hand how this payments thing worked. These steps did not however dissuade the EC from their preliminary conclusion that it would be possible to adopt a single set of rules covering the myriad of payment types falling under the Directive's scope, with as little variation as possible. The reality though was – and is – somewhat more complex, given that while it is true that 'a payment is a payment', there are nonetheless some major variations in the flows, technical architecture, user needs, liability models and risk characteristics between the different payment types that were about to be regulated. This inconvenient truth did not fit well, however, with the 'one size fits all' approach envisaged here, and was ultimately to be the cause of considerable angst and painful discussions and compromises to arrive at the final text, which (as we will see later on) was still to prove something of a Pandora's box.

Additionally, of course, it was relevant for the legislator also to understand the commercial model under which payments are being offered – including the different components of risk, which may (or may not) be factored in when banks set out their pricing strategies in a competitive market place. One early assumption made by the EC here was that the payments market would price in the same way as the insurance market – in other words that a complex set of actuarial calculations would ensure that the possibility of a risk event interfering in the execution of a payment would be factored directly into the tariff (or premium) charged for that payment. This, not entirely appropriate assumption, was to re-surface when the debate on whether to include 'one-leg' transactions under the scope of the PSD's conduct of business (COB) rules took place between the EC and the industry and later to continue in the discussions with EP and Council.

Finally, in addition to the technical and commercial background that the EC services needed to acquire to be able to produce a sensible piece of legislation, there was surely also a case to be made for investigating whether other jurisdictions on planet earth had produced specific payments legislation and if so, what it looked like and whether ideas here or there could be leveraged for the European market. And indeed there were examples waiting to be unearthed! For example the US Uniform Commercial Code (UCC), a collection of codified laws for commercial transactions in the US was developed as early as 1972 and over time grew to include specific rules on electronic funds transfers, or EFTS, under article 4A that are used by businesses. Article 4A extensively covers the payment process as well as the liabilities of each participant in the payment chain. For the purposes of consumer transactions the US had also developed legislation in form of the Electronic Funds Transfer Act, known as Regulation E, as early as 1978. This act defines liabilities and procedures for EFTs and establishes consumer protection in the context of using these systems. In fact it turns out that many of the areas that the PSD was looking to cover in its COB rules could already be found in existing US legislation. Curiously, however, not much of this appears to have been considered by the EC services for the purpose of inspiration or even terminological alignment, which would have made things a bit more consistent from a global regulatory perspective.

An official proposal and some additional reading

The 1st of December 2005 would go down in history as the day when the final Directive proposal (in fact NLF version 7!) was officially published[12] – a day that was certainly marked with a large red cross in my calendar! After an odyssey of negotiation, involving the input of many stakeholders and market experts, even though their views were not always listened to in the context of a highly charged political debate, the 'non-paper' had finally become 'the paper' – and the set of ideas contained therein were now finally released outside the corridors of the Commission!

But that was not all. The EC also added a few additional supplements to the already plentiful reading material in form of an Explanatory Memorandum and an Impact Assessment (IA).

Out of these aforementioned supplements, the IA merits particular attention as it will help to highlight the EC's rationale that underpins the PSD. First of all, it is important to understand that while IAs are not legally binding they are important in the sense that they should provide a 'sound analysis'[13] of evidence in support of the EC's decision-making process in relation to policy options by identifying impacts in the economic, environmental and social fields, advantages and disadvantages of each policy option and potential synergies and trade-offs. This means that the analysis presented in an IA is intended to give objective guidance on which policy option should ultimately be adopted in response to an identified situation, be it no action, a Recommendation or a legal intervention via a Directive or Regulation. IAs are a key pillar of the EC's Better Regulation policy as previously explained.

So, what did the PSD IA say?

The IA first of all explained that in line with the Treaty the overall objective of the PSD was to support the creation of the Single Market and increase efficiency of payment services in the EU.[14] In this context it is worthwhile recalling guidance from the Institute of International Finance,[15] which states that new initiatives should be considered systematically by clearly defining the failure of the market that is at the root of risks to systems, consumers and businesses and in this sense constitutes the basis for intervention. However our PSD IA didn't really follow this approach. Indeed, with no material market failure identified, the degree and depth of provisions that were proposed in the PSD might seem like a seriously disproportionate response on a dispassionate reading.

Now let's turn to the objectives of the PSD, which as we know were many, including consumer protection, modernisation of payment infrastructures, efficiency and economies of scale, competition and consolidation, cheap payment services, increased cross-border payment service supply, a level playing field between PSPs and the provision of standard information for consumers and streamlined legal conditions for all users and providers of payment services in Europe.[16] Even from the outset, it had to be questionable – and indeed remains so today – whether it is truly feasible to satisfy so many objectives simultaneously in one legislation.

When examining the analysis in the IA that leads up to its 'coup de theatre' – the unveiling of the preferred policy option – it becomes very clear that the choice was the result of a political decision, rather than one based on compelling empirical evidence, including the costs/benefits involved. Although the EC clearly acknowledges in its analysis that a Regulation would be the most appropriate instrument to provide legal certainty and simplicity, as well as being 'suited to ensure the elimination of legal barriers to the development of pan-European payment services', IA section 6.2 (2) also states that Member States, would in fact prefer a Directive, to avoid any impact or conflict with existing national rules on payment services (well, an impact was certainly envisaged by the PSD). So there we have it. Instead of preparing an impact analysis before getting into the policy making detail, the discussion of almost three years in fact gave enough time for Member States to ensure that their control in the process would not be lost. Going down the route of a Directive, offered plenty of opportunity for gold-plating and other non-harmonised caveats. However, if the creation of SEPA was indeed the original and true purpose of this exercise (as claimed by the EC), a Directive was surely not the optimum way to achieving this, due to the risk of different interpretations and national gold-plating that would compromise the creation of harmonised pan-European payment schemes. Of course it is also worth noting that an approach involving less detailed and more principle-based rules would have allowed for greater Member State buy-in for a Regulation.

Some of the statements made in the PSD's IA on the expected benefits from this legislative intervention deserve particular attention. While the IA identifies that the cost of EU payment systems is around 3 per cent of GDP, it is also stated that 60–70 per cent of this total estimated cost is driven by the cost of cash.[17] However, neither the NLF proposal nor the final PSD text included any provision that would reduce the use of this inefficient and costly payment instrument. On the contrary the proposal, as well as the final PSD text, arguably have the perverse effect of further encouraging the use of cash, having inserted a specific provision aimed at giving consumers and businesses certain additional rights when placing and withdrawing cash.

And then there is the EC's estimate of a nirvana-like €50–100 billion of savings per year for businesses across the EU[18] due to the development of integrated electronic payment propositions, including electronic-invoicing.

Unfortunately, these impressive estimates are not backed by detailed empirical analysis, plus there is also the tiny issue that electronic-invoicing, or e-invoicing as it is generally known these days, is not actually a payment service nor does it in any way fall under the scope of the PSD. Further, the EC chose to state within the IA that 'the economy needs efficient, consumer-friendly, low-cost and safe payment and billing solutions to foster trade and growth'[19] – and who could disagree with this? However, it is never explained why it is a priority for billing solutions (used primarily between businesses) to be consumer-friendly – nor why indeed the EC mentions this at all in connection with the proposed payments law that is not in the least concerned with regulating this area?

In relation to the economic, environmental and social impacts of a legislative proposal the IA guidelines require a proper analysis of costs and benefits. Annex 7 of the PSD IA claims to address these points by identifying the distribution of impacts among different market stakeholders as well as including a cost-benefit analysis. However, this crucial section is very descriptive, falling short of any quantified empirical assessment of costs versus benefits – and equally lacks an assessment of the potential growth of administrative burden that would result from taking the legislative proposal forward.[20] At various instances in the analysis, it emerges that an increase in transaction costs (not monetised) is expected by the EC to be passed on to the user (the consumer!) as a consequence of the proposed rules, in the name of transparency. It is hard to see though how this can also be argued to be in line with the EC's overall objective of providing 'low-cost'[21] payment services in the EU.

The conclusion of all this is clear. The process of drafting the PSD and analysing the potential impacts of its proposed solutions was not done in strict accordance with the EC's own Better Regulation principles and the IA was arguably more of an exercise of post factum justification. Expectations of benefits from PSD proposed solutions were not grounded in market reality and the financial estimates were high level at best. Even though each of the individual objectives of the PSD made sense, the clear risk was that the sum of them would not necessarily be greater than each one on its own given that they sometimes conflicted with each other.

So, where would we go from here?

(2) From the NLF to the final text

Following the publication of the EC's proposal, it was now up to the EP and the Council to take the next step – which was to begin the ordinary legislative procedure (aka co-decision).

Let's stay with ideology for a moment and recall that any legislation in Europe strives to be principle-based. While the PSD initially did consider itself as exactly that, and thus helpful to the market and the EU body of laws, the final text, as we shall examine later in detail, went far beyond the level of principle and instead dived deep into technical details, resulting in a thick soup of hidden riddles and complexities. This was recognised by the EC itself which commented in its December 2007 DG Markt Newsletter that 'some of the 96 provision of the PSD might remain not clear enough or even ambiguous'.[22] One of the key questions, then, is whether this outcome was (1) a result of the EC going into too much technical and procedural detail in its legislative proposal; (2) a result of the changes that were made during the co-decision process in 2005–7; or (3) simply a reflection of the fact that it was always going to be bordering on the impossible to balance the EC's multiple regulatory objectives successfully within one text. The truth is, perhaps unsurprisingly, a combination of all of these elements.

Against this background, the next part of this Title looks closely at the evolution of the different PSD versions compared to the final result – the official text of December 2008 – and also gives an overview of some of the key components and characteristics of this final version, together with a flavour of the debate which led to certain outcomes. As very few actors in this play have lived through all those versions, this book brings something of a unique inside perspective – something that is crucial to be able to comprehend the real objectives behind some of the PSD's rather confusing and meandering sentences. This memory of how things really happened should hopefully help industry, the customer and national legislators, and supervisors in Europe to use the PSD in line with its original and laudable intentions – as a solid building block for the creation of the Single Payments Market in Europe.

Let the negotiations begin!

The following table (Table 4.2) shows the timeline and key events that marked the bumpy passage of the PSD through the co-decision process.

Once the final PSD proposal was out, the payments industry, still bearing the scars of the negotiation process up to this point, wasted no time in sharing its views with the key decision-makers. On the 27 January 2006, I took the proactive step of inviting all financial attachés of the Council to the European Banking Federation's offices in Brussels in order to give them a firsthand presentation on the PSD proposal, including its positives as well as its negatives and putting this all into

Table 4.2 The PSD's co-decision timeline

Date	EU institution	Key event
01 Dec 2005	Commission	PSD legislative proposal issued
01 Jan 2006	Council	Austrian presidency begins
13 Dec 2005	EP	Rapporteur appointed by EP Economic and Monetary Affairs Committee (Jean-Paul Gauzès, EPP)
28 Feb 2006	EP	Draft report by ECON
26 April 2006	ECB	Opinion provided (welcoming the initiative, suggesting consideration to alignment of scope with E-money Directive, expressing concern at possible delay in adoption and suggesting an option to carve out and fast-track 'the most important parts necessary for the successful implementation of SEPA')
01 July 2006	Council	Finnish presidency begins
13 Sep 2006	EP	Report adopted by ECON
21 Sep 2006	EP	Legislative report tabled in Plenary
28 Nov 2006	Council	Discussion in ECOFIN (noted progress and invited current and incoming presidencies to build on progress made with a view to reaching a swift agreement).
01 Jan 2007	Council	German Presidency begins
27 Mar 2007	Council	Discussion in ECOFIN (General approach agreed based on a presidency proposal for a series of compromise amendments concerning issues such as capital requirements for PIs, activities PIs may undertake, waiver of smaller PIs, waiver of some provisions in respect of low-value instruments)
24 April 2007	EP	Plenary agrees compromise text in first reading
01 July 2007	Council	Portuguese presidency begins
13 Nov 2007	Commission/ Council/ EP	Final legislative act
04 Dec 2007	Commission	Directive published in the Official Journal

the context of the ultimate objective, the creation of SEPA. After all, these decision-makers needed to know. This event was, as well as being positively received and hugely valuable to these decision makers at such an early stage of the process, something of a revolutionary initiative. The next morning saw a repetition of this session in the EP, where surrounded by EU flags in one of the official meeting rooms the industry took its chance to inform the EP's decision makers about the objective and details of the PSD, therefore doing its part towards a better Europe with better regulation.

Following the political process of appointing the Rapporteur and the so-called Shadow Rapporteurs (representatives of the other parties), the EP's attention moved to its first detailed review of the PSD text. It is fair to say that the initial reactions from the team of officials charged with navigating the text through the ECON committee were 'mixed'. They could easily relate to the ambition of the EC's proposals, and see how the initiative supported the Lisbon Agenda plus the SEPA initiative (which was at that time just staring to appear as a topic in its own right on the Parliament's radar). However, on seeing just how wide the EC's proposal went and how very deep it ventured into detail, they immediately got rather concerned about the technical viability of the whole proposal. As is often the case, the officials reached out informally for technical input and assistance from a broad range of stakeholders to confirm or allay their fears, including industry experts and Council officials, as well as the EC itself.

So what was in the PSD proposal that created all this excitement?

The PSD is divided into broad sections, called Titles (which, by the way, explains why this book also comes in Titles rather than ordinary chapters in case you were wondering). Title I covers scope and definitions; Title II the prudential framework for payment institutions; Title III conditions for transparency and information for payment services; Title IV the rights and obligations of users and providers of payment services; with the implementation measures and final provisions covered in Titles VI and VII. Let's begin our short tour of the text with Title I: Scope and Definitions.

Title I – a question of scope

Before we plunge into the depths of this Title, a quick background note from my side. Not content with one scope, this Directive effectively has four (not to mention a number of bonus hidden ones), all of which partly overlap. As you can imagine, this has been a major contributor to making a clear reading and understanding of the PSD hard to achieve. Here are some examples ...

One-size-fits-all ... or does it?

As sketched out in the EC's proposal, the one-size-fits-all approach consisted of a single (but not necessarily simple) set of provisions for all types of payment services. Initially, the view of the EP officials was to question whether indeed it was possible to follow this one-size fits all approach, or whether a radical change would be required whereby the whole text would need to be re-written into separate chapters dealing with different payment types. Proposing such a change would have seriously prolonged the process on the EP side given that it would have represented a 180-degree shift from the EC proposal. This was the moment in the PSD story where the one-size-fits-all approach perhaps came closest to being overturned, which would have changed the fate of many of us. In the end though, the EP team decided, albeit with some (well-placed) misgivings, that the original structure of the text as proposed by the EC could perhaps be made to work and turned instead to the challenge of working out precisely what caveats and escape valves needed to be incorporated into the wording to make sure that this approach did not become a straightjacket causing major damage to the payment industry and stifling innovation.

Thresholds, opt outs and currencies ... a terribly moving story

An important illustration of the volatility that critical building blocks of the Directive were undergoing at that time – the PSD's equivalent of moving tectonic plates – is reflected in the discussions around the value threshold. In the early drafts of the NLF the scope of the conduct of business (or COB) rules was limited to payment transactions up to a maximum value of €50,000. This was considered appropriate in alignment with the final threshold of Regulation 2560/2001, and indeed that same threshold would still live on in Regulation 924/2009 years later. NLF version 5 in November 2004 removed the threshold, while the official proposal of December 2005 again reintroduced this cap.

Following the lively discussions on this topic between lobbyists and the EC in the pre-publication proposal stage, the issue was again to receive significant attention during the discussions with the other two EU institutions. The fact that the limit had gone in, and been withdrawn more than once during the drafting process was essentially a reflection of the EC's uncertainty around this topic. In great part, this was due to the crossover impact of one of the other key debates on how – or indeed whether – to include payments services for corporate clients within the scope of the COB rules. There was a clear argument that much of the PSD was really designed for consumer protection purposes (that is, for retail payments), and that it was not necessary to include corporates in the same regime given their greater level of financial sophistication and negotiating power. This line of thinking was the main argument in favour of having a value limit in the PSD as it was assumed that the vast majority of payments over €50,000 would be made exclusively by corporates. The main problem with this approach was that the PSD, as we know, had plenty of other objectives besides consumer protection, including the setting of maximum execution times, promoting the adoption of more efficient means of payment and supporting SEPA. In the context of these other objectives, it made no sense at all to include a value limit. The SEPA schemes, as a matter of reference, were not planning to include value limits and, from a systems point of view, operating different execution time regimes depending purely on the size of a payment would have been completely impractical. Also, in practice corporates do of course make payments under €50,000 rather often.

So, on that basis, the only logical approach was to have no value limit in the PSD while at the same applying core PSD rules to all payments, even if performed on behalf of large businesses. The only problem with this approach was the very consumer-focused nature of certain liability provisions. Hence the compromise of the 'corporate opt-out' was born, whereby the default position in the text was for corporates to be treated like consumers, but contractual freedom would be granted within the text permitting different arrangements to be agreed between corporates and their banks/PSPs in certain areas. As a consequence, the final text defines that payment services of any amount are subject to rules laid down in the Directive but grants a number of corporate opt-out clauses (all of Title III and certain provisions in Title IV as laid down in article 51).

If things were not yet difficult enough to follow for the onlooker, they were to get more confusing still when discussions started on the scope of the PSD in terms of what currencies would be covered. NLF draft versions 1–3 defined that payment services in all national currencies of Member States should be covered by the COB rules. However, NLF version 4 of August 2004 significantly expanded the scope to all existing world currencies 'equalling the amount of EUR 50.000'.[23] This raised significant concerns in light of the fact that final settlement occurs in the country of currency, for example, US dollars settle in New York. This final settlement and thus the success of such a payment ultimately rests with the third country, and so is outside the scope of the EU's regulatory reach. Potential conflicts of law as well as operational problems with currencies not traded on the global foreign exchange market would have been the unintended outcome. The EC maintained this position as far as their final proposal of 2005, but the co-decision procedure was to result in the reintroduction of the limitation to payments in EU/EEA Member State currencies, in line with the Single Market policy – and we could all relax a little.

So what exactly are payment services, instruments, transactions, accounts ...?

After sorting out thresholds, corporate opt-outs and currencies the next big question was to pin down the actual substance that was being legislated – the payment services themselves. Unhelpfully in this context, the definition of 'payment service' was to go through its very own evolutionary process, continuing in fact to be something of a conundrum even today. A 'payment service' was for example defined in NLF version 3 as 'the execution of a payment transaction, the provision of a payment instrument or the holding of a payment account'. NLF version 4 reviewed this definition and established the concept of the Annex to provide an exhaustive list of payment services covered by the PSD. The final PSD text defines 'payment service' under Definition 3 of article 4 (the Annex) as comprising services such as deposit and withdrawal of cash, operation of payment accounts, direct debits, credit transfers, standing orders, card transactions, issuing and acquiring payment instruments[24] and money remittance.

Furthermore, the EC added to the concept of 'payment services' a number of ancillary definitions such as 'payment instrument', 'payment transaction' and 'payment account' – additions that did not really have the desired effect of advancing the clarity of the legal text. For example, somewhat confusingly the definition of 'payment transaction' is sometimes employed interchangeably with 'payment service' in the Directive text, but itself actually refers to something else, which is the act of 'placing, transferring or withdrawing of funds' (article 4 §5).

A further controversy arose around the topic of deposit taking and account provision due to the EC's artificial definition of a 'payment account' (article 4 §14), which is described as 'an account held in the name of one or more payment service users which is used for the execution of payment transactions'. The need for the definition in the first place, as opposed to simply referring to accounts, can primarily be traced back to the EC's decision to use the PSD as the vehicle to cover off the prudential licensing of non-bank PSPs (PIs) as already explained. In this context, the EC realised that in order to be able to provide 'money transmission' services, a PI might well need to be able to provide a basic level of 'account' for the purpose of briefly holding funds before paying them away as part of the execution of a payment transaction. Given that the COB rules in the PSD were to apply also to these entities, it became crucial to distinguish such basic account services, designed for the very temporary holding of funds as a by-product of the payment service being offered, from an account offered by a credit institution, given that the latter class of providers is of course also licensed to take deposits under the heavy-duty Capital Adequacy Directive. Thus the definition of a payment account needed to be sufficiently narrow so as not to imply that a non-bank PI had any right or ability to take or accept deposits, but not so narrow that when the term was applied to credit institutions it would imply a limitation of functionality on the accounts that they offer.

Finding this balance was to prove a challenge. When the EP finally got the chance to debate the EC's text, it was immediately realised that a danger in the wording of this key definition as proposed was that by referring to an account 'exclusively' used for payment transactions there was a risk that this could be seen by national legislators as requiring them to force their credit institutions to open a brand new suite of dedicated specialist 'payment accounts' on the basis that a current account today can of course be used not just for the purpose of making and receiving payments, even if for most clients this is its primary function and attraction. This concern was shared by the banking industry on the basis that it would clearly not be a true level playing field if the PSD forced banks to have to additionally create such special-purpose accounts. The outcome of the debate was that the word 'exclusively' was proposed for deletion by an EP amendment, and this sensible proposal was carried through into the final text.

All therefore seemed to be fine for now. Clearly common sense had won the day and everybody's attention moved away from this issue (though only temporarily as it would turn out!) and onto the myriad of other issues in the text that needed fixing.

So who is regulated by the PSD?

Still on the quest to understand the PSD's scope, another question to consider is 'who is going to be regulated'? The different types of

PSPs were initially subsumed in a definition of NLF versions 1–3 as follows: a PSP is 'a natural or legal person who provides payment services to a payment service user in the course of his business. Such a person can be either a credit institution, including an electronic money institution, or a payment institution'.[25] The final list of PSPs was then expanded to covers six types of providers, including the ECB and national central banks for activities outside their capacity as monetary or other public authority, and Member States/regional/local authorities acting outside their public authority mandate. It is worthwhile clarifying the two different terms used in this context: the category of Payment Service Providers, or PSPs, designates all of the providers listed above, while Payment Institutions, or PIs, are one type of Payment Service Provider. For anyone that is by now intrigued enough to go ahead and actually read the original PSD text (and I might need to add a health warning at this stage), this clarification will be of major help.

The flip side of the first question was 'who is going to benefit from the PSD's rules', meaning who are the respective payment service users, or PSUs? Of course the PSD has its central focus on protecting every type of user, consumers and businesses, which is exactly in line with the legacy of payment laws in Europe – for example, the Directive 97/5/EC on cross-border Credit Transfers and the Recommendation 97/489/EC on electronic payments within the Internal Market. As part of the evolution of the legislative drafting the EC also introduced the option for Member States to decide to treat 'micro-enterprises' as consumers under the Directive. Use of this derogation at national level was clearly going to be the cause of additional complexity, and would also prompt the question of how the status of micro-enterprises that grow to SME size level would be reviewed as the Directive text (article 4 (26)) defines a micro-enterprise as 'an enterprise, which *at the time of conclusion* of the payment service contract, is an enterprise as defined in Article 1 and Article 2(1) and (3) of the Annex to Recommendation 2003/361/EC'. However, including this derogation was to prove to be a key element of the political compromise.

Which countries and locations does the PSD cover?

In terms of territorial scope, things would again turn out to get rather complicated. NLF draft version 3 had defined the scope as covering payments where both the payee's and payee's PSPs are located in the EU. From NLF version 4 onwards, however, the Directive proposal aimed at covering not only transactions within the Single Market, composed of the EU 27 and the 3 EEA countries,[26] but also the so-called one-leg (or leg-out) transactions, meaning payments between the Single Market and the rest of the world. The justification for including these one-leg transactions harked back to the EC's misplaced assumption that payments were – or could be – priced in the same way that an actuary prices an insurance premium.

It was quickly pointed out by the banking industry that this was an unsustainable position on legal and practical grounds. After all, how could a bank or any other PSP operating outside the EU/EEA have its conduct regulated by an EU Directive? (the old 'extraterritoriality' argument) Additionally, how could an EU bank making a payment outside of the EU on behalf of a corporate client and being asked to route the payment though a long correspondent banking chain over which it has limited control or influence be held strictly liable for the same type of operational performance requirements (for example, maximum execution times) as those for an intra-EU payment using a dedicated payment system?

Fortunately, EP and Council realised that the unintended but inevitable outcome which would be the result here – a significant increase in prices plus potentially a major reduction in competition if banks and other PSPs decided to stop making payments for their clients to certain countries as they were not willing to carry this level of liability – was not in the in the interests of consumers or corporate clients and had little to do with the PSD's core goals of creating a single payments area *within* Europe.

Accordingly, the coverage of one-leg transactions under the PSD was reduced to a single article number 73, which deals with value-dating. Still, not all Member States (nor the EC of course) totally supported this compromise. This lead to a further compromise whereby this scope topic (plus the related issue of which currencies the PSD should cover) were expressly referenced within the PSD's review clause as aspects that the Payments Committee would be invited to reconsider when undertaking the scheduled review of the PSD in 2012 (which as an aside, and by strange coincidence, turns out to be the same year apparently predicted by the Mayans for the world to end!). As will be explained later in this book, however, a number of Member States would subsequently choose to anticipate the outcome of this 2012 review by indulging in a little gold-plating on this topic during their implementations of the PSD in 2009.

So, what is not covered by the PSD?

The concept of a 'negative scope' was introduced with NLF version 3 and initially covered the exclusion of cash and cheque payments.

The final PSD text would end up listing 15 areas where the PSD does not apply.

The full extent of these various 'negative scope' provisions was to gradually take shape. For example, some of them were included when it was realised that certain payment types were not meant to fall under the PSD's scope; for example cheques, bills of exchange, documentary trade products or money exchange. While on a political level the EC had always stressed that cash transactions would be excluded as part of the general policy of reducing cash in the European economy, the negative scope in this area only excludes direct person to person cash transactions. This opened the door for the provision in Title IV (article 71), which explicitly regulates cash placements on 'payment accounts'. While this approach – specific protection for cash placements – is not in line with Recommendation 97/489/EC on electronic payment instruments, it also shows the inconsistent nature of the EC's proceedings in this matter. The key political argument for reducing the use of cash is the fact that the 'costs of cash to the EU economy are estimated between €45bn to €70bn per annum ... [corresponding to] 0.4% to 0.5% of GDP'.[27] While these figures represent empirically observed estimates, it is worthwhile to compare them again to those figures stated by the EC (recall the IA where the EC estimated the cost of payments to equal 3 per cent of EU GDP, of which 60–70 per cent are represented by the cost of cash).

In other cases, additional exclusions were developed as those involved in drafting the text increased their understanding of the payments world, for example leading to the exclusion of certain actors involved in a payment chain that only provide technical infrastructure and/or communication services (e.g. SWIFT) rather than payment services. Another example here was the decision to exclude independent ATM providers, on the basis that users maintain their payment relationship with their account-holding bank, not with the independent ATM provider.

Finally, there were the cases where the view was taken that certain activities, while involving payments, should not be within the Directive's scope. Key examples of that would be payment transactions carried out between PSPs themselves or payment transactions between a parent undertaking and its subsidiary without any intermediary intervention by a third party PSP.

Title II. Payment institutions: a new player on the horizon

Despite many challenges on this point, the EC stuck firmly to its proposal to keep the creation of a new entity of PSPs included in the text, rather than following the alternative and often repeated suggestion of various stakeholders and government representatives to park this issue in a separate supervisory law. E-money institutions (ELMIs) were given their very own e-money Directive (EMD), so why not do the same with PIs? But the circumstances have to be considered. With FATF SRVI[28] having been around since 2001[29] the EC was already late in complying and, running out of time, went for the practical approach of catching two fish with one fly. Of course, this was not exactly how the decision was presented to the onlooker who instead was told that in line with the Lisbon Agenda's goal to create the most striving and competitive business arena in Europe, the creation of new, non-bank, PSPs was a necessity to bring a fresh push for competition. After all, this entire PI story also created confusion in terms of the key objective of the PSD, which was – at least originally – supposed to be SEPA. Still, now that the elephant (or fish?) was confirmed as being firmly in the room, let's take a close look at it.

A special part of the PSD was reserved for these new kids on the block – the PIs. In the first legislative drafts in 2004 the EC opted for a very light touch regulatory regime by which PIs would be allowed to move funds on behalf of customers without any legal obligation to fulfil operational or risk-related capital requirements. Even the official EC proposal of 2005 considered it sufficient for a PI to present a business plan, tentative budget and administrative/accounting procedures, 'which would allow the presumption'[30] that such an entity operates soundly. In the absence of any objective risk analysis, the EC considered that a pure payment activity did not entail risks at a level that could potentially become systemic. Rather to the contrary the EC felt that 'the new license will increase the overall stability of the payment system ...'[31] and argued in return that there was a lack of empirical evidence that would prove that these non-bank players actually were risky.

The ECB did not buy into this rationale of light-touch regime and expressed serious concern over the lack of consideration of different risk categories and weightings in this context,[32] recalling in addition that for any payment services performed, banks are in fact subject to specific capital requirements as a result of the operational risk that is inherent to such services.[33] The Eurosystem also recalled its clear responsibilities for the stability, viability and smooth functioning of payment systems (today anchored in Article 127.2 of the Treaty on the Functioning of the EU/Lisbon Treaty) but did not get very far with its message. After all, empirical evidence was actually available with regard to the riskiness of some non-bank PSPs and the detrimental effect this had already had in certain cases on some of the poorest levels of society. Shared with the EC, this evidence nevertheless remained largely ignored as Europe was trying to build its image of a competition striving new economy.[34]

The reason for all this controversy was really down to the nature of the PI regime itself. So let us examine what activities PIs were allowed to perform and against which supervisory conditions.

The EC's plan: PIs should be permitted to provide all payment services even though they might have another key business focus in parallel. They should also be allowed to provide so-called 'payment accounts' to customers, extend credit for up to 12 months, have access to all payment systems around Europe as well as operate these by themselves, and all of this in the absence of any underlying capital requirements.

The outcome: PIs can indeed now offer all payment services, as stand-alone PIs or as hybrid businesses (for example, a telecom company can offer payment services in parallel to air time).[35] Open access to payment systems has been enforced as a requirement, with the exclusion of payment systems designated under Directive 98/26/EC (Settlement Finality) – a win for the Eurosystem. PIs can operate 'payment accounts' and extend credit of up to 12 months (a scary prospect for some Member States). However, any funds received in relation to a 'payment account' held by a PI, even though these look and feel rather like deposits, are not labelled as such. The reason? Because otherwise the strict rules of Directive 2006/48/EC[36] would have to apply to PIs, which would have meant that they needed the same capital adequacy as their best friends, the banks. This was, as you can imagine, rather like calling something 'green' when everyone really knew it was 'yellow' (and this was in fact confirmed verbatim by EC services).

While PI payment accounts have to be 'exclusively used for payment transactions'[37], the potentially indeterminate lodgement of funds with a PI pending their disbursement could subject the payment service user (or PSU) to additional risks, which would then reflect on the overall security of the system and consequently could endanger users' trust in the payments industry.[38] Through negotiation, additional measures were thankfully introduced that at least require some safeguarding or ring fencing of funds received in case of PIs that run a 'hybrid' business. For funds that are held longer than D + 1 (date of receipt of the payment order + 1 business day), PIs are required to deposit them with a bank, invest them in liquid low-risk assets,[39] or insure them. It should be noted though that some scholars would argue that PIs holding funds any longer than for immediate disbursement will create incompatibilities with EC banking law,[40] which makes the D + 1 timeline look somewhat liberal.

As a last, and rather necessary, measure, PIs were eventually subjected to some operational capital requirements to ensure a minimum buffer in case things did go wrong. Again, the perception that certain payment activities are less risky than others lingered on in the debate; for example the EC considered money remittance to be low risk and hence defined an initial capital of €20,000, while the provision of other payment activities, such as issuing a payment instrument (for example, a card) were considered more risky, and requiring up to €125,000 of initial capital. An interesting footnote here relates – again – to payment accounts. Only payment services 1 and 2 of the Annex include the operation of a payment account, while for example money remittance or card issuance/acquiring are listed as standalone services provided in the absence of a payment account (as otherwise this would have been stated in the annex). With the benefit of hindsight, this does slightly call into question why we felt the need to discuss for years the requirement for a neutral type of payment account in order to allow PIs to also offer payment services, if such an account is apparently not a key necessity for the business model of many existing types of PIs, such as money remitters.

As an insider's aside to the capital requirement discussions on PIs, it is interesting to observe that throughout the negotiation in EP and Council the UK had strongly opposed the establishment of capital requirements and even in the HMT consultation on the PSD (2007) it is considered 'that reliance on sound internal procedures and safeguarding requirements is a more proportionate way of managing the types of risk posed by payment institutions than capital requirements'.[41] Pitted against countries like Germany and France, who argued for much more substantial capital requirements on the basis that PIs take similar risks to credit institutions, the UK managed to line up sufficient allies from (mainly) Eastern European countries to achieve a final outcome comprising relatively low own-fund requirements. Whether these provisions will ultimately turn out to be sufficiently consumer protective remains to be seen.

A final building block for PIs was to develop the rules for setting up and operating a payments business. PIs would need to be registered or authorised and supervised by their national 'competent authority'. The latter is a great term for designating something important but unclear in its true nature – 'What or who is a competent authority?' Additionally, the fact that 'competent authorities' can waive authorisation procedures for PIs with smaller transaction volumes[42] (which restricts them to the provision of payment services in their home country) attracted significant criticism during negotiation, as it not only encourages forum shopping in relation to the degree of supervisory strictness but could even give the appearance of 'rewarding criminals operating illegal payment services in the underground economy'.[43] In the same vein, the fact that PIs that have operated in the past can just continue to do so without getting registered at all until April 2011 was another surprise and is rather inconsistent – the whole point was to regulate them. In addition, it also seemed rather odd from a level playing field perspective.

Furthermore, the passporting rights of PIs, while important from a competition perspective, do not fall under the integrated supervisory framework, which runs the risk of leading to future problems with mutual recognition, the interpretation of home country rules and the treatment of PIs by different types of 'competent authorities'. More on that topic to follow later on.

Having gently highlighted the multiple risks that could be associated with such a lightly regulated new provider, the banking industry very early on made the decision not to interfere more than absolutely necessary in this Title during its intensely political negotiation process. The only area of their intervention was around article 28 – access to payment systems – an area that would not only impact PIs but also existing bank networks and schemes such as the international card schemes and even the SEPA schemes.

At Member State level, discussions continued to be fervent and controversial around the whole PI topic. They were at one point even to lead to a proposal by the German financial attachés involved in the discussions within the Council to split Title II from the rest of the provisions and, as suggested above, draft a separate supervisory legislation for PIs. Suffice to say that this plan did not come to fruition and EP and Council continued for far too long to debate the pros and cons of Title II, which unfortunately meant that insufficient capacity was left to focus properly on the critical workability of Titles III and IV, something that providers and users of payment services would have to pay for in the future.

Title III – Conduct of business rules part 1

This part of the PSD is in essence a rather substantial list of things that users of payment services should be informed about before, during and after their payment transactions. Interesting really, given that the IA didn't identify the need for further information requirements beyond those stipulated in existing Community laws. There was also no evidence of market failure in this area requiring the imposition of such a comprehensive and detailed set of rules as defined in this Title. In addition, the degree of harmonisation achieved is also questionable as Member States are entitled to apply derogations or discretions in six[44] instances.

It is important to observe at this point that the story of the negotiations of these information requirements proved to be difficult and complex. For example, much debate took place early on in proceedings around the apparently innocuous question as to whether the various elements of information that a PSP was being asked to deliver to a user should be required to be 'provided' or 'made available' to the user by the PSP. At a quick glance, these terms sounded quite similar. However, getting the right wording here was more than a semantic nicety and in fact rather critical given the might of the liability provisions in the PSD which are always poised to swing into action if a PSP fails to meet his/her duties on any matter. In this case, the concern in the mind of the industry was that the 'provision' of information could be said to imply not only that it has been dispatched, but also that it has been successfully received (and processed!) by the recipient. Proving this in a way that would be able to satisfy a court of law would of course be extremely difficult if not impossible. 'Make available' on the other hand is a less strict requirement in the sense that it implies that the PSP has indeed given the user access to the relevant information in a certain agreed way, but cannot be held accountable for whether the user actually chooses to take advantage of this access.

The debate also moved on to the question of what was meant by 'durable medium', another term used in the text in connection with the provision of information. Given the PSD's supposed modernisation intentions, it would have been somewhat bizarre and indeed less than eco-friendly if all information was required to be sent out on paper, rather than taking advantage of modern alternatives such as email and the Internet.

Fortunately, a reasonably balanced outcome was achieved on both these topics during the course of the co-decision debate. On the 'provide versus make available' dilemma, both terms were in the end used in different places within the information requirements set of rules striking a balance between the various approaches that needed to be adopted in respect of the two terms. On the durable medium point, the EC was to confirm that a variety of modern media could be used to satisfy this requirement, allowing the various forests in the EU to expel a collective sigh of relief. However, a slight sting in the tale came in the shape of a derogation negotiated by some countries that would allow them to require PSPs to provide a monthly statement on paper to their PSUs (and for free, of course). So, two steps forward and one step back ... as usual.

It is worth noting, referring also back to the IA statement on Community law above, that this was not the first law that introduced rules on information provision. As an example, if a credit institution would like to provide a payment service in Euro via the Internet, four different EU legislations covering information requirements now apply: (1) the PSD, (2) Directive 2000/31/EC on Electronic commerce, (3) Directive 2002/65/EC on distance marketing of financial services and (4) Regulation 2009/924/EC on cross-border Euro payments. The sum of these laws represents more than 40 different information requirements – a complexity that does not really reconcile with the EC's stated intention of simplifying Community legislation. While the EC had notified in its Financial Services White Paper of 2005 that 'a broad study will be carried out in 2008 to review possible inconsistencies and appropriateness of information requirements in the existing EC rules',[45] the PSD was no attempt to fight this problem at its roots.

Such information overload would not only be disproportionate but also result in additional administrative burden, diverting PSP resources from investments in payment services and improved customer services. After the PSD went live, this was one of the first conclusions that had to be admitted. So many letters, carefully drafted with the help of armies of lawyers, had effectively ended up in the bin pretty quickly (with some users fishing them out of the said receptacle post-November 09 to understand what was suddenly going on, but more of that later).

Title IV – Conduct of business rules part II

Title IV of the PSD is designed as a set of procedures to be followed by all PSPs when providing payment services. The text aims to cover all relevant rules, starting with the user placing a payment order and ending with the receipt of funds at the beneficiary side, complemented by various types of information as elaborated under Title III. The rules can be subsumed under three headings: (1) rules relating to the authorisation of payment transactions, (2) operational rules around payment execution and (3) liability rules.

Even though the PSD governs the user-to-provider relationship, certain provisions of this Title, which in many ways constitutes the heart of the PSD, also touch upon the inter-PSP (or inter-bank) space (something not every bank is aware of or keen to accept).

Turning to the detail, it is worth mentioning that, not surprisingly, the scope of provisions under this Title underwent major modifications throughout the drafting and negotiation process. For example, while NLF draft versions 1–4 were designed to treat consumer and business users as equals, NLF version 5 (Nov 2004) introduced a specific definition of 'corporate user', subsuming all types of business users exceeding a certain defined size as per an existing EU Recommendation.[46] There is an argument that forcing these very small businesses – so-called micro-enterprises – to be treated as consumers, in cases where Member States make use of the derogation in article 51 §3 of the final PSD, would limit their choice with respect to tailor-made payment and information services. On the other hand a case could be made for consumers and micro-enterprises sharing a similar degree of information asymmetry, which could be addressed by the PSD rules. However, what is clear is that the situation is quite different for larger more sophisticated corporate customers that sometimes even operate their own in-house bank. This is why only *some* articles of the PSD should have by default applied to larger business users, while leaving the remaining articles out for scope for these users, instead of requiring providers to agree with these businesses on an opt-out of certain articles, as is the case in the final text.[47]

Rules around payment authorisation

Let us now turn to some of the key provisions in Title IV, starting with the rules around authorisation and execution of payments. In the spirit of consumer protection, these rules allow PSPs to agree the procedure by which their PSUs provide their consent to a payment transaction. Failure of the PSP to obtain consent will mean that a transaction is unauthorised. The method of agreeing consent and authorisation can be defined on a contractual basis with all types of customers, and even more freedom applying in the case of corporate clients (which becomes important in the context of related rules concerning refunding unauthorised payments as explained below) given that this provision (article 54) is one of the famous 'corporate opt-out' articles.

Continuing with our focus on consumers, authorisation is important because if the user denies having authorised a specific payment (and there might certainly be some users that could consider abusing this legal protection) the PSP must prove that the transaction was authenticated, accurately recorded, entered in the accounts and not affected by technical breakdown. If that wasn't enough, the options for PSPs to prove whether his user actually says the truth are significantly curtailed because 'the use of a payment instrument recorded by the PSPs shall in itself not necessarily be sufficient to prove either that the payment transaction was authorised by the payer or that the payer acted fraudulently or failed with intent or gross negligence to fulfil one or more of his obligations under article 56'. In this context it is also interesting to note that the concept of gross negligence is not known to all Member States' legal systems[48] and so the implementation of this article on a word-for-word basis will not give the same practical result.

For unauthorised payments the PSD then requires the payer's PSP to refund 'to the payer *immediately* the amount of the unauthorised payment transaction and, where applicable restores the debited payment account to the state in which it would have been had the unauthorised payment transactions not taken place'. In the event that the payer is a consumer and there is no suspicion of possible fraud, the EC has the clear view that this immediate refund obligation takes effect as soon as the PSP has received the refund request. Fortunately, given the larger amounts involved, and combined with the granting of the 'corporate opt-out' for article 54 §2 second sub, it is accepted that in the case of a corporate transaction there is a greater need for investigation into the circumstances of the claim before any refund is considered.

But we are still not finished here. The PSD also gives a right of refund in case a transaction is initiated by or through the payee, for example, by a direct debit or a card transaction. In those instances, consumers (this provision can be disapplied in the context of corporates and actually has to be in relation to SEPA Business to Business Direct Debits) will benefit from an 8 weeks refund period starting from the date of debit upon fulfilment of two cumulative conditions (see PSD article 62): '(a) the authorisation did not specify the exact amount of the payment transaction when the authorisation was made; and (b) the amount of the payment transaction exceeded the amount the payer could reasonably have expected taking into account his previous spending pattern, the conditions in his framework contract and relevant circumstances of the case.'

This refund rule will resurface again in Title VI and VII when we look at the discussions around SEPA as well as the challenges that some countries will have with the consequences of such a regime in practice.

Moving on, the PSD also established almost down to the cent what the liability should be for a user who has for example lost his credit card or who has been negligent enough to leave his online banking portal open and his PIN lying around in a public place while going for a coffee, allowing others to skim the details to move money illegally. For those purposes a maximum liability of €150 is applied to the user, while the provider has to bear the full liability and can only waive this obligation if he can actually prove that the PSU acted fraudulently or failed his obligation to notify the PSP with intent or as a consequence of gross negligence.

In light of these strict provisions it was however welcomed that PSPs can at least opt-out of this provision with their non-consumer PSUs, as risk premiums associated with business users, who tend to execute larger payments, would have been too high to make the continuation of the service viable. Here an example would be an employee of a big corporate who commits internal fraud using the online payment system of the company. In case the company claims that the payment transaction under dispute was not authorised, the PSP might have little practical chance to prove that a particular employee has committed fraud.

Operational rules in the PSD

As part of the PSD's deep dive into the world of payment services, specific rules are provided in order to define exactly how payment orders are received and how long payments should be allowed to travel before they reach their destination, what principle should apply payment transaction charging (?each PSU should pay their own PSP) and what rights and obligations apply in case of initiating payments as well as in the context of obtaining a refund.

One of the primary goals of the EC was of course to push the payment industry to deliver much faster average (and just as importantly maximum) execution times for payments within the Single Market. The starting point here was the very mixed situation reported in Title III of this book, which left the EC convinced that for cross-border payments much needed to be done. Brandishing the output from the various surveys conducted in the previous few years, designed to test the success of the 1997 Directive and of Regulation 2560/2001, the EC launched itself into the PSD drafting process armed with the clear objective to improve things greatly in this field. In the EC's eyes, their intervention on this topic needed to be far more radical than they had attempted with previous legislations. A timeline for the full end-to-end execution process, rather than just the time taken to get a payment from bank A to Bank B, was required. Consequently, there was a determination to remove float (the practice of sitting on funds for a while – effectively lending them – before making them available to the customer) at the receiving end of the payment, which was still popular in some markets and had not been ruled out by the 1997 Directive.

Additionally, the proposal emerged to regulate the moment at which the clock had to start ticking in terms of the execution time for a payment. By this stage, it looked like there was consensus between the EC, EP and Council that the right goal was to set an initial maximum execution time of three or possibly four days, with the goal to push this down to one day in due course, giving the market time to progressively adjust to the new regime. So, to move this plan ahead, it also needed to be clear how to establish the first Day, or 'D'. For the banks, the answer to this question was easy – 'D' obviously referred to the Day of Acceptance of the payment instruction. 'Day of Acceptance' was a well known term, referenced in fact in the 1997 Cross-Border Credit Transfers Directive, where 'D' was essentially defined as the day by when a payment instruction had been received and various checks had been completed, such as whether the payer had sufficient funds and/or whether there were any fraud or money-laundering concerns. However, the EC, backed strongly by many elements within the EP, had an inherent distrust of this concept being re-used for their new Directive. Their argument was that the 'Day of Acceptance' concept gave the banks – and other PSPs – far too much licence for inefficiency – as it would not in theory prevent a bank from receiving its client's payment instruction but not acting on it for days. Arguments came back from the banking industry clarifying that while this was indeed a theoretical possibility such a bank would hardly remain competitive and hence would not be able to actually pursue such a practice. This largely fell on deaf ears, leaving decision makers more determined than ever to establish a new and much tighter definition. Accordingly the EC proposed an approach under which the execution time cycle would start running automatically from the day on which the payer's payment instruction was 'received' by his PSP.

At first sight, this new suggestion sounded sensible – what a nice and clear approach! However, when EP officials started to look at the text more closely, taking soundings from the industry as to how such a provision could be made to work, it rapidly became clear that this seemingly simple approach masked a wide range of practical issues which would need to be addressed with skilled drafting if this critical component was to be operable. The issues included the fact that payments are not typically made on a 24 x 7 x 365 basis – most payment systems operate on weekdays (excluding bank holidays) and only during working hours (such as 9.00–4.00pm). At the same time, a payment instruction can be received potentially on any day and at any hour (think for example of someone undertaking their internet banking over the weekend or late at night). Additionally, it also had to be factored in that not all payment instructions are intended for immediate execution, as they might relate to a requirement for execution on a future date.

Worse still, further drafting challenges arose courtesy of the EC's desire to include one set of rules for all the different payment types caught under the scope of the Directive – the now famous 'one-size-fits-all approach'. As we know, the characteristics of a credit transfer are very different from those of a direct debit, and different again in comparison to a card payment. In the first case, it is generally always the payer who sends the payment instruction to her/his PSP, but this is not at all true for the other two 'pull instruments' where the request to make the payment will in fact be initiated by the payee and 'received' first by the payee's PSP not the payer's PSP. Resolving this significant set of drafting issues was to lead to much frustration on all sides and many drafting discussions involving EP officials, EC, the payment industry and later the Council under the German Presidency.

Even at the 11th hour when the EP had already agreed its report on the text and the Council was putting together its final package of changes, negotiations and discussions continued behind closed doors on this topic. One particular key meeting involving the EC, the Presidency and selected experts from the payment industry is worth mentioning. The (clearly by now very nerdy) individuals involved in these negotiations arranged to be locked up in a four hour trilateral meeting, with the aim of reaching agreement on the drafting of certain provisions so that they could meet the political objective of not allowing banks to take advantage of any vagueness in the way the start of the execution cycle was defined, but at the same time to resolve the various practical issues mentioned above. During this meeting the EC kept on advancing rather left field additional concepts, including the idea that the PSD should really talk about the 'point in time' of receipt not just the 'day', thus requiring the clock to start running immediately. This of course was slightly at odds with the already established principle of an execution time to be counted in days – meaning that what mattered really was whether the receipt happened during a processing day (or business day as it is called in the text) – not at what precise moment in time the receipt had actually occurred. Fortunately, what came out of that key meeting was a set of drafting principles on how the concept of starting the execution time with receipt could be made to work – striking a reasonable balance between the various different issues that had been at play. In the event, the reference to the 'point in time' of receipt was to survive into the final text, but its precise meaning is not all that relevant in a time-cycle counted in days.

Turning back again to SEPA, it was also necessary that the PSD would support efficient automated processing of payments by ensuring that the new liability regime did not penalise banks who had accurately processed a payment based on the account number of the payee as provided by the payer. This contrasted with the former position in some EU countries, really dating back to the time when payment processing was not automated in the way it is today, whereby the name of the account holder was deemed to have legal precedence over the account number itself. In turn this meant that banks in those countries should, in theory at least, have to check that name and number matched before crediting the payee's account – something that was simply not compatible with the future vision of a single domestic payments area and increasingly faster execution times. In this context, article 74 – which allows a PSP to specify a 'unique identifier' that will be used as the basis for processing a payment – can be considered as a true lobbying success. For SEPA credit transfers and direct debits, the relevant 'unique identifier' is the International Bank Account Number (IBAN).

The good news here is that the IBAN is a more reliable way of storing and representing account numbers than other methods. Unlike domestic account number structures, where in some cases multiple formats are acceptable and some information may be omitted (for example, the sub-account number or Unterkontonummer in Germany), each country's IBAN is in a single format and includes a special check digit to ensure the integrity of the rest of the IBAN and its link to one, unique, account number. It is therefore a much better standard than many previous methods of referring to bank accounts, for example the four pieces of information used in France, the single account number in the Netherlands and the bank code/account number structures used in Germany and the UK. Given the benefits of using an IBAN, the initial drafts of the article 74 provision in fact referred only to the IBAN rather than the more open definition of a 'unique identifier' which ended up in the final PSD text. The reason for the broader approach being adopted in the end was the realisation that, ahead of migration to SEPA, even within the Eurozone usage of national account number structures would continue for some time (maybe a chance was missed here in terms of pushing SEPA migration forward). Additionally, there was the need to cater for non-bank PIs who would of course not typically route their payment transactions based on IBANs. As the final result, the term 'unique identifier' was coined, leaving every PSP to agree with their PSUs what this would mean in practice for each payment type. Going back to the benefits that the IBAN provides relative to many existing national bank account structures, particularly its potential to reduce errors due to the presence of the check digit, this of course does represent one further benefit that will be realised when moving over to SEPA based instruments.

Once a payment is successfully executed in accordance with the maximum time lines and using the appropriate unique identifier, the next steps legislated in the PSD are the procedures that apply for transaction charging and rules around receipt, availability and the crediting of funds. In this context, let us remind ourselves of Annex 4 and 14, which are reflected in the following provisions. First of all there is the question around charging – in other words, who is entitled to charge and for what? The PSD is very clear in this respect as it stipulates that the sending and receiving PSUs should be responsible for paying their respective PSPs under the 'sharing principle', while at the same time the full amount of the payment transaction should always arrive at the payee's PSP.

Even though this might sound a little complicated, it is actually quite a simple rule. The PSD aims to ensure that the payer that wants to (or is obliged to) send a certain sum to the payee, let's say €1000, can place his payment order knowing that his PSP will send the full amount of €1000 to his payee's PSP. The payer will separately be charged, directly or indirectly, by his own PSP for sending the payment. For consumers, such charges are often included as part of their account maintenance fees, while for business/corporate clients a separate payment processing fee is more common.

Once the €1000 payment is on its way, no intermediary bank (or other PSP) is allowed to touch this principal amount until it arrives at the beneficiary bank/payee's PSP. From there onwards, it is left to the payee's PSP and his PSU to agree on how much and in which way the payee will be charged for receiving this payment. The guiding principle here is that no deductions should be applied before crediting the amount received unless these have been specifically agreed with the customer in line with PSD article 67 §2 (and from experience consumers should not expect deductions).

This sharing of charges – please note that it does not mean 'shared' in the sense that charges between sending and receiving PSP would need to be split 50/50 – introduces a fundamental departure from the principle in the 1997 Cross-Border Credit Transfers Directive, which to the contrary took the view that the favoured process should be for the payer to pay all charges and hence for the payment always to be applied in full to the payee's account by his PSP without (ever) triggering any additional charging or deductions.

For the banking industry, this complete volte face by the EC was (and still is) a little hard to grasp as it requires a radical change of practice in the context of both inter-bank and customer-to-bank procedures. For example, thanks to the PSD, the usage of the payment message charge codes is now limited to 'SHA' (sharing of charges between sending and receiving PSP), removing the OUR option (the payer pays all charges) as well as the BEN option (the payee pays all charges). In addition, inter-bank procedures that used to focus on reimbursement of the payee bank by the payer bank (via an OUR claim) have needed to cease. Payee banks do not and cannot ask for reimbursement by the sending side as they are now to seek compensation from their own customer instead. We will return to this topic again in Title VII, as this change of principles was destined to become one of the biggest PSD-transition-induced headaches for transaction banking in Europe.

Upon arrival of the funds (on a business day), a payee PSP, as previously highlighted, is obliged to credit the funds to its customer's ('payment') account and make them immediately available. In other words, if the payee holds an interest-bearing account, the funds that are credited should be able to gain interest from the day they arrive, but the payee should also have the choice to instantly use the money for other purchases or withdrawal. This rule, already highlighted in Annex 4, was clearly designed to remove inefficiencies and non-transparent procedures and will greatly benefit customers, but at the same time of course reduces the revenue of banks that in some instances were making money by lending or investing funds received before crediting them to their payees.

And finally, the PSD caters for refund rights (articles 62 and 63), which are crucial for the effective implementation of SEPA Direct Debits. As explained earlier, these rules needed to be harmonised, in particular regarding the timeframe during which a PSU can ask for a refund, to ensure coherence of rights and legal certainty across Europe. Due to the freedom given to PSPs under article 86 'to grant more favourable terms' there is however still a possibility that the eight week refund timeline for authorised transactions as defined in article 63 could be extended, creating potential inconsistencies at a pan-European level. Furthermore, Euro country domestic direct debits could compete with the SEPA scheme in case refund timelines to PSUs are longer than the eight weeks, which would create difficulties for the overall political project of migrating those payments to SEPA. Additionally, it should be noted that the PSD's refund rules also apply to all other electronic payment instruments that allow initiation by or through the payee. This therefore includes credit cards transactions, which of course already had a well-functioning chargeback process – being the method used for refunding all or part of a settled transaction to the cardholder, for example if he is overcharged or if goods are not delivered. The chargeback mechanism ensures that consumers with suspect transactions on their credit card, such as those that could trigger article 62, can resolve any problems through their card provider, rather than having to deal with the suppliers directly. The PSP is also protected as it has a method of recourse to the payee, as laid down in the card scheme rules. The PSP should therefore not end up unfairly out of pocket. Due to the existence of this well working process, it has never been really clear why the PSD felt the need to impose its own rules in this area.

Beyond those concerns, the approach taken by the EC went (unsurprisingly) much further than the identified SEPA harmonisation requirement and introduced a strict liability framework under which the refund liability is fully placed on the payer's PSP. While this makes sense at a practical level from the payer's point of view, it is odd to pull the PSP into the underlying business relationship between payer and payee (this is not its business at all). In addition, the burden of proof is again shifted from the claimant (payer) to the payer's PSP, significantly changing current legal practice in a number of countries such as, for example, the UK.

Liability rules in the PSD

In addition to the operational rules expressed in this Title, the PSD also introduces a comprehensive liability web for payment service provision in Europe. PSP liabilities cover four broad areas: liability for distribution of a payment instrument (article 57), liability for unauthorised transactions (article 61), liability for non-execution or defective execution (article 75) and burden of proof (article 59).

Having touched upon the specific liability scenario in the case of refunds above, the following section will highlight the overall liability shift that is triggered by the PSD. The EC initially intended to stipulate end-to-end strict liability on the payer's PSPs for the execution of payments within Europe (and in fact, as mentioned earlier at one point they contemplated extending this principle even to 'one-leg' payments). Placing liability on the PSP regardless of the circumstances and of their own actual culpability is rather in conflict with the fundamental principle of equity, which can, for example, be found in English law. While the concept of liability linked to one's own fault is fully accepted, the proposal here was to go much further than that, making the payer's PSP liable for the successful execution of a payment, right up to the crediting of the payee. The rationale advanced for this view was that from a consumer perspective it was reasonable to expect a bank/PSP to offer this protection on the basis that this would appropriately motivate the bank/PSP to ensure that nothing did go wrong, and also that the operation of the law of large numbers would mean that only relatively few transactions would actually go wrong and hence the liability involved could surely be factored into the bank's/PSP's pricing strategy (yet another instance of the EC drawing dubious parallels with the insurance industry). Aside from the potential lack of equity it is questionable how the imposition of 'strict' liability for matters that are clearly outside the PSP's remit would reconcile with other Community legislation and with consolidated jurisprudence of EU Member States regarding the assessment of responsibilities of a third party.

Other factors that badly needed to be given much more attention before finalising any requirements in this area included the potential implications should such an extreme consumer-protection measure be also applied to corporate-initiated payments, given the large sums involved. The EC additionally thought about requiring PSPs to cover any consequential loss, another potential legal can of worms. And finally, there was the need to consider the different functions performed by the payer's PSP in, say, a direct debit versus his role in a credit transfer.

After a strong debate during the co-decision process thanks to significant opposition by a number of Member States as well as considerable lobbying by the banking industry for a workable proposal on this critical issue, the final article 75 read as follows (see Table 4.3):

Table 4.3 Article 75 of the PSD

Article 75
Non-execution or defective execution
1. Where a payment order is initiated by the payer, his payment service provider shall, without prejudice to Article 58, Article 74(2) and (3), and Article 78, be liable to the payer for correct execution of the payment transaction, unless he can prove to the payer and, where relevant, to the payee's payment service provider that the payee's payment service provider received the amount of the payment transaction in accordance with Article 69(1), in which case, the payee's payment service provider shall be liable to the payee for the correct execution of the payment transaction.

(continued)

Table 4.3 Continued

Where the payer's payment service provider is liable under the first subparagraph, he shall without undue delay refund to the payer the amount of the non-executed or defective payment transaction and, where applicable, restore the debited payment account to the state in which it would have been had the defective payment transaction not taken place.

Where the payee's payment service provider is liable under the first subparagraph, he shall immediately place the amount of the payment transaction at the payee's disposal and, where applicable, credit the corresponding amount to the payee's payment account.

In the case of a non-executed or defectively executed payment transaction where the payment order is initiated by the payer, his payment service provider shall regardless of liability under this paragraph, on request, make immediate efforts to trace the payment transaction and notify the payer of the outcome.

2. Where a payment order is initiated by or through the payee, his payment service provider shall, without prejudice to Article 58, Article 74(2) and (3), and Article 78, be liable to the payee for correct transmission of the payment order to the payment service provider of the payer in accordance with Article 69(3). Where the payee's payment service provider is liable under this sub-paragraph, he shall immediately re-transmit the payment order in question to the payment service provider of the payer.

   In addition, the payment service provider of the payee shall, without prejudice to Article 58, Article 74(2) and (3), and Article 78, be liable to the payee for handling the payment transaction in accordance with its obligations under Article 73. Where the payee's payment service provider is liable under this subparagraph, he shall ensure that the amount of the payment transaction is at the payee's disposal immediately after that amount is credited to the payee's payment service provider's account.

   In the case of a non-executed or defectively executed payment transaction for which the payee's payment service provider is not liable under the first and second subparagraphs, the payer's payment service provider shall be liable to the payer. Where the payer's payment service provider is so liable he shall, as appropriate and without undue delay, refund to the payer the amount of the non-executed or defective payment transaction and restore the debited payment account to the state in which it would have been had the defective payment transaction not taken place.

   In the case of a non-executed or defectively executed payment transaction where the payment order is initiated by or through the payee, his payment service provider shall, regardless of liability under this paragraph, on request, make immediate efforts to trace the payment transaction and notify the payee of the outcome.

3. In addition, payment service providers shall be liable to their respective payment service users for any charges for which they are responsible, and for any interest to which the payment service user is subject as a consequence of non-execution or defective execution of the payment transaction.

The article is well worth repeating here in full – and reading very closely – as it is in its own small way a perfect case-study of how convoluted the drafting of some of the PSD's articles had to be in the end in order to accommodate the consequences of the one-size-fits-all approach covering all possible payment types and scenarios within one text.

In terms of the key elements that had to be discussed in minute detail between the banking industry and the legislators in arriving at this particular text, it is worth highlighting some of the measures that had to be incorporated to make the result (more-or-less) workable.

Most significantly, the principle of primary liability on the sending bank for a credit transfer has been faithfully maintained to keep the EC happy. However, it is clear now that this liability terminates at the point where the funds have been successfully delivered to the payee's PSP (still the payer's PSP does have the burden to prove that a subsequent problem was indeed caused by the payee's bank/PSP before the liability transfers across). Equally, it is made clear that the primary liability of the payer's PSP is to the payer and for the payee's PSP to the payee (read that sentence again – honestly it does make sense!). The issue that the payer's PSP is still nevertheless essentially being asked to bear liability for the actions of all parties in the payment chain (including therefore any intermediaries or clearing third parties) until the payment reaches the payee's PSP has been recognised by the fact that an additional Article 77 was added which states that 'Where the liability of a payment service provider under Article 75 is attributable to another payment service provider or to an intermediary, that payment service provider or intermediary shall compensate the first payment service provider for any losses incurred or sums paid under Article 75.'

Furthermore, the fact that an external event outside of the payer's PSP's control may sometimes result in a payment taking longer to arrive was picked up by the inclusion of a *force majeure*-type provision that would limit the liabilities under unforeseeable circumstances.

It is also significant to note that the article did, as the EC wished, include something on consequential loss, although it sensibly limits this to 'any charges for which they are responsible, and for any interest to which the payment service user is subject as a consequence of non-execution or defective execution of the payment transaction'. Still, article 77(2) talks about 'further financial compensation', which in addition to the amount that is lost or wrongly executed, could relate to more than the interest rate forgone. Unfortunately in situations where neither the payer's PSP nor the payee's PSP is close to the intermediary providers are involved, the requirement of establishing proof on the payer's PSP side is even more difficult. In such cases article 77, which aims to define a procedure for those particular instances by requiring any PSP or intermediary liable under article 75 to 'compensate the first PSP for any losses incurred or sums paid', will not readily alleviate the PSPs situation.

In summary, the final drafting discussions on this issue did much to ensure that the PSD regime does not totally tip the balance of risks against the payer's PSP which would, for example, have had the effect of reducing the EU's attractiveness as a 'payments hub' for international banks and thus would have negatively impacted the competitiveness of the EU at a global scale. However, the final outcome still impacts PSPs' balance sheets in terms of the need to cater for the significant increase in consumer protection, specifically in the context of the liability shift.

(3) A last sanity check against SEPA requirements

Through close analysis of the PSD it emerges with crystal clarity that the EC did rather let its attention get diverted from the initial *raison d'être* of the PSD, i.e. SEPA. Since the beginning the banking industry had identified that a small number of key provisions were required at EU regulatory level to ensure that a pan-European standardised payments landscape could be built.

Those key provisions were:

1. the abolition of Balance of Payments (BoP) Reporting requirements for Euro transactions within Europe
2. the introduction of clear and fully harmonised refund rights for consumers and businesses in the context of direct debit transactions
3. the confirmation of the primacy of the IBAN as the account identifier of the beneficiary over the beneficiary name to allow for faster automated payment execution.

Having by now extensively analysed the PSD it could be argued that the success rate in terms of hitting these three targets is very low – cynics might say almost nonexistent.

Firstly, BoP Reporting fell prey to political haggling within the Council, where a number of National Central Banks (NCBs) entrusted with this task were clearly uneasy about losing it (sparking rumours that this had more to do with employment policy than balance of payments ideology). The failure to remove BoP Reporting has therefore allowed the significant existing burden on corporate customers and their banks to continue, even in the context of SEPA. Instead of facilitating the free flow of Euro payments under SEPA, some countries continue to invoke this reporting obligation for payment values exceeding €50,000, which in some instances (such as Spain) can even force the executing bank, if intending to avoid this requirement, to send such payments via the local Automated Clearing House (ACH) rather than being able to centralise the clearing of such payments at EU level using a PE-ACH (see also Title VI on this topic).

Secondly, the refund rules defined in the PSD still risk being compromised, as explained earlier, by national implementations under article 86, where Member States are invited to provide more generous terms of protection to their citizens. If a country were to decide to allow for longer periods during which consumers could claim for authorised debits to be refunded, such an inconsistency in relation to other national rules would allow practical problems with a SEPA Direct Debit if when used cross-border. This risk has already manifested itself with the example of the UK, which pre-PSD provided a life-long direct debit guarantee to its consumers and will continue this practice under the PSD with the help of article 86. If the UK were finally to become a Eurozone country, and admittedly that might never happen, there would be a non-level playing field between the rights of UK consumers versus other EU consumers and additional contractual solutions might need to be considered in order to fill this gap.

And finally, the primacy of a 'unique identifier' as stated in the PSD, rather than mentioning the IBAN as the specific one, in practice appears so far to be an insufficient solution to the problem of slow and non-automated payments in Europe – despite its apparent success in answering the valid argument of the industry that requiring name/number checking would slow down the execution of payments in a single-domestic-market context. Legacy differences in tradition and practice between EU Member States still seem to create more problems with this unique identifier/IBAN primacy rule than solving them. Consumer organisations in countries such as Italy and Germany are demanding that name and IBAN should still be checked as this practice existed in the past and their customers appreciated this additional assurance. Other countries are of course more relaxed as such practices did not exist in their markets.

What does seem clear is that it will be almost impossible once SEPA migration is completed to have any realistic means of checking the validity of name and IBAN of beneficiaries in a multiple cross-border context within the current 32 SEPA geographies. While national databases of names and IBANs could exist or be built, SEPA is after all a harmonised environment applicable across the whole plethora of countries and it would be a serious challenge to establish a common name/IBAN database to allow for consistency checks in an automated way before payments are sent into the clearing. Therefore, these current debates are expected to fade away into the mist once SEPA has become the standard for payments in Europe.

A final provision that did make it into the PSD and that has to do with SEPA, even though the link may not be so immediately obvious, is the already mentioned 'sharing principle of charges'. Refraining from mentioning specific charge codes (OUR, BEN, SHA) in the legal text, the PSD took its approach from the SEPA CT Rulebook. The reason for not being more specific in SEPA is of course down to the fact that the XML schema does not include the 'old-world' MT message style charge codes that we still use today. In SEPA, the general principle therefore is that customers pay their providers separately and the full amount travels up to the beneficiary bank.

Of course, in 2010 we are still far away from SEPA migration, despite the assumption to the contrary that was made when writing this principle into the PSD text many years ago. This dilemma, as we shall later see, was set to unfold beyond what could have collectively been anticipated at the time of writing.

Title V
From Publication to Transposition: The Directive Dilemma

Introduction

After the odyssey of negotiation, amendments and re-negotiation, there were mild signs of euphoria in the industry when the final PSD text was published in the Official Journal of the EU on the 5th of December 2007. With so many years of hard work involved in getting to this point, there was a strong feeling that surely not much more could go wrong now. Even the timing of publication encouraged this feeling, given that the standard time lag with which EU Directives come into force – 20 days after their publication – meant that the PSD truly arrived on Christmas Day. What a delightful present for the banking industry in Europe!

(1) First reactions from the market

With the final text out in the market, little did any of us realise at the time that our shared sense of relief was not entirely well founded, and that against all our expectations Pandora's Box had just been opened! As soon as Member States had received the green light to begin their 23-month transposition process, during which time the PSD's rules had to be woven into their national legal structures by primary or secondary legislation (or a mix of the two), the first hints of the trouble that would lie ahead started emerging.

In hindsight, of course, this should have been predictable. It was always going to be a challenge to understand the PSD's key principles in the same way across all 30 EEA countries. Just remember how very different the payments markets are across this region in terms of their maturity, sophistication and payment systems; including the array of payment services offered, the degree of consumer protection and so on.

To start things off, the dreaded 'lost in translation' phenomenon kicked in almost immediately. Examples of this could be observed in the very fresh PSD translations that shortly after started appearing, with for example the Swedish draft version translating 'business day' as 'banking business day'. At first sight, not such a material change – until you remember that one of the PSD's goals was to encourage innovation and competition by opening the market to non-bank providers who might choose to operate very different 'business days' to those of banks, and that another goal was to stimulate banks into developing innovative services offered outside traditional banking hours and days. Not a very auspicious start then!

A further key concern that emerged only just after the final text had been published was that many Member States appeared to have failed to understand the imperative for all of them to bring the PSD into force on a common date, rather than on a set of convenient interim date(s) of their choosing. A scattergun approach – with Member States adopting a broad range of different dates – would have been completely unworkable for PSPs in the context of cross-border transactions, given the end-to-end nature of many of the Directive's provisions. It would also have made the compliance project for a multi-country bank far more complex and costly. This in turn would have potentially risked the introduction of the SEPA Direct Debit Scheme (SDD), the launch of which was dependent on the common refund requirements defined by the PSD. Of course, at the time no one was considering the possibility that some Member States might even miss the 1 November 2009 deadline ...

Adding to the challenges, article 86 gives Member States the freedom to derogate (to do something differently) in relation to twelve provisions of the PSD. Further to this set of derogations, there are another eleven instances in the text where Member States are also permitted to diverge from a standard application of the rules (it remains curious as to why those provisions were not also referred to under article 86). In any event, the fact that there were now two categories of derogations, one explicit and one rather more implicit, was inconsistent with the objectives and definition of full harmonisation and created some confusion as to which provisions were definitely fully harmonised. Article 86 also included a second significant potential source of divergence as according to § 3 PSPs can 'grant more favourable terms to payment service users'. While this is in many ways a very positive measure, designed to stimulate competition and innovation, it could – if used the wrong way – hold back the development of coherent payment propositions across the EU or even support protectionism.

Following on from this early realisation that not everything was as clear and straightforward as had been initially assumed, the remainder of this Title will take a close look at the various challenges that now lay ahead and illustrate the different initiatives undertaken by regulators and industry participants in pursuit of the (mostly) common goal of a harmonised and consistent legal implementation.

(2) The Transposition Working Group and the PSD Expert Group

The EC's services in DG Markt realised very swiftly that there was a need for EU level leadership to co-ordinate the transposition of the PSD if there was to be any chance of achieving a harmonised result. Consequently, representatives from each Member State (initially from Finance Ministries, but to be expanded in due course to include 'Competent Authorities' once appointed) were invited to participate in a series of regular meetings chaired by the EC with the purpose of clarifying the obligations and rules in the PSD to ensure national legislation would capture these in an appropriate and consistent way. The creation of this so-called PSD Transposition Working Group (PSD TWG) was also motivated by the fact that the PSD required the establishment of a 'Payments Committee' comprised of Member State representatives, with a mandate to oversee the results of the PSD's implementation and in due time propose further changes in line with the PSD review scheduled for the end of 2012. Accordingly, the EC had in mind from the outset that the PSD TWG would eventually morph into the Payments Committee.

To increase market transparency surrounding the PSD transposition process, the EC services also decided to establish a public website that would focus on giving all interested parties regular updates on the implementation status of individual Member States, together (once available) with a consolidated view of derogation usage and details of Competent Authorities. Additionally, to give the process a rather more interactive dimension, the EC decided – as was the case when the legendary Markets in Financial Instruments Directive or MiFiD was being implemented – to include the functionality for interested parties to submit their questions on transposition issues, which the EC, with the support of their legal services, would respond to periodically via FAQ answers on their website.

The first task for the PSD TWG was to discuss – again – the entire text of the PSD, for the purpose of identifying ambiguities and agreeing a common line. This in itself immediately presented some challenges in terms of methodology and approach. Given the massive interdependence between the scope and key definitions in Title I of the PSD and the conduct of business rules in Titles III and IV, it was hard to see how the work of the PSD TWG could best be prioritised. In the end, the EC settled on an approach that was to focus on discussing the individual Titles one by one in successive meetings over a period of many months – an approach that might in part explain why it was to take plenty of meetings, hundreds of website FAQs and enormous amounts of further intervention from the payment industry to finally resolve some of the key points of ambiguity.

In parallel, banks and banking associations in Europe, particularly those who had been closest to the negotiation process, also read the final text afresh, partly in order to start preparing for their own compliance. In doing so, it gradually became clear to them that while the text was massively improved – and much more coherent – than had at times ever looked possible during the dark days of negotiation, it was nevertheless riddled with ambiguities and inconsistencies. Additionally, given that not everybody had been directly involved in the often rather intimate lobbying efforts during the creation of the PSD, there was a practical risk of a carefully crafted compromise wording now proving too complex and subtle for the new readership and thus being misunderstood. The significant risk of diverging Member State approaches both in terms of their usage of derogations and more generally their understanding of the complex set of rules and obligations served to enrich this already explosive cocktail.

In any event, it was clear that central coordination was also needed to support the banking industry's compliance with this legislation. This was necessary not least because of SEPA, despite the fact that only a minority of PSD rules were in the end dedicated to this initiative. With the EPC tied up in the last preparatory touches for the scheduled launch of SEPA credit transfers in January 2008 – a launch which interestingly was not conditional upon the PSD being in place at all – the EPC Secretariat had no spare resources at that point in time to support broader industry efforts relating to the PSD implementation process. As a consequence, the European Banking Federation (EBF) stepped into the breach and invited the other two European Credit Sector Associations – the European Co-operative Banks and the European Savings Banks Association – as well as the EPC and the International cards schemes Visa and MasterCard – to join forces and form the European banking industry's PSD Expert Group (PSD EG).

Chaired by the author of this book, and comprising representatives from a broad cross-section of banking association and practitioner representatives that had been involved in the PSD since the early years, the PSD EG was charged with the critical mission of working with the EC, Member State authorities and other industry working groups at national level to identify ambiguities in the text, propose balanced interpretations, and lobby for these to be adopted on an EU-wide market basis. While banks had always had a variety of views on whether the PSD was actually necessary, now that it had arrived the banking community had an (almost) united agenda in wanting to ensure it would be implemented in a way consistent with the original spirit of the law. A non-harmonised outcome would be in complete conflict with the SEPA agenda as well as being a cause for huge amounts of additional compliance costs and red tape, risking the realisation of the core potential benefits around efficiency and a competitive level playing field.

The PSD EG began its work in December 2007 and quickly submitted a number of papers and questions to the EC and the PSD TWG. Within the first few months, the group rapidly established itself with those bodies as a significant and credible stakeholder in the transposition process, with the first success coming when the EC recognised the validity of the PSD EG's arguments for all Member States to agree to adopt a common target 'In Force' date of 1 Nov 2009 – an approach that was then ratified by the TWG in one of their first meetings.

After this first victory, the work of the PSD EG was about to develop into a set of complex negotiations with the EC and Member State authorities, conducted throughout 2008 and 2009, which would result in the adoption of many of the Group's proposals by the authorities, as well as the development of self-regulatory industry PSD implementation guidance and best practice proposals.

(3) PSD interpretation: a web of ambiguity emerges

As a result of the drawn-out process that the PSD went through during the negotiation phase, including the original EC proposals, the review by the EP, the multitude of changes proposed by successive Council presidencies and finally the tripartite negotiations between those three key bodies, it is hardly surprising – given the lack of a single overall owner with an end-to-end view of the text – that the final version is not entirely coherent. The actual scope of the PSD itself changed so frequently during this process that it is rather natural to see so many ambiguities and even fragments of ancient text relating to long-forgotten previous drafts and policy agreements in the final version.

In the EC's quest for the 'right' interpretation of the PSD, speed was of the essence. Historical evidence shows that the EC has a general tendency to provide guidelines 'after the process of transposing the directive has begun and the necessary legislation is already being drafted, adding to transposition problems'.[1] This unfortunately also happened in the case of the PSD, where the slow trickling of recommendations from the EC and the PSD TWG in some cases arrived too late for countries that were already well advanced with drafting their national transposition laws. Indeed, certain countries had already started their transposition process before the EC's first PSD TWG meeting took place in February 2008. Once ready for the task, the EC services chose a two-level approach, trying to exercise maximum control over PSD interpretations. On the first level the EC gathered continuous output via the PSD TWG while on the second level many public questions were directly answered by the EC as FAQs on their public website.

The website turned out to be the element that in the end was to attract most attention, as well as most criticism in some respects. But how could a website FAQ for a payments Directive ever become controversial? Partly this was because of the fact that the website process was intended act as a 'feeder' to gather topics of sufficient importance to warrant discussion and debate at the PSD TWG. However, this debate did not always happen in advance of a reply being posted on the website, and this could – and did – lead to clashes with the industry on some occasions.

Additionally, a number of the responses to website questions turned out to be contrary to the previous common understanding of the PSD's requirements, and sometimes answers to very similar questions asked a number of times over the period that the FAQ process operated were to vary significantly. In the end, the FAQs were said by some to have a passing resemblance to the creation of Dr Frankenstein – being a monster of more than 350 parts, bolted together using various components, not all of which would fit together terribly well.

Against this background the disclaimer on the EC's website relating to its FAQ responses is quite illuminating; the following excerpts in particular:

> The information contained on the site: is of a general nature only and is not intended to address the specific circumstances of any particular individual or entity; should not be relied on in the particular context of enforcement or similar regulatory action; is not professional or legal advice (if you need specific advice, you should always

consult a suitably qualified professional); is in no way constitutive of an interpretative document.

This disclaimer, which was perhaps not as widely read by interested parties as it should have been (including by some of the more enthusiastic Competent Authorities who have been fond of quoting from the answers), is key, as it makes clear that the responses are the EC services' own interpretation of each issue raised and cannot be considered as interpretative guidance. They are not legally binding in their own right and a court can make up its own mind as to how much weight to attribute to them. Nevertheless, coming from the EC services team, their weight should not be underestimated, and on many occasions the answers had a major bearing on how a number of Member States chose to interpret and implement the PSD text in their national markets.

The first gold-plating ... and at EU level!

Having set the scene for the PSD transposition process, we now turn to the area of gold-plating, a phenomenon generally discussed in the context of a Member State making a conscious (or sometimes unconscious) decision to go beyond the core text of a Directive when implementing it into their local law.

Although gold-plating is an inevitable side effect of Directives generally (as discussed in Title II) it had the potential to be particularly problematic for the PSD given its goal of establishing a single competitive payments area for Europe – something that could easily be compromised by scope-creep on the part of individual Member States.

While individual Member States were in due course to do some PSD gold-plating of their own at national level, unusually on this occasion the first appearance of this phenomenon happened at the European level and was, believe it or not, seemingly induced by the EC itself. So much for all those maximum harmonisation rules.

Of the many possible examples that could be highlighted, two that are worth exploring in some detail are the treatment of payments in which one leg of the transaction lies outside the EEA area (the so-called one-leg transactions) and secondly the intense debate that arose when the EC and the TWG started discussing the innocent-sounding definition of 'payment account'.

As our first example, let's look at an early action of the EC, which consisted in recommending to all Member States to apply a number of PSD rules to transactions that are initiated or received in the EEA, but have the second leg of the payment transaction in a non-EEA country, for example in the US. As explained in Title IV of this book, the PSD is a European law designed to improve the efficiency, competitiveness and transparency of payments that travel within the Single Market. Seeking to go further than this would be impossible to enforce in many respects due to the lack of the EU's jurisdictional reach and practical feasibility. In addition, it would result in a disproportionate liability for European providers versus the parties of the payment chain that are located outside the EEA.

Accordingly, it came rather as a surprise to the payment industry when one of the EC's first moves in the context of PSD TWG discussions on Title I of the Directive was to open up this whole question again and to go as far as recommending to Member States to apply 35 different articles from Titles III and IV to one-leg transactions via a voluntary implementation at national level. The argument used by the EC was that a number of Member States had indicated bilaterally that they were thinking of using their national transpositions to extend the scope of the Directive to one-leg transactions – and even in some cases to non-EEA currencies – and hence if they had not responded by proposing a standard set of articles for scope extension, the resulting free-for-all would have resulted in a non-level-playing field across European markets.

The industry, via the PSD Expert Group, pointed out in response (with impeccable logic!) that a harmonised approach could more easily be achieved by Member States simply not going beyond the agreed text in the Directive on this issue. However, in the end this proved to be one of those topics where some Member States were determined to do their own thing. Examples included Germany, which during the TWG discussions pushed for inclusion of one-leg transactions. A number of other countries also ended up extending certain provisions to one-leg transactions and to non-EEA currencies, often motivated by a desire to ensure that their PSD transposition gave a similar level of rights to consumers as was already enjoyed at the domestic legal level.

In the end, after many months of debate, the EC decided to leave Member States to decide for themselves the extent to which they wanted to go beyond the PSD's clear limitation on the one-leg issue, as illustrated by their answer to website FAQ 277 where they concluded:

> Member States remain completely free to regulate 'one leg' transactions in which at least one of the payment service providers is located in the EEA. Some of them have considered that the implementation of

the PSD would be a good opportunity to apply some of its provisions to one-leg transactions.

Our second example of EU level gold-plating triggered by the uncertain drafting of the PSD appeared in the form of the multiple-tree-felling debate which concerned the innocuous sounding question of what was meant by the term 'payment account' within the definitions of the Directive in article 2.

The 'original' version of this definition – from the EC's legislative proposal of 2005 – had referred to 'an account which can exclusively be used for payment transactions'. As explained in Title IV, this had ended up being modified in the final text to 'an account which can be used for payment transactions', which was felt to be a satisfactory outcome by the payments industry as it removed the risk that new special purpose accounts would have to be created by banks just because of the PSD and also given there was a general understanding that a 'payment account' provided by a bank was clearly a current account.

However, a few months after the final text was published, the EC started expressing the view that, while this was clearly an unfortunate unintended consequence they were forced by inescapable logic to adopt the view that the phrase 'an account used for payment transactions' would cover all types of accounts offered by credit institutions, rather than just the current accounts that the legislators had originally had in mind.

This suggestion was met with disbelief, turning quickly to dismay, on the part of the banking industry once it was clear that this was not an example of humour on behalf of the EC services. What was at risk, if this incredibly wide reading was to prevail, would be having to apply the PSD's full information requirements and COB rules to all types of savings, loan and mortgage accounts.

At a practical level, this would have meant having to review and potentially re-issue the terms and conditions for all these accounts to ensure full compliance with the PSD's full information requirements regime – at the cost of a few more equatorial rain forests and to the benefit only of countless law firms across Europe.

At a more fundamental level though, key elements of the intrinsic features of these types of accounts that made them most appropriate for depositing/saving or borrowing money (rather than making or receiving payments) were worryingly in conflict with the PSD's COB requirements with regard to execution times and value dating. For instance, many popular savings accounts offer the depositor a higher rate of interest in return for their agreement that funds will be left with the credit institution for a certain period of time, or that they will be required to give notice of say 30/60 days before making a withdrawal. The PSD, however, has a requirement that payments being made from 'payment accounts' are to be made to the beneficiary bank within one business day of the payment instruction being received by the payer's PSP. Were savings accounts to be deemed as payment accounts and hence this requirement were to apply, the consequence would be that a credit institution could no longer offer its clients higher rates of interest as an incentive to leave the funds longer on the account – which of course in the pre-PSD environment had been a genuine win-win for both parties.

These and many other issues were raised rapidly by the industry in response to the EC's statements on this topic. Additionally, some Member States also quickly recognised the issue, for example HM Treasury in the UK which advocated regulatory clarity to ensure that 'the definition of payment account should be strictly related to the objective of regulating payment services.'[2]

This then became a priority topic for discussion by the PSD EG, who knew that it needed to come up with a solution that would stay true to the principles and objectives of the PSD but avoid the destruction that the EC's hard line interpretation would cause to the competitive market for savings in the EU. It was no good looking simply to the name of an account, as different countries use different terminology for essentially the same product – so a principles based solution would have to be found.

What emerged from the PSD EG was a recommendation that the EC and Member States should adopt an approach that focused on the purpose of an account and its underlying functionality. In response, the EC services confirmed in early 2008 that on reflection they considered 'pure' loan accounts and 'pure' mortgage accounts (that is, except hybrid mortgage accounts) to be excluded and stated that 'savings accounts where the holder can place and withdraw funds without any additional intervention or agreement of his PSP should be considered as payment accounts within the meaning of the PSD', identifying fixed term deposits as clearly being excluded by this test.

The PSD EG then built further on this approach by suggesting the adoption of a principles-based approach that:

1. Would focus on the *underlying purpose and functionality* of an account (not its 'type' or 'denomination') on the basis that the underlying legislative intent of the Directive is to focus only on those accounts whose main purpose is the execution of payment transactions.

2. Would take into account the *presence of contractual terms* that confirm the nature of the account – and therefore demonstrate whether or not it should be treated as falling under the definition of 'payment account'.

Fortunately, the EC services saw the logic of this approach – including the fact that it should be down to Member States to set the principles and to leave PSPs the freedom to self-assess the status of their own account types, with the local Competent Authority being well placed to verify whether this had been done appropriately.

As a consequence, the EC was eventually able to confirm back to the PSD EG that a principles-based approach was 'exactly what has been discussed within the PSDTG' and additionally, in their answer to website FAQ 150, they confirmed that for an account to be considered as a payment account 'the PSU should be able to withdraw funds whenever he likes *without any restrictions*'. With this clarification, the EC's position came at last fully in line with the PSD EG's proposal for using a subjective self-assessment test based on purpose and functionality to determine whether a specific account would fall within the scope, or whether instead a few small rainforests could be saved.

(4) PSD national implementation: the Midas touch

The full harmonisation aspect of the PSD is crucial to the success of SEPA and to help stimulate competition in the European payments market. It means that Member States are meant to refrain from maintaining or introducing any other rules than those defined by the legal text. But as we now know there were many loopholes to be found in the PSD, which if directly or indirectly used could create inconsistencies between countries and potentially open the door to 'regulatory arbitrage'.

The stage was thus set for a range of difficult discussions at the level of the PSD TWG. A further challenge was caused by the fact that many of the national officials now responsible for the transposition negotiations were not the same as those who had negotiated the original proposals. The newcomers were naturally less aware of the background history, which added to the risk that the original legislative intentions might get lost (inadvertently or conveniently) along the way.

Part of the price of PSD consensus had been the inclusion of 23 'official' derogations (on top of all the 'unofficial' ones caused by textual ambiguity). These provisions were included at the request of certain groups of Member States so that countries could preserve some elements of their existing national legal environment. The following table (see Table 5.1) provides a brief overview of all 23 derogations.

Table 5.1 List of Member State derogations within the PSD

Article	Nature of derogation
Article 2(3)	Waiver of the application of PSD provisions with regard to institutions under Article 2 of the capital requirements' Directive.
Article 7(3)	Not to apply ongoing capital requirements where a payment institution is included in the consolidated supervision of the parent credit institution.
Article 9(2)	Calculation of safeguarding requirements when funds can be used for future payment transactions and for non-payment services.
Article 9(3)	Application of safeguarding requirements to genuine (non hybrid activities) payment institutions
Article 9(4)	Threshold of EUR €600 for applying safeguarding requirements
Article 22(3)	Option to take into account professional secrecy rules under the relevant provisions of the capital requirements Directive.
Article 26(1)	Waiver of authorisation/supervision requirements of payment institutions.
Article 26(4)	Limitation of payment activities carried out by waived entities under Article 26.
Article 30(2)	Application of information requirements to micro enterprises.
Article 33	Burden of proof on the provision of information requirements lies with the payment service provider.
Article 34(2)	Low-value/e-money payments: reduce/double amounts under Article 34(1) and increase them for prepaid instruments up to €500.
Article 45(6)	More favourable provisions on termination conditions.
Article 47(3)	Provision of information to the payer on paper once a month for free.
Article 48(3)	Provision of information to the payee on paper once a month for free.
Article 51(2)	Non-application of out-of-court procedures to non-consumer PSUs.
Article 51(3)	Application of right/obligations under Title IV to micro enterprises.
Article 52(3)	Limitation of the application of the surcharge rule.
Article 53(2)	Low-value/e-money payments: reduce/double amounts under Article 34(1) and increase them for prepaid instruments up to €500.
Article 53(3)	Limit derogation under this provision to accounts or instruments of a certain value.
Article 61(3)	Reduction of payer's liability for unauthorised use of payment instrument taking into account the nature of personalised security features of the payment instrument.

(*continued*)

Table 5.1 Continued

Article 72	Shorter maximum execution times for purely national payment transactions.
Article 88(3)	Transitional provision in favour of legal persons under certain conditions.
Article 88(4)	Transitional provision for natural or legal persons eligible for the waiver under Article 26.

It will be noticed that many of the derogations unsurprisingly relate to Title II of the PSD, the authorisation regime for non-bank payment institutions, in reflection of the particularly delicate nature of the political compromise that surrounded the negotiation of this part of the text. However some key provisions in Titles III and IV were also left up for grabs – ranging from the ability to class micro-enterprises as consumers for the purpose of extending consumer-protection to these under the Directive, to the ability to set tighter execution times (than those stipulated in the PSD) for national transactions and also the ability to ban surcharging or require PSPs to provide monthly statements on paper.

To provide clarity, the industry's PSD Expert Group prepared a detailed overview of the use of some of the more interesting derogations in Titles III and IV of the PSD, sourced from information provided by national banking communities, supported by commentary on any notable features relating to their use. This information can be found in Appendix I (PSD Member State Derogation Status).

In some cases, how a particular derogation is used turns out to be just as important as the fact that it has been used. A good illustration of this point is the derogation to article 52(3) which allows a Member State to limit or ban the use of surcharging. This is the practice where a merchant requests an additional fee from their client for the use of a particular payment type, such as for the use of a card. Given that one of the stated aims of the PSD is to help modernise the European payments market and encourage the use of more modern electronic payment types this is a key derogation, because the use of surcharging may actually have the effect of discouraging the use of more efficient payment types. However, a related practice which can help increase the use of electronic payments is the use of discounting, whereby a merchant offers a lower price for when a particularly efficient method of payment is being used (for example, a direct debit or a debit card). The fact that the use of this derogation would appear to have the effect of banning both practices, discounting as well as surcharging, was to cause a number of Member States to choose not to apply it. Italy though is a good example of a country that neatly solved this issue by implementing the derogation in an elegant way that bans surcharging but still gives the necessary flexibility under Italian law to allow discounting to continue.

Even though the use of some of the PSD's national derogations has caused practical issues for PSPs, particularly for multi-country banks offering services to clients across a mix of jurisdictions, at least the 23 derogations are all known quantities and in the main their usage does not damage the ability of the PSD to achieve its objectives. The same cannot always be said of the other type of divergence in Member State implementations – namely the practice of 'gold-plating' that we explored conceptually in Title II and have already mentioned in this Title in the context of two EU-led examples.

The position on national gold-plating and other non-standard implementation aspects at the time of writing is summarised in Appendix II (Examples of Cases of Gold-Plating, Non-Conforming Transposition and other Interesting Transposition Features at Member State Level), based on information provided by national banking communities. The outcome is clearly not as uniform as the original PSD had foreseen, but thanks to the dialogue that the industry provoked on this topic some of the more extreme initial proposals by some Member States were moderated in their final form into a set of scope-extensions that while not uniform are at least operable.

Member States went about their gold-plating activities in a variety of different ways, some favourable to all stakeholders – such as the decisions in Italy and Ireland to extend their PSD transpositions to incorporate provisions enabling the legal continuity of Direct Debit mandates across to the new SEPA scheme – and some rather less favourable, at least from the payment industry's perspective. There have also been a number of cases where gold-plating within one Member State lead to subsequent discussions within the PSD TWG and in some instances the adoption of the same practice by other countries.

The varying types of national gold-plating experienced with the PSD can best be illustrated with a number of brief examples. At its simplest and potentially non-too damaging form, some Member States chose to encourage their PSPs to go beyond certain PSD standards, for example by reducing the amount of maximum loss a consumer can suffer in case he loses his payment card, or by extending the PSD's standard 8 week refund period for authorised direct debits (Note though that this latter example, innocent as it might sound, has the potential to cause major implications for migration to the SEPA DD scheme, which by definition has to work to a single set of standards and refund rules across the whole SEPA region). In other cases, Member States and their Competent Authorities, who sometimes were coming fresh to the text of the PSD and armed with a string of supplemental national policy objectives, chose to extend the scope of the PSD's information requirements to non-payment accounts. In one particular case they even tried to go beyond the PSD's execution time requirements by arguing that a same-day maximum should be applied to all payments where the payer's and payee's PSP happen to be the same institution – a previously unimagined reading of the value dating provisions in the text. This latter example was particularly puzzling in the sense that Member States already had the option to ensure shorter execution times for national transactions under another derogation which was precisely designed for that purpose (article 72).

A further gold-plating incidence surprisingly emerged in the UK around the topic of the reporting of interest paid and received by a PSU. It had previously been accepted by all – in line with the fundamental point that the goal of the PSD was to regulate payment transactions rather than accounts – that the reference to notification of interest rate changes in Title II solely related to cases where interest rates were being charged to customers in relation to payment transactions, (perhaps as an alternative to the application of a separate transaction fee) and where these rates had increased. However, in the UK the FSA developed the view that this information requirement also covered the charging (or paying) of any interest relating to the balance maintained on a 'payment account' – therefore including savings and overdraft rates. This view caused consternation in the UK market due to the additional communication costs that would result for no obvious customer benefit (potentially leading to disadvantages in some instances if some popular products had to be withdrawn as a result). Despite the fact that the business and legal community in the UK came up with a strong set of arguments to the contrary, and even the Queens Council gave an opinion, the UK went ahead to issue specific regulatory guidance in line with their specific view. Such a story illustrates how a small number of Member States (or even just one!) can develop an extreme view on a particular interpretation on an EU Directive based on a national perspective and use their powers to impose this within their local market, while the majority of Member States see no need to take action on the subject. So much for competition and a level-playing field ...

(5) Industry guidance to help smooth the path

One of the original objectives of the PSD EG was to record and formulate practical PSD implementation guidance for banks based on the outcome of the dialogue with the EC services and national authorities, in the spirit of ensuring a consistent and efficient PSD implementation across Europe.

Version 1.0 of the PSD EG's 'PSD Guidance' was officially launched to the market on 8 September 2009. The document did not attempt to be exhaustive in the list of topics it addressed, but rather focused on specific issues that had been the subject of discussion during the course of the PSD EG's work, including frequently asked questions from the market. The launch of the document – which essentially recorded the outcome of much of the PSD EG's activity on behalf of the EU banking industry over the preceding 18 months – was marked by a press release and a high-profile launch event in Brussels. This event was well attended by the EC services team, who took the opportunity to praise the document and the work of the PSD EG generally, highlighting its activities as best practice in terms of cooperation between the banking sector and the EU Regulators – despite their different priorities and interests – to ensure the smoothest possible transposition of this key example of EU Financial Services Legislation.

The below table (see Table 5.2) shows the high level structure of the PSD industry guidance document:

Table 5.2 PSD industry guidance overview

I. Structure and overview of the PSD
II. Scope and definitions
1. Introduction
2. Key Definitions – best practice guidance
3. General FAQs
III. Information requirements
1. Introduction
2. Best practice in relation to key PSD information requirements
3. General FAQs
IV. Payment transaction processing
1. Introduction
2. Inter-bank best practice in relation to key PSD operational requirements
3. General FAQs
V. Annexes

The PSD Guidance was – and continues to be – used widely across the EU, and a number of national banking communities were inspired to write similar guidance documents by adapting the PSD EG's work to fit their local market conditions.

The guidance remains a living document, as work continues to bring in additional best practice and answers to further commonly asked questions at a time when the banking industry across Europe gradually comes to terms with the legacy that the PSD has bestowed on them.

Efforts within individual banks and banking communities to ensure full compliance by 1 November 2009 were generally strong, but this did not in all cases mean that the same was necessarily true for those who were ultimately responsible for meeting this deadline – namely, the Member States themselves. The UK and Bulgaria proved to be the frontrunners in terms of PSD readiness (already achieved by March 2009). While other countries were clearly moving much more slowly at this point in time, none was prepared to admit that they were in danger of missing the transposition deadline. The first country to crack and officially confess that they were going to be late was Sweden, as they realised that their resources were too thinly spread thanks to also having to prepare for their turn at taking the Presidency of the EU in the second half of 2009 – an excuse for late transposition of an EU Directive that caused a few eyebrows to lift within the payment industry.

In the context of these two countries, there is still a risk that clients may experience a period of inconsistent treatment as the 'old' legal regime practices might still be applied.

Against this background, it was realised by the PSD EG in mid 2009, by which time the risk of late transpositions was becoming very apparent, that an ideal self-regulatory 'best practice' would be if banks in 'late countries' could voluntarily adopt key PSD payment processing provisions (particularly by respecting the full amount principle) until their transpositions were completed, wherever possible and practical.

To this end, the PSD EG encouraged discussion on this topic within the national banking communities of those countries where their transposition was known or expected to be delayed. In response, the Swedish Bankers' Association in particular came forward with a collective 'best practice' proposal, whereas other affected communities, such as those in Finland and Poland, chose to leave it to individual banks to make their own decisions.

The current situation – as at August 2010 – is that we are now left with two EEA countries that have still to get their legislation in place.

Our friends in Iceland had their own issues to deal with in 2009 and are not yet live, however hoping to become compliant before the end of 2010. They even had a volcanic eruption in the meantime – far more exciting than the PSD somehow!

Finally Poland, another big EU Member State, is also not PSD ready and has still not committed to a specific date for 2010. The EU community is hoping that this country will be live before the end of 2010, but maybe the Polish banking industry or the regulator, or both are rather not so much in favour of the PSD.

(6) Review of related legislation

The PSD turned out to be quite an intrusive law in the context of existing payments legislation and as a consequence elements of Regulation 2560/2001 on Cross Border Payments in Euro and the Electronic Money Directive (EMD) had to be reviewed and adapted as the PSD did not fit with them but demanded primacy. As both these laws and their successors still form an integral part of the overall legal landscape for payments in Europe, a short analysis is worthwhile to place them in context.

So what happened to the 2001 cross-border Pricing Regulation?

As we all know, Regulation 2560, the famous (or maybe infamous) Euro payment pricing regulation arrived in 2001, essentially as a means to spur the banking industry into developing cross-border retail payment mechanisms for Euro payments that would be as efficient as those used for large scale domestic payments (see further details on the origins of Regulation 2560 in Title III of this book).

Towards the end of the PSD preparations, it became clear that a significant revamp to Regulation 2560 would be necessary to ensure sufficient alignment with the new regulatory framework for payments in Europe. A series of consultations took place with the market and Member States during 2008 and early 2009 to determine what would need to be changed and what additional objectives might need to be incorporated.

From a banking industry perspective, this presented a clear opportunity for the EU Regulators to deliver on an objective that had originally been a part of the PSD plan – namely the abolition of cross-border Balance of Payment Reporting (BoP) other than of a sample-based nature. This was a necessary condition for the realisation of a single domestic payments area. Note that the EPC during the SEPA scheme design phase was so convinced that the PSD would ensure the abolition of these reporting requirements, that they did not even design fields into the SEPA technical message formats to accommodate BOP reporting requirements. This of course made it even more vital to get the issue fixed as part of this Regulation as otherwise serious barriers to SEPA would continue.

With the EC conceptually agreeing with the banking industry on this point – continued BoP reporting at a national level was indeed illogical in the context of developing a new multi-country domestic payments market paradigm – a proposal was drafted to ensure the abolition of BoP reporting in two stages, with the lifting of requirements for payments under €50,000 by 2010, followed by a sunset clause for all such reporting in 2012. However, to the industry's disappointment, this view was not supported by a sufficient number of central banks and authorities at the Member State level, and in the end this proposal was seriously diluted to the simple requirement of removing any remaining reporting for payments up to €50,000 from 1 January 2010 plus a commitment of the EC to re-examine and review the question of whether BoP was still indeed required by end of October 2011. The banking industry and the corporate community were in shock: the sunset clause had gone.

Another of the EC's ambitions for the revised Regulation 2560 turned out to be more successful, however – providing 'support' for SEPA by extending the pricing regulation aspect of the revised text to cover cross-border direct debits, thus removing the ability to price SDDs differently in a cross-border way compared to when offered domestically. This was a fully understandable objective from a regulatory perspective, and not something that the industry objected to – other than by pointing out that enforcing this principle by law was arguably rather unnecessary, as any bank that attempted to introduce split pricing (domestic/cross-border) for its SDD services would have undoubtedly found itself with an uncompetitive offering anyway.

Arriving at this outcome of a requirement for price parity was not that straightforward, however. In some of the EC services early work on the revision they came up with some questionable drafting proposals, such as the suggestion to delete the 'corresponding payment' test which had been at the heart of the original Regulation 2560 text and instead to state simply that cross-border and domestic Euro payments of the same amount should be priced the same. This rather missed the point that payment services come in a variety of flavours, not just plain vanilla. Typically a wide range of cross-border and domestic options will be available, varying for example by speed, channel and the amount of information which can be transported to the beneficiary alongside the payment itself – in other words, just such features that had made it important to find the 'corresponding' domestic payment type to match against each cross-border payment product in order to be able to apply the necessary pricing parity. Fortunately, as the debate with the market on the revised proposed text continued, this was explained clearly to the EC and the vital 'corresponding test' was reinstated.

So, apart from the compromise solution on BoP Reporting, the alignment of various terms and definitions with those used in the PSD, and the expansion of scope to cover the pricing of cross border direct debits, what else was new about this Regulation?

There was indeed more to it. In fact, a very positive more. Upon further discussion with the EC services, the payments industry conveyed successfully the need to include two key measures which were specifically designed to support the launch of SDD. These are dealt with in detail elsewhere in this book, but in brief saw the inclusion of a provision allowing a default MIF of €0.088 for cross-border direct debits for an initial period up to 1 November 2012, and the inclusion of a provision designed to ensure that banks throughout the SEPA area would make themselves reachable via the SDD Core scheme – something that the industry, EC and ECB realised was absolutely fundamental if the SDD scheme was ever to be able to take off in any meaningful sense. Accordingly, a provision was included in the text mandating banks who are members of existing DD schemes in the Euro area to make themselves reachable via the SDD Core scheme by 1 November 2010 at the latest, and for banks providing services in non-Eurozone countries to do so by 1 November 2014.

After a reasonably short passage through the EP and Council, a final version of the revised Regulation – now known as Regulation 924/2009 – was published in the Official Journal of the EU on 9 October 2009 and the Regulation came into force on 1 November 2009. Obviously, once countries fully migrate to SEPA (which now looks likely to be regulated by a forthcoming EU SEPA Migration Regulation), the threshold of €50,000 should logically be removed with regard to BoP as well as in the context of the pricing parity rule.

As an interesting footnote to this particular tale, one of the hot debating points which arose once the text had been finalised was around the apparently innocuous question as to exactly which institutions would actually be covered by the 1 November 2010 SDD Core reachability requirement, given the reference in article 8(3) that this key provision relates to PSPs 'located' in the Euro area. This immediately prompted the question of what 'located' actually meant in this context. The initial EC view, supported by their legal service team, was that this obviously had to mean the location of the respective institution's head office. Sounds reasonable at first, until you realise that if you extended this interpretation out across the whole Regulation it would mean that the reach requirement (either 1 November 2010 or the 1 November 2014 for non-Eurozone) would never actually apply to a non-EU headquartered bank that offered payment services in the EU, and indeed maybe other core provisions in the Regulation could be argued not to apply to these types of institutions either. Quickly realising that this all sounded hugely unintended and not at all pro-SEPA, the industry politely pointed out this interpretative flaw and suggested that 'location' in this instance surely had to refer to the place where the payment service was being offered from (branch location), irrespective of where the head office might sit. After months of internal discussions within the EC, white smoke finally emerged in April of this year, when the EC issued a clarifying note on their website advising that having thought it all through again 'the deadline for the application of the reachability obligation ... is determined only by the location of the branch (inside or outside the Euro area), regardless of the location of the parent company' and also that 'no distinction should be made between the braches with head offices located outside the EU and those with head offices in the EU'. So, all's well that ends well on this point at least – but this small sub-tale nevertheless serves as a salutary reminder as to how the interpretation of one little word in a legal text can have fundamental and rather disturbing implications.

Next steps for the E-Money Directive

The EC clarified in the early stages of the PSD transposition process that despite the inclusion of e-money institutions (EMIs) in article 1 of the PSD, those actors would be restricted to the provision of e-money issuance. This was a rather confusing statement for the market, as regulating EMIs under the PSD suddenly didn't make sense at all if they were not to be allowed to provide any of the payment services defined by the PSD.

Furthermore, initial capital requirements on EMIs within the original E-Money Directive amounted to €1 million (article 4, 2000/46/EC) as opposed to the significantly smaller capital requirements applicable to PIs (€20,000 to €125,000) while PIs in fact were entitled to provide a broader array of services including payments based on e-money.

In addition, the restrictions of activities placed on EMIs in article 1(5) of the EMD seemed not in line with the PSD's non-exclusivity approach, whereby PIs are permitted to engage in other non-payment service business activities. Again, this seems unfair.

Discussions with the EC during the PSD drafting period repeatedly raised these – and many other – points of inconsistency between the two regimes. A Review Report on the EMD had in fact already been published in July 2006, but this had focused on the conclusion that there was a need for revision due to the fact that some provisions hindered rather than stimulated the take-up of the e-money market and that this revision should only take place after the PSD's formal adoption. (At the time, there was the expectation that the PSD would be approved by the end of 2006). Further discussions were to lead to the EC undertaking a comprehensive review of the text of the EMD. Initially, their view was that they would like to revise the text completely and combine it into an enlarged PSD, but it quickly became apparent that it was now simply too late in the process. Accordingly, the EC in the end adopted a more pragmatic two-stage process. In stage one, the plan was to revise the existing EMD with a series of tactical adjustments to bring it more in synchronisation with the PSD's authorisation regime, while stage two would possibly be a full integration of EMD provisions with the PSD, once the PSD itself came up for review in 2012.

After consultation with the market – including existing EMIs and the Payment Systems Market Group (PSMG), the EC issued a proposal for a revised EMD in October 2008. Key changes were applied to the definition of e-money as well as to some of the elements of the prudential regime. Most importantly it had to be made clearer to the market what e-money really was supposed to mean. As you might have guessed, this rather essential definition had been rather unclear ever since the EMD had been introduced in 2000 and it was high time to provide guidance on this.

After the usual process of negotiation, the EP adopted a slightly modified version of the proposal on the 24 April 2009, and on the 16 September the final version of the text was published in the Official Journal as EU Directive 2009/110/EC, with a requirement for all Member States to complete their transpositions by 30 April 2011.

After the recent (considered largely positive) experiences of a more interactive transposition process with the PSD, the EC proposed a similar set up for the EMD with the creation of EMD Transposition Workshops at EU level as well as the utilisation of the now (in)famous EC FAQ website tool approach. Indeed, the EC has recently been carefully studying some of the 'lessons learnt' from implementing the PSD, for example the importance of having a single common date from which the legislation would enter into force in each Member State – and even ideally a common date by which Member State transposition texts should be completed to give the market in each country a reasonable adjustment period prior to the In Force date.

The Capital Adequacy Directive: what's it got to do with the PSD?

On the face of it, the Capital Adequacy Directive (Directive 2006/49/EC), in short CAD, has no obvious correlation with the PSD, and even though it was going through its own periodic revision process in the famous Lamfalussy style, there was no reason to suppose that it would require amending in a way that had any relevance for the PSD.

Unfortunately the PSD website response to a seemingly innocent question posed in October 2008 this time raised more than just eyebrows when the EC published its answer. The question was straightforward: does a credit institution with headquarters located in a non-EEA country, but operating branches within the EEA that are subject to EU legislation and supervision, need to incorporate these branches within the EEA before being allowed to continue providing payment services in Europe after the PSD deadline?

The answer that anyone would have expected was of course a firm 'no'. However, what the EC services concluded in FAQ 137 was that the drafting of Article 1(1) of the PSD was accidentally such that it did not expressly authorise all credit institutions to continue offering payment services within the EEA, only those who were doing so via a legal entity established within this geography. As such, their conclusion was that although this was never intended by the PSD, the effect of the accidental drafting was now that any credit institution operating with a non-EEA branch in Europe would either need to incorporate this branch in Europe or otherwise apply for a payment institution licence (wholly counterintuitive).

In addition to the disproportionate consequences this interpretation would trigger, it also posed a significant risk to the attractiveness and competitiveness of the European market in comparison to the rest of the world. This would have been a very ironic outcome, given the PSD's stated role in helping to fulfil the Lisbon agenda's goal of making the EU more competitive on the global landscape!

Action had to be taken as a regulatory solution at the EU level would be needed. But unfortunately the time for applying easy changes to the PSD had long passed; this text was now cast in stone. So an alternative solution needed to be found, and this is where the review of the CAD turned out to have a key role to play. The solution would lie in a very small change in the CAD, which at the time was going through one of its many review processes. A carefully negotiated amendment, developed by myself in discussion with HMT and FSA of the UK, was proposed to the EP with the effect of amending article 1(1) of the PSD. Fortunately, and after considerable behind the scenes discussions, this rather neat solution was supported by the Council as well as the EC, and hence disaster was, on this occasion, averted.

The result was that Directive 2009/111/EC, when it appeared in the Official Journal of the EU on 17th November 2009, included the following text in Article (3) (see Table 5.3):

Table 5.3 Article 3 of Directive 2009/111/EC

Article 3
Amendment to Directive 2007/64/EC
Article 1(1)(a) of Directive 2007/64/EC is replaced by the following:
(a) 'credit institutions within the meaning of Article 4(1)(a) of Directive 2006/48/EC, including branches within the meaning of Article 4(3) of that Directive located in the Community of credit institutions having their head offices inside or, in accordance with Article 38 of that Directive, outside the Community';

While technically Member States have until 31 October 2010 to transpose Directive 2009/111/EC into their local law, in practice the EC was able to re-assure affected banks that this new provision could effectively be deemed to be in force, and hence non-EEA headquartered banks could continue providing payment services via their EEA branches in an uninterrupted way.

Title VI
SEPA From Design to Launch: Finding Your Way through the SEPA Jungle

Introduction

Returning now to the other story within our story, by March 2005 things were at last starting to kick off for real for SEPA. After all, this initiative needed to move quickly now as otherwise it might come too late to play its part in fulfilling the Lisbon Agenda's master plan of turning the EU into the 'most competitive and knowledge-driven economy by 2010'.

As an initial statement of intent, the SEPA Roadmap, endorsed the previous December by the EPC Plenary, was proudly proclaimed to the market via the famous 'Crowne Plaza Declaration' of 17 March 2005. Intended to demonstrate the strong commitment of the EPC community, this declaration conveyed the message that tangible results for SEPA would now be delivered according to the set timetable and that the EPC was fully empowered to make things happen in order to turn the SEPA vision into reality. The declaration confirmed a commitment to having all four SEPA deliverables (the SEPA Credit Transfer Scheme, the SEPA Direct Debit Scheme, the SEPA Cards Framework and the SEPA Cash Framework) completed by the end of 2005, with an operational start date of January 2008 to coincide with the anticipated delivery date of the PSD. (Don't forget – at that time the PSD was still expected to be adopted before April 2007.)

This Title traces the evolutionary path of these four SEPA deliverables, from their initial design through to their launch into an expectant market, and assesses the impacts they have had so far on the European payments landscape. The journey into the land of SEPA will hopefully provide some context to help ensure that the currently ongoing debates around SEPA adoption and migration can be correctly framed and thus depoliticised – or at least a little.

Following an overview of the SEPA scope and the standards framework, we will examine each SEPA deliverable in turn. To conclude, this Title will also take a brief look at the infrastructure space, and highlight developments around ACH consolidation and inter-operability – together with the overall impact of a harmonised standards framework on the payments processing landscape in Europe.

Before we delve deep into the payments undergrowth of the SEPA schemes, let us briefly recall where the various responsibilities sat for the design, implementation and supply of SEPA payment services to the market. The primary role of the EPC was intended to be (and still is) the design, support and ownership of SEPA schemes and frameworks. Anything that has to do with the competitive space, which is essentially what any of the adhering PSPs create out of the SEPA primordial soup when fashioning their own capabilities and products, and what happens in the infrastructure provider space, has little to do with the EPC as scheme owner and governance body. The EPC is only able, to the degree possible – which is of course dependent on the willingness of participating PSPs across the current 32 constituent Member States – to ensure the schemes are made available to the market and that they evolve in line with the needs of users (something which turns out to be not as easy as it sounds, as we shall see later).

Ultimately, this Title aims to explore some of the popular misconceptions and myths surrounding the SEPA initiative, with the ambitious but sincere goal of encouraging a more constructive and factually based discussion on the topic.

(1) SEPA standards, design principles and geography

As discussed in Title III, the ambitious goal of SEPA is to try to create a united Euro retail payment system for Europe. As we also discovered earlier, while such harmonisation was achieved relatively quickly in the area of wholesale payments with the introduction of TARGET and Euro1, retail payment systems remained fragmented along national borders, running on separate domestic technical standards and schemes. In parallel with the anticipated switching to the single set of harmonised SEPA standards across the Eurozone, the expectation was that this would naturally trigger a significant consolidation of infrastructure processors down to a handful of pan-European ACHs handling Euro flows. If the point ever came where the Eurozone and the EU were to share the same geographic scope – meaning all EU Member States would have adopted the Euro (will the UK for example ever do so I still wonder?) – SEPA would then encompass the execution of retail payments across the entire market and the full integration of the Single Market for Payments would finally be a reality.

However, let's not forget that for the sake of this narrative we are now firmly back in 2005, and as such still miles away from realising any of these grand objectives.

The SEPA rulebooks and standards development

To introduce SEPA, we shall start by exploring how the design phase was structured. This will be helpful background to better appreciating the overall approach and the challenges that were going to be encountered further down the line. The design of the SEPA schemes for credit transfers and direct debits is of particular interest here, given the decision to construct entirely new inter-bank schemes from the ground up, while the SEPA cards and cash projects were instead envisaged as frameworks to be superimposed on the existing landscape.

Designing brand new schemes capable of meeting the needs of such a variety of players with so very different market characteristics, as highlighted in Title III, was quite a tall order. So, a bit of process structure was needed first to ensure that the many ideas and requests of national communities could be streamlined and filtered. Therefore the approach agreed for developing the SEPA schemes was to concentrate on three discrete layers of deliverables: the SEPA rulebooks; the SEPA data model; and finally the technical standards.

Layer 1 had to be started first, as this was essentially the place where the business requirements and processes needed to be agreed. If the definition of business requirements for a national payment instruments can be a difficult process – and believe me it can – imagine the challenge of a situation where a large group of bankers from as many as 31 countries at a time were locked in debate in a big meeting room in Brussels competing to sell the benefits of why their respective national schemes, processes and standards were of course the natural solution to adopt for the whole of Europe (NB no one really wanted to change ...). Accordingly, before any business requirements could start to be written down the EPC had to make it very clear to all participants that it was not feasible to simply clone an allegedly 'perfect' scheme from any single country and that existing schemes needed to be subjected to a thorough examination to determine the 'best of breed' characteristics which should feature in the creation of something new for Europe. A one-size-fits-all solution was required. (Now where, I wonder, have we heard that before?)

With many warm-up discussions and meetings having already taken place in the previous three years, the time to deliver tangible output had come and the fresh set of EPC working groups established for the task quickly grew an intricate web of subgroups, each charged with their own part of the mission, resulting in an outbreak of monthly, bi-monthly and assorted ad hoc meetings.

So, the design engine room was at last hot and running. Time, and lots of it, was spent sitting in said meetings of said working groups, visiting and revisiting endless drafts of rulebook elements. An unexpected by-product of my personal participation in these gatherings was an ever increasing awareness of the finer arts of compromise and mediation, which were necessary indeed to achieving agreement on virtually any point within such diverse groupings of nationalities, institutional backgrounds, and personality types.

Once the essential business characteristics for each scheme were agreed – a process which took quite a number of months in the case of credit transfers, but even longer for direct debits – the next deliverables were the data models that had to capture the information for the SEPA inter-bank messages. Only when both these two layers were completed was it possible to hand the set of SEPA specifications over to the standards maker, in this case SWIFT, with the request to translate the message information into appropriate technical message formats.

While 2005 saw the creation of Layers 1 and 2, the question with regard to what type of standard should actually be used for SEPA was left till the end of that year. The final choice approved by the EPC Plenary in November 2005 was to go for the UNIFI ISO 20022 and XML standards, subject to SWIFT's ability to deliver these within the required timescale. Given the necessary lead time that banks and other parties would need to prepare once the final standards were in place, this effectively left only a year to get everything ready from a standards development perspective.

Before going into the details of the SEPA schemes, I would first like to answer a question which I'm sure must be on many readers' minds at this point, namely: What exactly is UNIFI ISO 20022 – and what the hell is XML?!

ISO and XML are topics that are increasingly 'en vogue' to be dropped into conversations across the globe, starting initially in industry panel discussions, but also considered as a respectable subject for cocktail chatter (at least in some marginally strange gatherings). However, I'm sure that many users of these ubiquitous abbreviations may not be entirely aware of what is really behind them. Let's enlighten ourselves.

XML turns out to be short for Extensible Mark-up Language and has been around since 1996 when it was developed in response to the need to improve the functionality of web technologies by creating more flexible means to identify information. As such, XML is therefore not a simple processing language but in fact a *Meta* language – a language that describes other languages. While one consequence of this is that XML is a rather verbose syntax, a resulting second consequence is that it turns out to be terribly useful as a supporting structure, enabling communication between different systems that could otherwise not communicate with each other. This is something, as we shall later see, that turns out to be very relevant for companies in the context of a systems and process integration with regard to their transaction services.

As a matter of further background, the history of the ISO XML can be traced back to 2003 when four standards organisations (SWIFT, TWIST, IFX and OAGI[1]) teamed up in their effort to create next-generation electronic payment messages that would use an XML format – an effort that was dubbed 'IST Harmonisation' or 'ISTH'. In parallel to their efforts a set of standards bodies in the financial services sector put together an alignment project under the auspices of ISO's financial services standards committee (Technical Committee 68). As a background, ISO is the International Standards Organisation, known in various other market contexts, for example in relation to product safety standards. The next year saw the release of the ISO 20022 standard – the UNIFI ISO 20022. The first part of this mouthful is a reference to the Universal Financial Industry Message scheme, which is the international standard that defines the ISO platform for the development of financial message standards. The ISO 20022 standard provided a common methodology that can be used to define electronic financial messages (whether these are for payments, trade or securities transactions) in a structured – and machine-readable – way and established a structure for a common repository and relevant procedures for its administration. SWIFT was chosen as the ISO 20022 repository. Both stories aligned when IST joined the ISO 20022 project and helped in developing a set of payment messages called the 'Payment Kernel'.

In the development of SEPA these design tools were used to reflect a limited (but over time broadening) subset of information to be included in SEPA messages.

In a nutshell, the combination of ISO 20022 and the XML syntax gives the benefit of working in a structured way with a potentially much larger set of information than 'old' message types – a benefit that is clearly being leveraged in SEPA. Indeed, this is one of the key attractions for customers in the business world as carrying a broader set of information within a financial message supports their treasury and allows for improved payment reconciliation. European banks would be the first in the world to deploy this new global data format for mass payments in a daring evolutionary break from the traditional world of the more limited MT formats provided by SWIFT.

Even though the extensive set of SWIFT MT (message type) standards is used globally, these are still proprietary standards used by banks, securities houses and other FIs (plus today an increasing number of corporates) within the private SWIFT network. Upgrading a bank's payments applications to the ISO 20022 XML message standards has the potential to facilitate faster, more efficient and finally harmonised transaction processing and, given these standards are not proprietary, global compatibility is now a real possibility. The ideal world is really XML because it is fully standardised. As a reminder, MT messages are formatted in the way the bank (or any other of the above users) chooses before being sent out to the market, which means that they are never standardised. As we shall see later on, all these advantages of the ISO 20022 XML were also going to trigger significant interest in markets far beyond the European space.

After many months of hard work and equally hard compromising, the EPC Plenary adopted the SEPA credit transfer and direct debit scheme rulebooks, covering the business process layer and appropriate elements of the logical layer, in December 2006. In addition the SEPA data model and implementation guidelines were adopted at the same time, with the SEPA data model setting out in detail the three layers described above. While these were not yet the exact rulebook versions that would be implemented for market launch, the essence of what the SEPA schemes would look and feel like was now ready and presentable.

The cards and cash frameworks, much less complicated to construct as they did not delve into as much detail as the rulebooks, were already approved by March 2006, together with the PE-ACH framework, the latter setting out the requirements for CSMs in SEPA (more on all of that later on).

The Four Corner Model

The 'Four Corner Model' (see Figure 6.1) enabling the key parties (the Originator, the Beneficiary and their respective banks/PSPs) to contract and transact with each other, is fundamental to the SEPA schemes. From a technical perspective, the ISO 20022 XML standard is required to be adhered to by banks/PSPs. These have the option of

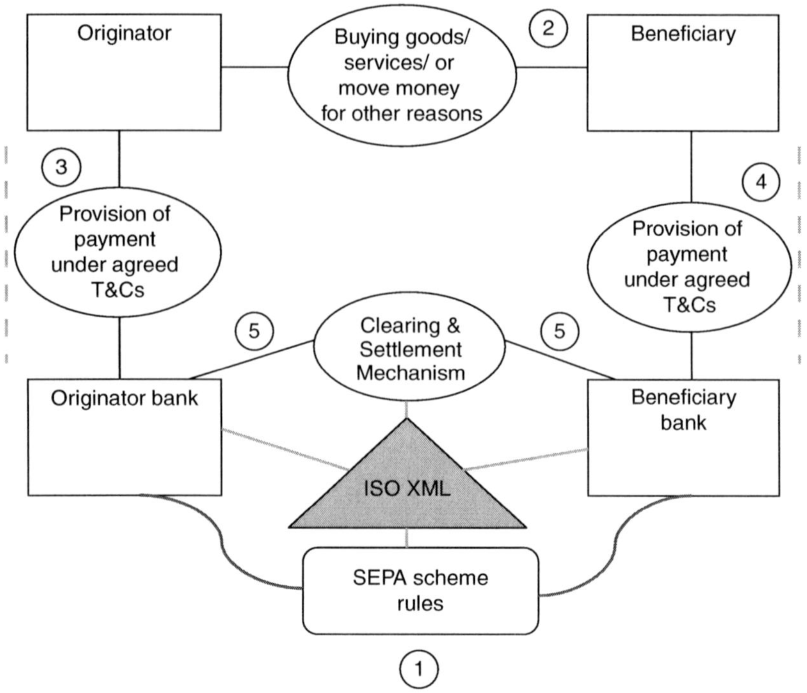

Figure 6.1 The SEPA Four Corner Model

using a SEPA-compliant CSM, or other SEPA-compliant clearing methods such as bilateral clearing. Customer-to-bank/PSP SEPA implementation guidelines were also developed, but the use of ISO XML between customers and their providers is optional (hence the dashed lines to the left and right of this figure).

Adherence to SEPA schemes

One of the key features of the SEPA schemes (this applies equally to SCT and SDD) is that banks/PSPs wishing to participate (NB non-bank PSPs are granted non-discriminatory access to the SEPA schemes by virtue of PSD article 28) are required to formally 'adhere' to the schemes, a process whereby they are bound in a contractual way to the scheme rules. This adherence process includes the provision of a legal opinion and a confirmation that the bank/PSP or group of banks/PSPs in question will ensure that they are 'reachable' under the scheme from a practical perspective. The Scheme Management Entity, part of the EPC

AISBL legal entity (under Belgium law), is the contracting party. While the decision to participate in a SEPA scheme is a voluntary one (initially at least), once the adherence agreement is signed and accepted by the EPC, the rulebook(s) become binding on the participant. Even though participants retain the freedom to choose between processing SEPA transactions themselves or using intermediaries or outsourcing parties, the responsibilities defined in the rulebook continue to apply to them.

SEPA: a borderless concept for (currently) 32 countries

The whole idea of SEPA is that whether a credit transfer executed under SEPA is domestic or cross-border should cease to matter, as the rulebook is providing a standardised procedure. The starter group of countries defined as the borderless SEPA geography was composed of the EU-27 plus the three EEA countries (Norway, Iceland and Liechtenstein) as well as the non-EEA country Switzerland. This area was enlarged in 2009 – a bit like EU enlargement – to include Monaco, another non-EEA country. Other banks/PSPs from non-EEA neighbouring countries are getting more and more interested in joining SEPA, and active discussions are currently being held, for example, with the Channel Islands and the Isle of Man.

Adherence criteria for EEA member country banks/PSPs are fairly straightforward as banks/PSPs across this area are bound by common EU-wide financial legislation. However, SEPA adherence criteria for non-EEA country banks/PSPs are slightly different, because as a general rule EU legislation does not automatically apply in those countries. The key point here is that there needs to be some form of legal level-playing field between EEA and non-EEA players. Where EEA countries were automatically eligible to join the SEPA initiative and thus allow their banks/PSPs to submit adherence applications directly or via a National Adherence Support Organisation (NASO), non-EEA countries need to be first considered eligible to join the SEPA club (as stated, so far Switzerland and Monaco have managed to do so). For example, they must ensure that their credit institutions are regulated by domestic legislation that is functionally equivalent to the Directive 2006/48/EC and that their non-bank PSPs are regulated via domestic legislation that is functionally equivalent to Title II of the PSD. Furthermore, these applicants need to demonstrate that domestic legal provisions relevant to payments made via SEPA are substantially equivalent to relevant provisions in the PSD (Titles III and IV), Regulation 924/2009 and Regulation 1781/2006 and that their PSPs are subject to anti-money-laundering processes in respect of SEPA participants that are functionally equivalent to EU Directives

2005/60/EC and 2006/70/EC. Provisions functionally equivalent to Articles 81, 82 and 93 of the Treaty establishing the European Community (competition law!) should also be in place in those jurisdictions and it is important that applicant countries have nothing in their domestic law that would be contrary to Article 3 of the Rome Convention regarding the Freedom of Choice of Law. Applicant countries have to demonstrate a strong relationship with the EU, ensure that no domestic legislation prohibits or impedes cross-border dealings between its (future) SEPA participants and existing SEPA participants, and that no tax or operational issues make payment services provided by the non-EEA applicant's (future) SEPA participant unfairly competitive vis-à-vis other SEPA participants. Of course financial regulators in non-EEA applicant countries will have to be able to share confidential regulatory information on SEPA participants and otherwise cooperate with SEPA country regulators once admitted.

While the above list of issues to keep in mind as a non-EEA country applicant is not exhaustive, it is worthwhile noting in the context of the challenge of aligning relevant conditions to create as much of a level playing field as possible across SEPA. In my opinion we are not yet at the end of the SEPA growth phase and certain players, such as the Channel Islands and the Isle of Man, would naturally fit into the SEPA geography.

Separation of schemes from infrastructure

Another key feature of the SEPA project is the clear split between infrastructures and scheme rules and principles. This split is intended to encourage competition and choice in the infrastructure space as well as – of course – in the bank-to-customer (or PSP-to-PSU) space. In line with the PE-ACH/CSM framework highlighted in Title III (and elaborated further later on in this Title) a number of options are permissible for exchanging SEPA transactions. Various CSM providers exist in the market and a bank/PSP has the choice of which CSM to use or whether indeed to use a CSM at all (bilateral clearing is still allowed so long as it is done in a SEPA-compliant way). The big idea here is that the pre-SEPA lack of choice for national or pan-European mass payment processing for euros will be a thing of the past.

Additional optional services in SEPA: from AOS to CHAOS?

As one of the necessary devices to ensure a sufficient level of consensus among the variety of stakeholders across the European payment landscape, the EPC was forced to invent an escape valve for banking communities and individual banks who wanted to do something slightly different to the standard rules within the SEPA schemes. The solution – the carefully labelled 'Additional Optional Services' (AOS) concept – is an attempt to recognise the 'human rights' of individual banks and communities to provide additional services to meet specific customer needs in a local or regional context, but to do so in a way which should avoid anarchy.

As you can maybe already imagine, the concept of AOS bears the intrinsic risk of acting as an accelerator for fragmentation in cases where banks would secretly (or indeed openly) really rather like to recreate their existing domestic circumstances despite having a harmonised payment scheme at their disposal. At the same time some banks and communities see it as the key to create more advanced SEPA solutions that not all of Europe is ready to adopt from the beginning (the old story of 'SEPA as a lowest common denominator' and how to avoid being trapped). The challenge therefore, as a former Secretary General of the EPC once put it, was in ensuring that 'AOS should not become Chaos'.

While an AOS between a bank/PSP and its customer in the context of a value-added proposition isn't an issue so long as the core transaction is based on the SEPA schemes – this type of service is a desirable outcome and very much in the competitive space – there is a clear concern in relation to AOSs that impact the inter-bank/PSP space and/or the other customer in the transaction chain. An example of an AOS impacting the inter-bank/PSP space might be a requirement on the beneficiary bank in an SCT to check that the ISO creditor reference present in the remittance information has the correct check digit. For an AOS impacting both the inter-bank/PSP relationship as well as the customer relationships on both sides, an extended remittance field longer than the standard 140 characters in SEPA could be quoted as an example. The challenge for the industry going forward will be to ensure full disclosure and where relevant approval or rejection of AOSs that fall into the last two categories and to consider which innovative enhancements should be built into the schemes themselves to avoid fragmentation. Any AOS that compromises the inter-operability between providers under the scheme triggers the risk of creating so-called 'mini-SEPAs' – a fashionable term that highlights the danger that a large-scale harmonisation project could accidentally end up where it started, in a fragmented domestic (or single bank/PSP) interpretation and definition of rules and procedures.

The market has already seen the development of some initial AOSs, where Finland has been the forerunner thus far. The question to ask here is: how could a bank offering SEPA services to a Finnish business customer compete with other Finnish banks if it has not implemented the local message-add-ons as represented by the AOSs? The simple answer is 'it cannot'. Surely this does not support pan-European competition, but appears to reinstate local barriers instead.

Furthermore, at individual bank level there is already ample evidence of certain players choosing their very own definition and implementation of the SEPA messages. For example, if a corporate goes to three different banks in Country A, asking for a SEPA credit transfer, and receives three different implementations, none of them being in line with the standardised SEPA rulebook version in terms of the definition of optional versus mandatory fields, there is clearly fragmentation – and this happens completely under the radar of the AOS discussions!

(2) The SEPA schemes: What's inside?

With the theory and some of the praxis now explained, let's take a closer look at the SEPA schemes themselves, starting with an examination of the most straightforward example of the species.

The SEPA credit transfer scheme – or SCT for short – is an inter-bank/PSP standard for processing non-urgent Euro credit transfers at domestic and cross-border level across the whole SEPA geography. As previously examined, the retail payments area in Europe already had some kind of method for sending a certain type of cross-border Euro payment, thanks to the Convention on Credit Transfers in Euro that was developed for Euro payments falling under Regulation 2560 (discussed in Title III). As a consequence, the creation of SCT was more of an evolutionary next step with an added emphasis on harmonisation and integration, rather than a totally new concept. However, for the banking industry it was still strange and new in many ways due to the fact that SCT was to be a formal scheme, with detailed business rules, message attributes and standardised formats. This scheme approach was very different from the usage of MT messages where banks map information and populate fields in a non-harmonised way, as highlighted earlier. The usage of the XML schema was for the first time going to allow for full harmonisation in this space. And let's not forget that the ISO and XML standards were in any case an innovation in their own right!

Key features of SEPA credit transfers

Looking at the functionality of SCT, every payment user who is transacting with an institution that has adhered to the scheme can as a minimum receive SEPA payments. Users are also able to initiate SCTs if their bank/PSP has created an SCT-based product and supports this in at least one initiation channel, for example online banking. This immediately shows the difference between the scheme and the product – a bank/PSP that has not developed an SCT product for its users can only provide reachability under the scheme, or in the absence of SEPA scheme adherence, not even that. This distinction will come in handy when we look at SEPA migration later on.

To execute an SCT, the sending party needs to provide the IBAN and in some cases the BIC of the beneficiary party, as all credit transfers processed via the SCT scheme require this type of account identification. Having a single standard for identifying and validating an account with a bank in Europe based on IBANs allows the storage of trusted information in a standardised way – another key benefit of SEPA.

Due to the fully standardised inter-bank/PSP message and processing rules as well as the ancillary optional standards in the customer-to-bank/PSP space, SCT, when fully implemented, will facilitate streamlined payments initiation, processing and reconciliation in a straight-through-processing (or STP) fashion. For larger business clients this degree of standardisation and automation is a very appealing proposition as it will save time and money – but more of that later on.

Customers using an SCT are also able to include specific remittance information of up to 140 characters within the payment message, on a structured or unstructured basis depending on the agreement between themselves and their bank/PSP (for consumers a structured field is usually not required, but consumers can of course also insert up to 140 characters in the payment message). While 140 characters were also supported in the old-fashioned MT 103 (and 103 +) SWIFT messages, the important additional obligation in the SCT is for scheme participant banks/PSPs to pass all the information included by the sending party through the payment chain. For example, banks/PSPs acting as intermediaries or on behalf of the beneficiary are not permitted to truncate information provided by the sending side. The beneficiary bank/PSP should also offer support to their business customers, such that the recipient can properly reconcile this information. This is of course again very relevant in the business space where bill payments need to be able to be reconciled correctly by the receivables department of a company.

Another key feature of the SCT scheme is the full amount principle (ring any bells?), which requires the full amount of a payment to reach the beneficiary bank/PSP. Additionally, banks/PSPs are only allowed to apply charges for a transaction if these have been agreed with their customers – at either end of the transaction. This concept, which is quite a revolutionary feature of SEPA, was essentially leveraged and extended by the PSD to cover any domestic or cross-border intra-EEA payment in any EEA currency. While the PSD in this respect envisaged itself as a legal framework for SEPA, it might also in turn have the effect of further increasing the attractiveness of the SEPA schemes as banks/PSPs are increasingly forced to confront the question of whether the use of a more efficient setup, such as SEPA, is not now becoming an essential requirement in the brave new world where non-transparent pricing is no longer allowed. Further speculation on cross-over issues such as these can be found later on in Title VII.

In addition, the processes around handling any rejected or returned payments are also fully standardised in the SCT scheme, providing certainty on what will happen in the event that a payment does not arrive at its destination. Rejects occurring in the relationship between the sending bank/PSP and its customer – for example, if the customer has insufficient funds on his account – are outside SEPA inter-bank/PSP rules, because the payment is never sent out in the first place. For other circumstances, the SCT provides a clear set of rules. Rejects in the inter-bank/PSP space, in case the beneficiary bank/PSP rejects receipt of the funds, need to be processed on the same day and the reject message must be sent back along the same path that the original credit transfer took, with no alteration of the data. Obvious stuff, perhaps, but certainly beneficial to the sending customer.

The rules for 'returns' (necessary where, for example, the account of the beneficiary is closed or blocked and cannot be credited) are also clearly defined. The beneficiary bank/PSP has to return the full amount and, as with a reject, to do so along the same path that the original credit transfer took, with no alteration of the data. This certainty around the full amount arriving back with the sending customer was not a given under existing cross-border payments. As a SEPA best practice this rule was even adopted by the EC when deciding what to include in the PSD's bag of tricks. For the 2010 next version of the SCT rulebook, the EPC will also include 'recalls' enabling a sending customer to ask his provider to revoke (before settlement) or recall (after settlement) a payment.

Moving on, the time it can take for an SCT to arrive at its destination is also clearly defined in the scheme rules and underpinned by the PSD. Here customers in some countries have seen an improvement in a cross-border context compared to the previous option available under the Convention on Credit Transfers in Euro as SCTs currently have to be executed in a maximum timeframe of D + 2, where D is the day the payment order is received by the sending bank/PSP. The beneficiary bank/PSP, in line with the PSD, is then required to credit the customer on the same business day that it receives the funds. As we already explored in previous Titles, the PSD will require all electronic transactions, including SEPA, to be executed no slower than D + 1 from January 2012 onwards.

As a small side note, while the EPC was busying itself designing the SEPA CT scheme, the banking community also saw the development of the 'Prieuro' service by the EBA. This additional credit transfer service was developed – with encouragement from the ECB – as a faster alternative to the SCT, but did not adopt the same design model or standardisation path as the SEPA schemes. Prieuro, which is more an inter-bank Service Level Agreement (SLA) than a full scheme, allows for Euro credit transfers to be executed within a four-hour time frame, with the choice of the CSM (essentially TARGET2 or EURO1 in this context) left to the initiating party. The service runs on the 'old' MT message formats and was essentially designed as a stop-gap answer to calls for a same-day Euro payment service, without yet going the extra mile of developing a fully fledged contractual scheme with a supporting technology platform for making real-time retail payments. Further developments in this area can be expected in SEPA in the future, particularly in the context of interesting technical developments seen at a local level already within some national communities, such as the UK's famous 'Faster Payments' scheme (with its promise that a sterling payment message can be exchanged between two direct member banks in only 15 seconds).

SEPA direct debit design challenges

The creation of the SEPA direct debit or SDD scheme was a far more significant challenge than the credit transfer piece and this for a number of reasons. For one, direct debits are in general perceived as more risky – and are certainly much more complex – than credit transfers. After all, a payer is giving another party the right to debit his account, thus giving up the level of payment-by-payment control that he would have in the context of a credit transfer. Furthermore, the existing European landscape for direct debits showed significant variations across national markets in terms of the characteristics, formats and message standards under which domestic direct debit schemes operated – while at the opposite side of the spectrum some Member States did not even have domestic direct debit schemes at all but relied on bilateral agreements between banks and creditors (for example, Malta, Cyprus). Unsurprisingly, therefore, the compromise on a pan-European harmonised scheme took much longer than initially expected.

On this point, it will be recalled that both SCT and SDD were really intended to have been ready for market launch in 2007. At the time it was optimistically assumed that the PSD would have already been in place across Europe as the legal foundation for SEPA. As we already know from earlier Titles, the PSD negotiations turned out to be much tougher than expected and only finally made it for adoption at EU level in December 2007, to be followed by the Member State transposition period. After much scratching of heads within EPC circles, it was decided that it would still be possible to move ahead with the launch of SCTs in January 2008. For SDD however, it was a very different story, as the banking industry really did need harmonisation of certain legal rules, particularly with regard to refund rights which prior to the PSD's harmonising influence varied wildly between Member States. Offering a cross-border direct debit for consumers therefore depended on the PSD being in place.

In another departure from the approach adopted for SCT, the SDD scheme was in fact developed as a twin proposition. In December 2005 the EPC Plenary had made the decision to formulate a specific second scheme for business-to-business DDs. As a consequence, two DD schemes were developed: one that can be used between consumers and businesses – the so-called SDD Core scheme – and one that is solely reserved for business usage – the so-called SDD B2B scheme.

Relatively plain sailing so far then – but now on to the seriously tricky stuff. We're talking here about DD schemes, which means that one of the fundamental questions to be answered is: Who should hold the mandate, the creditor or the debtor's bank?

Countries were seriously divided on this point. In relation to consumer DDs some were used to having the mandate, once signed by the debtor, stored by the debtor bank – the so-called Debtor Mandate Flow (or DMF). In those scenarios the debtor bank is able to use the original mandate to check that the authority to be debited has indeed been given by the debtor and that the amounts subsequently collected correspond to the agreement between debtor and creditor.

Other countries, though, had grown up with a very different tradition where once the mandate is signed by the debtor it is retained by the creditor – the so-called Creditor Mandate Flow (or CMF) approach. Under this approach, neither the debtor bank nor the creditor bank ever actually see the physical mandate (at least in normal circumstances) and the inter-bank flows and checking procedures are based on using electronic representations of relevant elements of the mandate's contents as this is exchanged between the parties at a transactional level.

Three camps emerged in the EPC community concerning what to do on this fundamental issue for the SDD scheme. Countries used to the DMF approach were rather keen to keep it – citing the high levels of consumer protection that they suggested this provided. Countries in this camp included for example Finland, Greece, Slovenia, Slovakia, Czech Republic, Hungary, Latvia and Lithuania. Other countries held the polar-opposite view, having grown up within the CMF tradition. Countries in this camp included some of the heaviest users of direct debits, namely Germany, Luxembourg, Netherlands, Spain, UK and Ireland. Third, there were those countries whose existing schemes combined elements of both DMF and CMF approaches – including Austria, Belgium, Italy, Portugal, France, Sweden, Denmark and Poland.

After what turned out to be a marathon discussion and negotiation lasting years rather than months, the final model chosen for the SDD scheme constitutes a compromise between the two models. In order to accommodate those countries that most widely used the direct debits at domestic level (for example, Germany), the CMF model was announced as the winner. However, in order to maintain the attractiveness of the SDD scheme for DMF countries a way needed to be found to make the mandate-related information readily accessible for all parties in the chain in the interest of debtor protection. While the original EPC proposal was to achieve this by formulating a proposal for a second-mandate flow option (that is, a possibility for a mandate flow from the debtor to the debtor bank), the final decision was the creation of the 'e-mandate' option within the SDD rulebook. This 'e-mandate', yet to go live in the market, is designed to support debtor protection by proposing that creditors should offer an electronic e-mandate function to their debtors. Once the e-mandate is created this information could then be automatically uploaded into the debtor's online banking profile. There, any changes to the mandate including blocking and cancellation could be performed by the debtor. Both debtor bank and creditor bank can then store the mandate-related information in an electronic form, so that in case of dispute the proof as to the status and content of the mandate can be delivered rapidly. Additional demands around the provision of such 'mandate-related information' even outside the context of the e-mandate option were to start surfacing in late 2009 and early 2010 in requests from countries such as Belgium and Italy, leading to some heated exchanges between the EPC and parts of the stakeholder community – to which we shall return to later in greater detail.

A second major design uncertainty that has plagued the development of SDD and continues to be a hot topic for debate in some circles concerns the lack of clarity from a competition policy point of view with regard to the legality of having a Multilateral Interchange Fee (MIF) – or, as labelled by the EPC, a Multilateral Balancing Payment (MBP) – as a component of the SDD scheme. As part of the historical diversity between existing national direct debit schemes it so happens that a number of countries in Europe have an arrangement whereby a creditor bank pays an interchange fee to a debtor bank for each DD collection that it sends to that debtor bank. The advocates of this approach argue that this is necessary to ensure an appropriate balance of cost and revenue between those banks that service larger corporate business clients and the (typically) smaller banks that focus on a consumer clientele and only act as debtor banks. The advantage of an MIF, they argue, is that it helps ensure that the consumer does not need to pay for receiving a debit entry on his account, while the corporate creditor should be happy to pay his bank for providing a collection service. In some countries the background story is even more intricate. Take, for example, the case of France where national legislation requires that cheques are issued and processed for free by banks and where the interchange approach for DDs was developed in part as a counter-balance to help debtor banks live more easily with the cheque situation. However, it also has to be said that the MBP or MIF practice does not exist in the majority of domestic European SDD schemes.

This very divergent set of current national practices was to lead to some of the most politically charged and tortuous discussions in the EPC's early life. From an internal EPC perspective, a compromise was eventually hammered out whereby the MBP-supporting minority were successful in negotiating the inclusion into the SDD rulebook for an MBP to be applied as a default for cross-border direct debits (only) under the scheme. However, having arrived at a fragile banking-industry consensus on this issue, concerns were then raised by DG Comp, the EC competition watchdog, who had as you can imagine been very carefully monitoring this debate. Their emerging view was that the EPC's proposed default MBP of 8.8 Euro cents, even though underpinned by carefully developed (and expensive!) pan-European economic analysis and competition lawyer advice, was still potentially violating EU competition law. Arduous and nail-biting discussions then ensued between the EPC as the scheme owner and DG Comp, with their pro-SEPA colleagues in DG Internal Market and the ECB largely having to watch from the sidelines. At risk was nothing less than the future of the SDD scheme, as none of the countries that had interchange in place in their existing domestic DD schemes were prepared to give in to a proposal that would remove this concept from the scheme altogether.

With a certain degree of irony (or maybe just symmetry) the breakthrough solution to the MBP log-jam was to come from the same source as the initial challenge – DG Comp itself. Conscious of the need to provide at least interim certainty sufficient to see SDD launched to the market, DG Comp discussed with DG Markt the possible options available in the context of the ongoing revision of one of our favourites, Regulation 2560/2001 (see Title III). In the end, as part of the new Regulation 924/2009, provisions were included to agree to the introduction of a default MBP for cross-border SDDs at 8.8 Euro cents per transaction, permissible until 1/11/1012. In practical terms, this meant that in the intervening period before 2012 a creditor bank (or PSP) could be required to pay a debtor bank (PSP) 8.8 Euro cents per cross-border SDD collection in SEPA (in the absence of a different bilaterally agreed arrangement). This would apply if the debtor bank is in a country that has a local MBP built into its national direct debit Euro scheme. Additionally, existing domestic levels of DD MBPs or MIFs are allowed to continue until 2012. However, it is still unclear what will happen after the 2012 date, for cross-border and domestic MBPs. An interesting point to note here is that the cross-border MBP story will not necessarily support low-cost harmonised SEPA DD pricing across SEPA as debtor banks in certain countries will ask for the cross-border default MBP, while others will not. At the same time, counterproductive situations could arise where a national DD is more expensive for a creditor than a cross-border SEPA DD, due to the existence of a national MBP of more than 8.8 euro cents. It gets even more interesting when looking at SEPA DD usage domestically versus a more expensive domestic non-SEPA DD scheme that includes an MBP (the assumption here being that the SEPA MBP will only kick in at a cross-border level). But then again, what happens to the pricing for a creditor in cases where SEPA DD is used domestically in a country that today has a domestic MBP? Will this MBP carry over into domestic SEPA DD pricing? And, after all, how can you offer harmonised SEPA pricing if domestic SEPA DDs have a different cost base than cross-border SEPA DDs. Many questions but not many answers ... for now.

With the CMF/DMF and MBP precipices more or less safely negotiated (despite not having fully resolved them), there was still a third tricky issue to fix in order for the EPC to have confidence in launching the SDD scheme into the market: How to ensure sufficient debtor bank reachability?

Years ago it was already clear to me that a low uptake scenario for SDD would prevail in the absence of regulatory pressure, partly because countries were still rather fondly attached to their local DD solutions, and partly because of the SDD 'Catch 22' problem (creditors won't wish to use SDD until they can be sure that all their customers' accounts can be reached through the scheme, but debtor banks won't want to make their customers' accounts reachable until they see customer demand and hence a business case for doing so). Accordingly, I strongly promoted the case within the industry and to the EC during the review of Regulation 2560 to also include a requirement that as a minimum those institutions that offer Euro direct debits today should be compelled to join the SDD Core scheme, at least in order to be reachable as a debtor bank. The logic of this approach was accepted by all and Regulation 924/2009 included just such a provision, making it a requirement for all banks/PSPs who were offering a domestic Euro direct debit to be also reachable through the SDD Core scheme by 31 October 2010. While a lobbying success and a good outcome, it should be noted that this was the first point at which direct regulatory intervention became necessary to ensure the successful delivery of a key element of the supposedly self-regulatory SEPA programme.

So, after our run-through of how the three major hurdles that could have stopped SEPA in its tracks had been tackled, let's now take a look at what is so special about SDDs by examining how these schemes actually work.

SEPA direct debit scheme features

The preparation of harmonised Euro direct debit schemes is of course a key element of the payments market integration, not least considering the fact that direct debits are widely used across the markets and constitute a significant benefit to the economy by ensuring that invoices are paid when due.

As with the SCT scheme, a customer intending to initiate a collection to debit his clients, for example a gas company sending its monthly direct debit collection to debit their users, needs to use the IBAN and BIC as the appropriate account identifiers.

From an inter-bank/PSP perspective, the collection is (of course!) handled via ISO 20022 XML standards according to the SEPA definition and these can also be extended out to the creditor (and in the B2B scheme also the debtor) level by making use of the optional customer-to-bank SEPA implementation guidelines.

However, while in a credit transfer things are rather straightforward as the person sending the money is clearly in direct control – he always

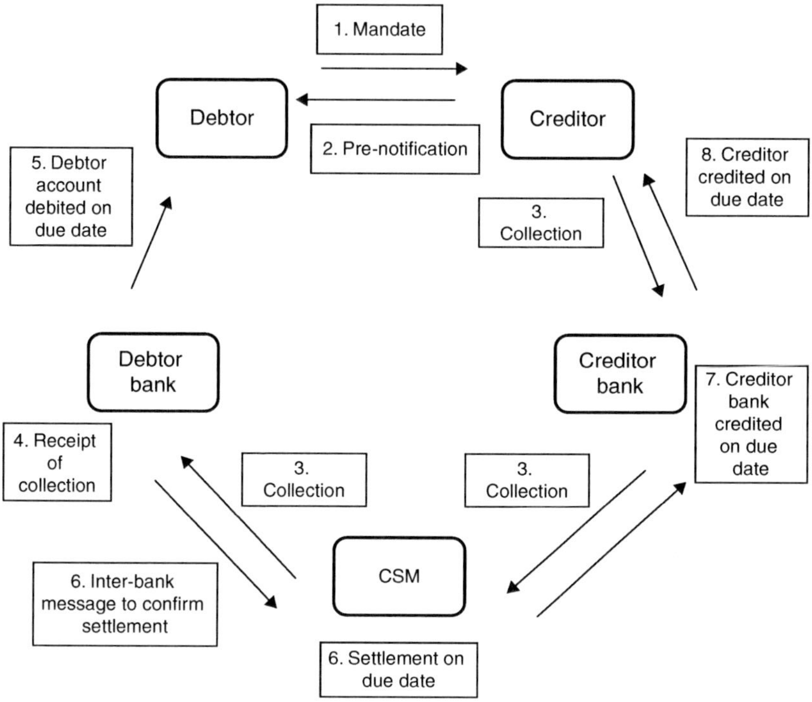

Figure 6.2 The SDD process flow

initiates the payment – the story in direct debits is more complicated. As previously highlighted, here, a payer is not directly paying to his counterpart, but – via a mandate – authorises another party to debit his account with the amount he owes. Giving someone the authority to debit your account requires trust on your side that this someone will legitimately follow the agreed steps and only debit the amount that you agree to or that you owe. With the final decision having been taken in favour of the CMF-inspired process flow, an illustration of how that works in practice is contained in Figure 6.2 above.

- *Step 1.* The direct debit process begins with the mandate, with which the debtor authorises a creditor to initiate a direct debit payment and by means of which the debtor can pay his bill. At the same time, the mandate includes the authorisation to the customer's bank/PSP to pay these collections. (Note: This so-called 'double consent' model differs from today's German consumer direct debit scheme (Einzugsermächtigungsverfahren/ELV) where the debtor just provides authorisation to the creditor to initiate a direct debit collection. This small but significant difference was going to prove a problem for SEPA migration later on ...). The mandate, duly signed, has to be sent back to the creditor. Once stored by the creditor the mandate related information has to be included in the collection message to the debtor bank every time the creditor wants to debit his customer.

- *Step 2.* When the time of payment nears – for example an electricity bill that is due to be paid by the 15th of the month – the creditor (the gas company) sends a pre-notification – often the invoice itself – to the debtor. In order to allow the debtor sufficient time to check the upcoming bill, and if irregularities occur to contest the upcoming debit, the pre-notification should arrive with the debtor well in advance of the collection.
- *Step 3.* The creditor initiates the collection. This can happen at the earliest at D-14, or fourteen calendar days before the due date/payment date. For the first collection in a series – for example the first gas bill payment of many to come, or in case of a one-off direct debit – the collection has to reach the debtor bank/PSP at the latest five inter-bank/PSP days before the due date. Once a direct debit is running, any subsequent collection can reach the debtor bank/PSP up to two inter-bank days before the due date.
- *Steps 4 + 5.* After the collection inter-bank/PSP message has reached the debtor bank/PSP, it will debit its customer on the day the payment is due. Having received mandate related information with the collection message in advance of the due date, the debtor bank also has the opportunity to provide a mandate checking service for its debtor in order to minimise erroneous debits.
- *Step 6.* Following this debit, the debtor bank/PSP will send a confirmation message to the CSM and settlement happens on that same day.
- *Steps 7 + 8.* The creditor bank/PSP receives the amount on the due date and credits the creditor – the bill is paid on time! Due date, debit date and settlement date all happen on the same day.

R-transactions in SDD

As with the SCT scheme, the EPC also defined clear rules for what should happen when transactions cannot be executed perfectly, for example, if the debtor disputes the amount that is being collected or if a debtor has actually closed his account and the creditor can no longer collect with the account information he has. As a further demonstration that the SDD process flows are more complex than their SCT relatives, there are in fact as many as seven scenarios where these so-called 'R-transactions' kick in. In no particular order, these are (take a deep breath) rejects, refusals, returns, reversals, revocations, requests for cancellation and refunds. For all of these exceptional transactions, the SEPA scheme has clearly defined processes and data sets to be used by the banks/PSPs involved.

The most famous R-transaction that was crucial to be harmonised from a legal perspective across Europe is of course the refund. Here the eight-week rule for authorised debits and the thirteen-month rule for unauthorised debits fully apply in the Core rulebook. In fact, the SDD is more generous than the PSD requires it to be, as it actually allows debtors an unconditional eight-week refund period, while (as a reminder) the standard PSD approach stipulates two criteria that need to be fulfilled in order to claim a refund: (1) the amount not being specified; and (2) the amount being unexpectedly high.

If a debtor, for any reason, wants to stop a debit on his account, the refusal process applies if the debit is stopped in advance. A debtor bank/PSP that acts upon its customer's request not to debit will execute a so-called reject, which means that the transaction is not processed at all. Furthermore, customers can always advise their banks/PSPs to ensure that no direct debits are applied to their accounts.

While we could spend many happy hours on the detailed rules that SEPA participants need to follow in case of any of the above exceptions, let's rather turn to something a bit more exciting.

The e-mandate

As mentioned earlier, one of the key measures eventually agreed as a way of ending the great CMF v DMF struggle was to create an 'e-mandate' option within the SDD rulebook as a quasi second-mandate flow option. This 'e-mandate' functionality, once implemented, offers a method to dematerialise paper-based mandates and to allow for automatic checks of the mandate validity throughout the entire processing cycle. The logic is that this will further help to limit the risk of erroneous debits and hence the level of potential rejects and returns. Obviously, the risk for debtors being potentially wrongly debited in a CMF context is perceived as being higher in some countries than others. From experience the CMF consumer DD scheme works perfectly fine in Germany, even though the creditor holds the mandate and never shares it with anyone – but then in this specific example it also happens to be the case that the creditor's bank is held liable to the debtor's bank for any damages caused by presenting a direct debit which has been incorrectly marked as authorised. However, as we know already, in some other countries today customers prefer the debtor bank to be responsible for holding the mandates (DMF).

The e-mandate is an optional service, which needs to be supported by all four parties in the chain. This means that a creditor would need to offer its customers an electronic channel via which they can complete and electronically sign the mandate. Once received by the creditor, the mandate is routed to the debtor bank for validation. Any creditor that offers the option to complete an e-mandate also needs to be able to ensure that the debtor can amend or cancel such a mandate and any amendments can only be undertaken by the debtor – such as an address change. To ensure a high level of debtor protection, the e-mandate-related data is shared between creditor, creditor bank, debtor bank and of course the debtor himself. As previously highlighted, debtor banks can choose to display these e-mandates in the debtor's online banking profile and allow for modifications and cancellations.

From a technical perspective, the e-mandate is also based on the ISO 20022 XML SEPA definition, and validation services provided by the debtor bank or an outsourced entity have to be able to verify the authorisation and perform an electronic signature – with the signing certificate issued by an approved EPC certification authority.

The big idea is that using an e-mandate will not only save time and cost – and trees! – but also allow the debtor to use this tool in the context of online transactions, for example establishing an e-mandate with an online merchant for a recurrent or one-off purchase as an alternative to using a card. A proof of concept for e-mandates is scheduled for 2010, but ultimately its success will depend on creditors' willingness to use this new method, and on banking and potential external routing providers' willingness to deliver the underlying technical services. Additionally of course there is the need to ensure the acceptability of a dematerialised mandate in place of a paper one – something which turns out not to be entirely straightforward in all countries (with Germany again as our example!).

The SDD B2B scheme

While most of our focus (and indeed the EPC's) has been on the development of the SDD Core Scheme, as mentioned earlier it was decided at the same time to develop a second parallel scheme for use in the B2B market. Most elements of the scheme are identical to the SDD Core Scheme, so all we will briefly touch on here are the key areas of difference. The most noticeable and important of these is that in the B2B scheme the debtor is not entitled to obtain a refund for an authorised transaction. The logic for this is that in the B2B domain debtors do not need the same levels of protection as consumers, and that given the amounts that may be involved it is essential to provide a high level of certainty of payment for the creditor. Of course, even under the B2B scheme the debtor still has the right to a refund in the event of an unauthorised transaction. As a result of this feature, the B2B scheme cannot be offered to a consumer customer as this would be in contravention of the PSD.

Other feature differences worth highlighting very briefly are that the B2B scheme requires debtor banks to ensure that the collection is authorised by checking the collection against mandate information provided with the collection (some debtor banks also perform this checking for SDD Core transactions), and requires debtor banks and debtors to agree on the verification to be performed for each direct debit. (Note: Interestingly, it turns out that the legacy German B2B direct debit scheme (Abbuchungsauftragsverfahren) requires the debtor bank to receive a direct debit mandate signed by the debtor in favour of the creditor (DMF-flow) – in direct contrast to the CMF approach used for the German consumer direct debit scheme (ELV), as referred to earlier. All of this was to lead to further complications in the context of SEPA migration discussions.) Additionally, in response to the specific needs of the business community, the B2B scheme offers a significantly shorter timeline for presenting direct debits and reduces the return period.

(3) So what benefits can the SEPA schemes bring to users?

The big picture – overall economic benefits

Both SCT and SDD have the potential to play a major role in facilitating cross-border trade of goods and services – and hence tie in very closely to supporting the key freedoms of the Single Market that we were discussing back in Title II. Over time, all customers, corporates, public administrations and consumers are expected to benefit from SEPA. So far, a comprehensive analysis of the macro, meso and micro benefits is not yet available, but nevertheless some interesting initial research has already been done.

For example, to investigate the extent of the potential benefits, the EC commissioned an independent SEPA benefit study in 2007, the result of which promised significant savings across the board. Looking at the economic cost of payments prior to SEPA, the analysis (based on 2006 figures) indicated an overall average level of 2.3 per cent of GDP based on research done across the UK, Poland and Sweden.[2] The study predicted a potential market benefit arising from SEPA of up to EUR 123 billion over a six-year timeframe, resulting in a 0.2–0.22 per cent gain of domestic GDP. In an even more startling prediction, the report also suggested that if e-invoicing were to take off, building on the back of the SCT scheme, benefits to customers could reach up to 0.8 percent of GDP per year on invoice-related processes.

A brief reference to an earlier (June 2005) McKinsey report is also relevant here as this had attempted to clarify the importance of payments for suppliers and providers. Their estimate was that at least 24 per cent of banking revenues, 34 per cent of banking costs and 9 per cent of profits are related to payments and the analysis observed that there are significant historical and structural differences in the revenue models and payment instrument mix in the Eurozone.

Looking at such high-level studies, what is immediately clear is that realising the economic benefits of SEPA will involve a coordinated effort by banks/PSPs and their customers, which will need to be carefully aligned with national implementation and migration plans, a topic we will come back to later.

Having looked at the big picture benefits, I will now review the potential benefits that SEPA, and in particular the SCT and SDD schemes, will be able to offer to the various types of PSUs.

So what's in it for consumers?

At the surface, the arrival of SEPA might not appear all that dramatically different or new to consumers. In the past, consumers, and for that matter every other type of PSU in Europe, could already send cross-border Euro payments using the IBAN and BIC and they even enjoyed regulatory protection when doing so, including on pricing given the Regulation 2560 requirement that Euro cross-border payments should be priced the same as the corresponding domestic service.

However, even though all of these things plus the Euro itself had been in place since 2002, the level of cross-border Euro payments had stayed at around 2 per cent of all Euro traffic in the market. In part this comes back to the argument that the actual motivation for cross-border payments is effectively down to the extent to which customers buy and sell services and goods across borders in Europe. It is therefore perhaps unlikely that simply by creating SEPA credit transfers as an alternative payment mechanism and regulating the pricing will in itself change this behaviour in any significant way. However, this would miss the point that SEPA is designed to take the place of existing domestic Euro schemes for credit and debit in the Eurozone in order to move from a fragmented landscape to a harmonised market. Therefore, consumers that today might have a sporadic need for cross-border Euro payments – for which they need the IBAN and BIC – will have to ultimately switch over to making the majority of their Euro payments in this way. For many this will mean a phase of adaptation from the relatively short domestic account number to the more comprehensive and safer IBAN.

In addition to the move to IBAN, there are key benefits within the SCT scheme, such as the principle of shared charges, which as we know was ultimately adopted as a general principle for all European payments in the PSD. This will ensure that the full amount of the payment travels to the receiving bank, while the charges for making and receiving the payment will be paid respectively by the sending and receiving customers and in line with clear agreements with their own PSPs (at least that's what should happen!)

The mass-adoption of SCT will also mean that a national payment in Germany can be initiated in the same way – with the same type of information – as a payment from Germany to Finland and vice versa. This will bring the long awaited harmonised solution for making payments, which can finally act as a real facilitator for buying abroad in Europe.

Overall, it is probably fair to say in relation to the SCT that the SEPA revolution mainly happens in the back-end systems of banks, with less visibility and excitement for the consumer, but that a tangible and positive change will come when Eurozone markets migrate their domestic credit transfers to the new scheme. This will then ensure a fully harmonised way of making credit transfers across SEPA, a point in time when the frontier between domestic and cross-border payments will finally disappear.

Looking at the SDD, the impact of SEPA is more intriguing for a consumer. Never before was there a possibility to use a direct debit instrument for cross-border Euro transactions. The ability to enter into a cross-border DD agreement with a business in another SEPA country will open up significant opportunities for enhanced cross-border commerce and trade. This is after all what the EU as a Single Market really stands to encourage.

In addition to the innovative feature of being usable across borders as well as domestically, the SDD also offers a higher degree of protection to consumers when compared to the PSD's benchmark rules.

As previously highlighted, the eight-week refund period is provided on a no-questions-asked basis rather than being conditional.

Additionally, the e-mandate option, once it has fully taken off, will allow customers a rapid and convenient method of entering a direct debit relationship with a supplier, while at the same time facilitating the SDD as a real alternative to using a card in an online shopping context.

And finally, for those that have a holiday home abroad in another European country the SDD offers now the opportunity to pay the regular fees for this second home from the consumer's home account, rather than obliging her/him to open and maintain local accounts in the place of the holiday residence. This will save cost and, more importantly, a lot of hassle.

There are many more examples of how consumers will be able to benefit from SEPA, but this should give you a flavour for now.

What about multinational corporates then?

Depending on their business model and size, businesses could see tangible benefits at many different levels. This is certainly the case for multinational corporations which tend by their nature to be permanently thirsty for standardisation, rationalisation and automation of their business processes.

The first step to improve corporates' business in the transaction banking context was the advent of electronic payments generated by ERP systems (Enterprise Resource Planning systems) that were enabled via corporate-bank connectivity. Furthermore, top-tier corporates already pursue opportunities to consolidate their Treasury and Cash Management services via so-called Shared Service Centres (SSC), or with help of an in-house bank, in order to achieve lower costs and economies of scale. However, the multitude of payment instruments (ACH, cross-border payments, wires, special high-value payments, cheques etc.) as well as the multitude of bank relationships and the fact that some banks have proprietary payment message formats or extend standard formats with proprietary elements, constitutes a significant set-up cost and maintenance burden for these businesses. Obviously national differences in payment message formats add another layer of complexity. The harmonisation of financial infrastructures and standards triggered by SEPA in this context is thus a tremendous opportunity for these businesses to implement fully standardised and automated solutions allowing for payables and receivables centralisation, thus removing the obstacles that exist due to different payment systems and formats across the European markets.

SEPA not only enables the move from fragmented local standards and formats to one European standard, including the option of a guaranteed remittance data set of 140 characters, but as a consequence also permits the rationalisation of accounts and banking relationships in terms of payment service provision, which will have a positive impact on the overall transactional efficiency.

SEPA ISO XML supports efficiency, reduces application development times, optimises the number of interfaces required and enhances security.

For example, consider the degree of automation, or STP. The higher the STP level the lower is the cost for a business. In the long run, SEPA will trigger an increase in STP over the whole supply chain, due to the option of end-to-end standardisation – from invoice to reconciliation of incoming receipts – as per the Customer-to-Bank implementation guidelines for SCT and the two SDD schemes.

Specific additional functionalities in the SCT scheme, such as allowing 'payment on behalf of' (POBO) using ultimate originator and beneficiary information will be very attractive for these customers as they enable them to make payments on behalf of their various group entities. Also, information on the purpose and type of payment – purpose field and code – will help the beneficiary business customer in the context of reconciliation. Furthermore, the development of a harmonised SEPA solution for salary payments, today executed mainly in a non-standardised way at domestic level, will be a necessity for markets to fully embrace SEPA. Otherwise, as we already see with ongoing local AOS developments, countries will look to find their own solution, introducing further fragmentation in SEPA.

SEPA supports the overall move for a business that today operates with resident entities in-country, using payment services at local level to pay local suppliers – a situation that is costly, complex, requires reconciliation processes for each account and liquidity tools to optimise local balances – to a situation where the business runs with one single operating account across all of its European franchise, where payments are initiated cross-border from that one central location and payment capabilities for SEPA are leveraged where available to allow for full POBO treatment. This will permit an optimised account and legal entity structure where supported information regarding the underlying purchasing entity is included in the payment message. Transparent and real-time information will facilitate liquidity management, a consolidated view of the supplier and buyer relationship can be put in place, and standardised low-cost transaction instruments – SEPA! – will enable the businesses' fast expansion into new markets.

Obviously, to achieve this ultimate state, it has to be noted that only SEPA currently offers the POBO functionality, which means that payments in non-Euro currencies will still need to be dealt with separately. At the same time, there is a medium-term risk that POBO fields may not be available in full to the beneficiary – remember the fact that not every bank has implemented the SEPA ISO XML. And finally, barriers such as BoP or other national legal, tax and regulatory rules could still interfere to a certain degree.

The creation of the pan-European B2B SDD brings the functionality of a dedicated business direct debit, known to only a few markets today but now available in all thirty-two countries. This B2B solution will in particular support the intra-European supply-chain management of companies, and is expected to boost trade across the Single Market. Businesses will have more certainty around their cash flows and can thus improve their liquidity/cash forecasting capabilities. In addition, the next SDD rulebook versions (due to be live in November 2010) will allow businesses to automatically reconcile outstanding invoices with incoming collections using the ISO Creditor Reference Standard.

In a nutshell, SEPA has the potential to support the next evolutionary step in a multinational company's treasury.

SEPA for SMEs

Looking at purely domestic SMEs (including micro-enterprises), such companies will find slightly less obvious immediate value in moving to SEPA solutions than their multinational big brothers. As such, the potential cost and complexity of implementing SEPA connectivity, despite the fact that SEPA will offer enriched transaction information, might initially outweigh the benefits for the individual business in question. Many smaller companies are not using sophisticated ERP systems and may even have a multitude of manual and paper-based processes to manage their treasury.

For those that have automated systems and processes in place, upgrading these to ensure their connectivity to SEPA will offer a number of immediate benefits and allow for a future-oriented long-term positioning of their business in the new payments world. The innovative end-to-end SEPA solutions based on global ISO standards will generate substantial efficiency gains, reduce costs and promote the trend towards automation and centralisation. Even for domestic-focused businesses, the streamlining of payment processing via SEPA will cut costs and increase transparency.

While the B2B SDD might be seen by some as more of a specialist business requirement for big banking entities to serve their large corporate clients, significant benefits are also supposed to be brought to the

SME community in Europe in order to facilitate the further increase and integration of trade within the Single Market.

The migration of Eurozone direct debit schemes and processes to SEPA will offer a common domestic solution and standard for businesses in Europe, whilst the feature of cross-border collections is, in the first instance, probably the most attractive trigger for businesses in the region that have an ambition to expand further into the Single Market.

The most important point is that banks/PSPs should support these customers with adequate SEPA solutions and mapping facilities as well as, for example, via SEPA multi-bank gateways to ensure that SMEs can effectively make use of SEPA. Of course, businesses could also decide to implement the XML themselves (like some larger corporates have done already). This would allow them to directly link into their PSPs' SEPA services (STP!).

SEPA for the public sector

The story of SEPA for these types of users is multifaceted. While the benefits of a harmonised scheme for Euro credits and debits are clear, the project itself – considered as one of the largest payment initiatives ever undertaken – is inevitably requiring political support. Public-sector bodies are considered as the key drivers of SEPA in bringing about critical mass, due to the fact that e.g. around 20 per cent of all credit transfers are executed by these entities. Accordingly, the EC is taking a close personal interest in monitoring and encouraging progress in this area.

Public-sector entities in Luxembourg are already 100 per cent SEPA CT users, followed by Slovakia with 60 per cent coverage and Belgium at 15 per cent. Other countries' public administrations (for example in the Netherlands) are planning for migration from 2010 onwards but the majority of countries have not yet set out clear migration timetables and deadlines – similar to the banking industry's migration plans that have generally also remained vague, with a few exceptions such as Finland, which will move to SCT by end 2010.

From the perspective of potential benefits for public-sector payment users, SEPA brings all the previously listed advantages including remittance fields and other aids to automation, certainty around max. execution times, full amount and the harmonised handling of rejects, returns etc. For a public-sector user that primarily needs to execute domestic payments, the changeover to SEPA might initially be rather limited in its appeal. However, public-sector entities that traditionally have more cross-border payment needs – for example the departments for work and pensions – will find the SEPA scheme an attractive proposition for their intra-European Euro flows.

Looking ahead, as much as SEPA is 'Euro' it is also 'Electronic'. The SEPA solutions will thus support governments in moving away from paper-based and cash-heavy processes towards electronic, paperless, more efficient as well as cheaper payment solutions, which will ultimately allow the improvement of public services. There is a clear expectation on the side of the EC that governments across Europe should rapidly embrace the e-government mantra where SEPA represents a facilitator and platform for e-government solutions such as e-invoicing, e-procurement, e-payments, e-signatures and e-services in relation to taxation, customs and social security payments. If, therefore, the start is made with SEPA, banks/PSPs can compete by offering multiple value-added e-solutions in this space that can support the public-sector agenda for efficiency.

(4) The launch of SEPA: reality versus expectation

SEPA credit transfers go first

As planned, and in line with expectations of the EC and the ECB, the launch of the SEPA credit transfer scheme took place on 28 January 2008. So, the big question is: What has happened since? How successful was the adoption and use of the new ISO 20022 XML standards by the banking industry in Europe? Did all stakeholders, consumers, SMEs, corporates and public-sector clients immediately start transacting their euro credit transfers, be it domestic or cross-border, high or low value, via SEPA? Well ... not exactly.

The seemingly good news is that as of July 2010 nearly 4500 banks in 32 countries have adhered to the SEPA credit transfer scheme – information which is publicly available on the EPC website where an up-to-date participant list can be downloaded. So, an impressive-sounding number, albeit still falling short of the 100 per cent reach level. Unfortunately, though, the reality so far is that the take-up of SCT has proved to be rather less enthusiastic than was hoped for. As of April 2010 still only around 7.5 per cent of the total volume of credit transfers generated by bank customers are being executed based on the SEPA standards, according to the SCT Indicators compiled by the ECB. The question then is: Why has the initial usage been so slow, and who is responsible for this?

A bank's participation in SEPA assumes the technical capability to be able to process an incoming ISO 20022 XML message. However, at this point the vast majority of SEPA CT adherents are not yet set up for internal end-to-end processing in XML. The continuous evolution of the SEPA rulebooks requires annual adaptation by banks/PSPs offering SEPA capability and also requires them to increasingly be in the position to be able to extend the advantages of the richer payment details to their customers. Considering that only very few of the global corporate payment customers are so far themselves running on XML, banks serving corporate and SME customers need for now to provide mapping solutions to allow these business clients to benefit from SEPA payments. But as said already, XML is still a challenge for the majority of banks themselves – meaning that to date many cannot provide the enriched payment messages to their clients as those banks use message conversion procedures instead.

At a general level, even though it could have been anticipated, the ISO 20022 XML also turns out to be something of a challenge from a technical, infrastructural and performance perspective. While domestic payment messages are usually very simple and short, thus absorbing little memory capacity (for example 1 or 2 KB for a UK BACS message), a SEPA message today is around 500 KB due to its breadth of information and the larger number of data fields. This richness, while bringing of course the aforementioned benefits to businesses, creates a real challenge for processing performance at high volumes if systems are not sufficiently equipped and engineered properly. Today, as shown by the numbers, these volumes are very low and thus there is not yet a challenge for banks and infrastructures. This will change ...

On a related point, banks that have a predominant business focus on domestic clients and domestic payment needs might consider SEPA not to be a priority as for them it only adds yet another way to make cross-border Euro payment in Europe. This might to a degree explain the reluctance of certain banks to provide anything but 'passive reachability' to date while others have not even joined the scheme at all (we still miss a few thousand banks in the SCT scheme today). Equally, it is important to remember just how fragmented and diverse the structure and goals of different elements of the retail banking market in Europe are to appreciate why seeking to get these players to take common cause – in migrating en masse to the SEPA schemes – is in itself a task which makes herding cats seem suddenly rather straightforward!

Just before we get too depressed, though, there are a few examples – albeit rather isolated at this point – of communities who have been able to make more positive commitments and are on course to embrace SEPA CTs a little more rapidly. Among these are our good friends from Finland. On 17 February 2010, a news release was issued announcing that

Table 6.1 Summary of the Finnish SCT migration plan

Timing	Requirement
From 1 July 2010	IBAN and BIC must be provided in invoices and credit transfer forms.
31 Dec 2010	The transitional period for credit transfers ends, after which date the existing domestic legacy payment data standards are to cease to exist as standards.
Jan 2011–31 Oct 2011	Banks and software houses are permitted to continue offering the services scheduled for termination as 'special services'.
From 31 Oct 2011	Banks will no longer accept payment data complying with the legacy standards.
From 1 Nov 2011	Payment orders cannot be submitted without an IBAN.
From 31 Dec 2011	Transmission of payment transactions and recurring transactions transmitted according to legacy standards in inter-bank payment traffic will end.

an approach to migration to SCT had been agreed between Finnish banks and the members of the Finnish SEPA Forum Core Group – and, critically, had also approved by the Bank of Finland and the Financial Supervisory Authority. The agreed plan takes the form of a number of progressive stages, as summarised in the above table (see Table 6.1). Overall, this approach – including the way in which the private and public sector have managed to work together – is a model that other countries might wish to study closely.

In Title VII, we will return to examine the wider question of SEPA migration and explore what can and needs to be done to make serious inroads into the remaining 92.5 per cent gap left towards full SCT migration.

The second launch with SEPA direct debits

1 November 2009 finally saw the launch of the first ever pan-European payment scheme to process Euro-denominated direct debits for consumers and businesses. Despite having been hotly anticipated for almost two years by businesses and politicians across Europe, the SEPA DD launch was not trumpeted as loudly as in the case of SCT in 2008. One of the many reasons for that may have been that the majority of banks and businesses were at the same time busy welcoming – or at least focusing on – the arrival of the PSD, which had equally been anticipated for some time.

In the run up to the launch of the SDD, the number of adherence agreements received by the EPC was rather less impressive than the level seen in the feverish excitement (well, sort of) during the build-up to the

SCT launch. There was almost a sense that the SDD had been now so long awaited that some banks had forgotten about it in the meantime.

Initial adherence statistics thus showed an average participation of around 30 per cent of eligible SEPA banks for both DD schemes, with around 2600 institutions signed up respectively. While these institutions are considered to be responsible for around 70 per cent of current Euro direct debits, the number still reflects a rather disappointing lack of initial interest in providing SDD based services to customers when compared to the SCT.

A few countries are particularly low in terms of initial adherence levels, due at least in part to the previously discussed MIF/MBP issue. As described earlier, all banks offering a domestic Euro direct debit service within Europe will be required to join SEPA by November 2010 (due to the Porsche Regulation, as Regulation 924 is now known in some circles), but this is only to ensure full debtor bank reach – an important step but not on its own enough to turn the trickle into the necessary flood.

The countries currently spearheading SDD adherence – at least on paper – include Germany, Austria and Italy. However, the adherence figures do not in practice show whether banks are actually proactively offering this service to their customers on either creditor or debtor side at this point, which would explain the fact that initial volumes across Europe were in the hundreds rather than the thousands or millions.

Resolving the reach issue is only part of the solution. The success of SDD is also crucially dependent on the active support of creditors. After all, if a consumer or a business is not asked by their biller to get paid via SDD instead of some legacy local DD, no debtor would ever be starting to use the SEPA solution or demanding it from its bank/PSP.

One of the other factors that need to be overcome is the need to avoid businesses having to send out new mandates to all their consumers as part of their migration to SEPA, thus mitigating costs and potential adverse business impacts. Apparently Germany – the biggest user of direct debits – still falls short of a solution to allow for existing mandates to continue their legal validity under SEPA.

Finally on our mini-quest to explore some of the initial barriers to widespread SDD adoption, recent discussions between the EPC community and consumer organisations at EU level indicated some discomfort with the proposed CMF model, largely based on the perception that having a situation where the creditor (not the debtor bank/PSP) holds the physical mandate would somehow not be safe enough for consumer debtors in terms of being protected from unauthorised debits. Many of the necessary checking features, which are part of DMF schemes, are in fact equally possible to be supported within a CMF flow. Indeed a number of these are already built into the SDD scheme rules as 'optional' features to be used at the discretion of debtor banks/PSPs. At the same time, an additional option for creditor banks/PSPs to provide mandate-related information to the debtor bank/PSP before the collection has been now embedded into the next version of the SDD Core scheme. And finally, the use of the e-mandate will in due course provide further ability to check the validity of the mandate at all stages in the transaction chain.

Pulling all these various SCT and SDD adoption issues together, in Title VII we will go on to explore what can be – and is being – done to overcome these and get the SEPA migration super-tanker finally pointed in the right direction as well as to travel at proper speed.

(5) SEPA for cards: pump up the volume

Introduction

The SEPA project in the area of cards is an altogether much less tangible affair. In the light of the EPC's decision to develop a framework rather than to write specific rules that need to be adhered to by all participants, the launch of the SEPA cards framework (SCF), on 1 January 2008, was therefore a much quieter event than that of the SCT scheme 27 days later. No customer around Europe suddenly came into the possession of a SEPA card, and no new cards scheme, domestic or international, suddenly appeared. Hence no issuer began issuing cards that would be proudly showing off a SEPA logo.

To understand what the SCF and the SEPA card actually are today and are intended to be in the future, we will now take a brief look at key issues, challenges, benefits and the possible future of this important SEPA instrument.

SEPA for cards – the vision

For a number of years now, cards have been the fastest-growing electronic payment instrument across the globe, linked closely to the growth of retail financial services. As a means of payment, cards are nowadays the primary alternative to cash and cheques, offering convenience for consumers and merchants with a much higher level of security. It is hardly surprising, therefore, that cards are seen as a core component of the SEPA project – in fact a central element.

The main types of actors in the cards market are the card issuer and card acquirer (both roles traditionally performed by banks, at least before the arrival of a certain EU Directive), the card holder, the merchant, and of course the card scheme itself. The role of the card scheme is to set the rules, including acceptance and transaction processing standards and requirements designed to ensure the operational integrity and security of its processes.

The majority of payment cards already have some form of international inter-operability with wide ATM and point-of-sale (POS) acceptance; for example, via Visa and MasterCard's credit and debit card schemes. However, domestic payment cards in SEPA countries might lack this functionality if they are not branded, co-branded or integrated into a wide-acceptance card scheme initiative.

Against this background the conceptual aim of the EPC in this area was to establish a common set of standards for the multiple card schemes operating in the Eurozone and any other participating countries and, in doing so, enable more of a level playing field for the actors to expand or otherwise improve the efficiency of their businesses.

In terms of potential benefits this would bring, the concept is that acquirers would then be in a position to be able to acquire transactions from any SCF-compliant scheme (meaning an end to the concept of a national monopoly acquirer, or rules that prefer domestic acquirers over acquirers from other countries). Additionally, it would increase the freedom and ability of merchants to be able to do business with a wider range of acquirers.

From a consumer perspective, the intended benefits were as summed up in the following brief extract from the opening preamble to the SCF itself:

> This SEPA Cards Framework ... will enable European customers to use general purpose cards to make payments and cash withdrawals in euro throughout the SEPA area with the same ease and convenience as they do in their home country. There should be no differences whether they use their card(s) in their home country or somewhere else within SEPA.

So to recap, the focus of the SCF was not to create a common scheme but rather to concentrate initially on matters of card acceptance and inter-operability ...

What is a SEPA card – and what is actually in the SCF?

The SEPA card, which by the way is not a SEPA-branded item, can be a debit, credit or ATM 'cash only' card and can – or rather should – be able to be used in any of the 32 SEPA countries for payments in Euro currency.

However, the EPC very strongly underlines that neither acceptance nor issuance is mandated by the framework. In fact, market forces are deemed to do the necessary to ensure the ultimate success of the SEPA card. What is really focused upon in the SCF context so far is the fact that any card scheme, domestic or international, should join the framework and follow the rules for inter-operability and safety. Any institution interested in joining the framework should be able to do so, due to transparent and non-discriminatory criteria.

Any issuer or acquirer of a SEPA card should be able to operate freely in the 32-country space. Again, the PSD plays a key role here in allowing non-bank PSPs to obtain a licence to issue or acquire cards in Europe, and once fully authorised in one of the EEA countries to make use of a European passport. This will allow those institutions to issue and acquire cards freely across the EEA markets (admittedly missing out on Switzerland and Monaco – the current two non-EEA countries in SEPA) and thus to further contribute to competition in this space.

In the SCF, the EPC defines the principles and rules needed to underpin SEPA-wide acceptance of cards. The idea in the SCF is that SEPA for cards would be reached through a two-stage process. Step 1 involves banks and PIs taking measures to ensure that the payment scheme(s) they participate in become SCF-compliant. Stage 2 is then ensuring that banks and PIs deliver SCF-compliant payment products to their customers.

To this end, the SCF defines that each bank or PI involved as a participant in various SCF-compliant card schemes has a choice of a number of options (see Table 6.2):

Table 6.2 SCF-compliant options

Option 1: Select one of the SCF compliant schemes to replace its current use of a non-SCF-compliant scheme.
Option 2: Act in such a way as to evolve one or several non-SCF-compliant schemes so that they become SCF-compliant.
Option 3: Brand its cards with more than one SCF-compliant scheme provided that these schemes accept such co-branding.
Option 4: Develop its card business into its own SCF-compliant three-party scheme by issuing/acquiring directly or through licence agreements.

SCF-compliant cards must have the potential to be effectively accepted at ATMs and/or by merchants in all SEPA countries. However, the SCF does not mandate any level of geographical coverage within SEPA – and does not guarantee that all cards will be accepted by all merchants.

The aim, though, is to ensure that all general-purpose cards in circulation in SEPA, whether co-branded or not, will be SCF-compliant from 31 December 2010 onwards – and also that they all operate in accordance with the EMV (originally Europay MasterCard Visa) standard as the common security approach, thus complying with CHIP and PIN security for card transactions.

Initial adoption and EMV roll-out

Accordingly, an important indicator on the progress of creating SEPA for cards is the number of cards, POS and ATMs now in the market that require the use of PIN and CHIP for the authorisation of a card payment. As of Q1 2009, the statistics showed that in terms of ATM cards, 15 of the SEPA countries had reached the magic 100 per cent figure for EMV penetration, including countries such as France, Portugal, Finland and the UK. Other markets were climbing towards this level, for example Germany 85 per cent, Italy 75 per cent and Belgium at 93 per cent, with countries like Poland (44 per cent), Malta (53 per cent) and Lithuania (39 per cent) bringing up the rear. Iceland at that point was still recording 0 per cent.

At the same time, EMV compliance for cards reached 71.10 per cent across the SEPA region with 82.57 per cent of POS terminals being EMV-compliant as well.

Existing national card schemes are being adapted as required for SCF compliance, governance, processing and other functions. Already compliant, for example, are Banksys (Belgium), Girocard (Germany), GIE CB (France) and SIA SBB (Italy).

The standards issue

It needs to be recognised that the acceptance of a card at any given terminal is ultimately dependent on the decision of a merchant to accept that particular card, which in part also depends on the acceptance of a common set of standards by all parties. It was therefore recognised by the EPC that the SCF on its own was not sufficient and that additional – and highly technical – work would have to be undertaken in the standards area. The EPC cards standardisation programme, still very much 'work-in-progress' at this point, is aimed at establishing minimum requirements in the following 'domains': cardholder to terminal, card to terminal (EMV), terminal to acquirer, acquirer to issuer.

The SEPA Cards Standardisation Volume (what a grand name!) developed by the EPC defines the functional and security requirements (including requirements for the evaluation and certification methodology and architecture) recommended for adoption by players throughout the card payment value chain to ensure inter-operability within SEPA.

The standards proposals themselves are due to be fully defined by the end of 2010, having already gone through several rounds of consultation. The key challenge, of course, apart from defining these standards in the first place, will be to ensure that they are not only implemented by banks and other PSPs but also actively taken on board by merchants, which means that merchant terminals will need to be configured to ensure SEPA compliance, allowing for a true 'SEPA Cards Experience'.

The Eurovision card contest – a third scheme?

If you look briefly at the global cards market, you will quickly observe that the six largest card schemes account for roughly 75 per cent of all cards in circulation worldwide, albeit the fact is that a majority of cards are being co-branded with national schemes. Four of these six are US-routed and two emerged from Asia. Noticeably absent from the list of market leaders, though, is any European card scheme.

So, unsurprisingly, another lively aspect to the SEPA cards debate has been the question of whether the SEPA area needs its own European card scheme. This has certainly been the view of the ECB and the EC for a number of years now, which fear that the dominance of existing international schemes could actually reduce competition for cards when the SCF is fully implemented. Accordingly, the European authorities have been arguing that the European banks should pick up this challenge – considering that the SCF offers banks an opportunity to combine their capabilities to create a major new European cards scheme. It is debatable whether for the European markets adding a third player to a global duopoly will really change much in terms of competition, but I shall leave that to a future analytical excursion.

Discussions continue in the market with various groupings of banks and other providers considering launching initiatives in this space. The best known of these are the initiatives of Euro Alliance of Payment Schemes (EAPS) to interlink six card schemes from Germany, Italy, Spain, Portugal, the UK and EUFISERV (an initiative of the European Savings Banks); the Monnet initiative which is investigating the creation of a new scheme and was originally launched by French and German banks, and the Payfair retailer-driven initiative aimed at delivering a merchant-oriented debit card scheme.

At this point it is not yet clear whether any of these initiatives will be successful in creating a scheme able to rival Visa/MasterCard – and then of course there is also the added complication around the business case for a new European card scheme in the light of the level of EC scrutiny concerning multilateral interchange fees.

The final piece of the SEPA cards jigsaw – the MIF debate

The economics and financial model for a four-party card scheme (cardholders, issuers, acquirers, and merchants) include key elements such as the fees paid by the cardholder to the issuer, the interchange fee paid by the acquirer to the issuer, and the merchant service charge (MSC) paid by the merchant to the acquirer to pay for processing and the interchange fee.

In the context of consumer cards the level of interchange fees has for a while been under close scrutiny in some card markets, with the EU certainly being no exception, as regulatory bodies are putting more and more pressure on the banking community to reduce fees, operating on the somewhat hopeful expectation that an improvement in the economics for merchants would of course be passed on to cardholders. (Note: experiences e.g. in Australia suggest that life may not be as straightforward as that!)

In any event, this has certainly meant that MIFs have been a hot topic of discussion in the EU at the same time as the SCF has been taking shape and the 'Third Scheme' arguments have been raging. In late 2007, the EC prohibited MasterCard's multilateral intra-EEA interchange fee for cross-border consumer cards transactions. MasterCard appealed, but then decided in April 2009 to adopt an interim solution based on the so-called tourist test theory – which seeks to ensure that merchants do not pay more for a card transaction than for a cash transaction. As a result, it has fixed its cross-border intra-EEA MIF at 0.2 per cent for consumer debit card transactions and 0.3 per cent for consumer credit card transactions. The EC has accepted MasterCard's revised approach, at least for now, and also came to an accommodation with Visa in April 2010 in connection with its MIF on intra-EEA cross-border debit transactions. However, it remains to be seen whether the 'tourist test' approach (recently renamed 'merchant indifference test') is relevant in every case – and the banking industry is certainly not keen to see it used too heavily across Europe.

In the context of our story, though, the key point is simply that none of this is helping to speed up the process of migrating to SEPA for cards – with or without a new European scheme champion. In addition to that banks may generally need to rethink their business models depending on how the interchange issue is finally settled.

(6) Infrastructures in SEPA: a fresh look

With the evolution of new standards in payment processing in Europe – and ultimately, hopefully, at a global level – the role of infrastructure providers becomes an additional and important key variable in the SEPA equation. Domestic ACHs (or automatic clearing houses) are today players in a very fragmented landscape across Europe. More than 30 exist across the SEPA region, mostly working on proprietary standards, and it is surely a legitimate question to ask whether we really need that many in a harmonised payment landscape of the future.

While processing credit transfers, direct debits and cards transactions has traditionally been taken care of by ACHs or in some cases the NCBs, whereas in certain countries bilateral clearing dominates, the progressive vision offered by the SEPA harmonisation project is to centralise processing, clearing and settlement into a small handful of pan-European providers capable of reaching all banks/PSPs in the SEPA zone. This would save cost and complexity and bring countries closer together with the objective of market integration. Furthermore, most infrastructures are bank-owned entities, which should in theory make it relatively straightforward to bring about a consolidated space where all banks can start saving costs and reaping the benefits of centralisation and guaranteed reach.

The EPC's approach – the CSM framework

The EPC Roadmap 2004–10 articulated a key principle, which states that in the new SEPA world schemes should be entirely separated from infrastructures through which they are operated.

Within the infrastructure space, three sub-layers were identified in the EPC's PEACH/CSM Framework document, as approved in 2006. At the first level there is a set of Principles for SEPA scheme-compliant CSMs. At the second level, individual scheme participants are free to select the CSMs that meet their requirements, provided that they comply with these principles. At the third level, processors and networks then play their role in supporting the operations of participants and CSMs, under contracts agreed between the parties concerned.

As set out earlier in Title III, CSMs fall into a number of categories, all of which are possible candidates for selection by scheme participants wishing to execute their SCTs and SDDs in accordance with the schemes. By way of a brief reminder, these range from a full PE-ACH, right through to bilateral SEPA scheme-compliant clearing and settlement.

The most interesting (and most rare!) animal to be seen in the SEPA CSM jungle is a full PE-ACH which according to the EPC is 'A business platform which will include the provision of the clearing and settlement of SEPA Scheme payments with full reachability throughout SEPA and made up of governance and operational rules, the necessary technical platform(s) and related services.' The key point to note here is that a PE-ACH has the daunting challenge of providing full reach, which is an essential requirement of SEPA.

The PE-ACH/CSM Framework anticipated the need for at least one PE-ACH, but also the possibility for coexistence of more than one. Just to confuse matters further (in case they are not confusing enough already), a PE-ACH-compliant ACH can be one integrated PE-ACH-compliant ACH acting alone, or composed of several SEPA scheme-compliant CSMs working with each other in an integrated environment.

Progress along the path to consolidation

In September 2007 the EPC invited infrastructure providers to disclose their intention to become SEPA scheme-compliant CSMs in order to obtain assurance about who would be there in the market to support SCT – the answer being that no less than 15 infrastructures decided to make declarations to that effect.

In its fifth SEPA Progress Report, the ECB defined four criteria to assess the SEPA compliance of infrastructures: processing capability, reachability, inter-operability and choice. The ECB went on to publish more detailed terms of reference on this subject in April 2008, inviting infrastructures to use these as guidance for self-assessment and to make the results publicly available from September 2008.

The following table (see Table 6.3) shows the current list of SEPA scheme-compliant CSMs and PE-ACH providers, including (where relevant) their country of origin.

As you can clearly see, while there are now a significant number of processors qualifying as SEPA CSMs, only the EBA Clearing's STEP2 SCT system currently operates as a PE-ACH – reflecting the low and largely cross-border volumes seen to date. The STEP2 system has some 300 banks connected directly and in July 2010 processed 663,259 SEPA-compliant credit transfers on an average day, representing a value of 3.84 billion Euro.

The good thing is that, given that the STEP2 system (of course!) insists on IBAN and BIC being used, in line with SCT Rulebook requirements, any decision to start using STEP2 for domestic transfers – with Luxembourg as perhaps the best-known example to date at country level – represents a positive step in the direction of SEPA migration.

To give you another specific example of initial progress, in Slovenia, while all the banks are connected to EBA STEP 2 (either directly or

Table 6.3 SEPA scheme compliant CSMs and PE-ACH providers

SEPA scheme-compliant CSM	SCT/SDD	Country
Banca d'Italia	Yes/Yes	Italy
Bankart	Yes/No	Slovenia
Bankservice JSC	Yes/Yes	Bulgaria
CEC	Yes/No	Belgium
Deutsche Bundesbank	Yes/Yes	Germany
Equens	Yes/Yes	Germany/The Netherlands
EuroGiro	Yes/Yes	Denmark
Iberpay	Yes/Yes	Spain
Interbanking Systems (DIAS)	Yes/Yes	Greece
KIR S.A.	Yes/No	Poland
National Central Bank of Austria	Yes/No	Austria
ICBPI-ICCREA	Yes/Yes	Italy
SIA-SSB	Yes/Yes	Italy
SIBS	Yes/Yes	Portugal
STET	Yes/Yes	France
VocaLink	Yes/Yes	UK
PE-ACH-compliant ACH		**Country**
EBA Clearing	Yes/Yes	n/a

indirectly via Banka Slovenia), to ensure the necessary pan-SEPA reach the market decided at the same time to establish a multilateral net clearing payment system to enable processing of domestic payments in accordance with the SEPA data format. The system, known as SEPA Internal Credit Payments system (SEPA IKP), went live on 4 March 2009 and has already facilitated the orderly migration of payments from the legacy Giro Clearing system – to the extent that in the final days of the operation of the old system, participants sent a daily average of just a few dozen payments to the system. This means that Slovenia is already on SEPA for domestic credit transfers.

A further interesting example of the early adoption of STEP2 to enable domestic SEPA processing can be found in Finland. The EBA Clearing has undertaken a number of functionality enhancements to the core STEP2 SCT service since its launch to better meet the requirements of communities such as Finland, and has also been able to accommodate a number of AOSs agreed on between banks operating in Finland, such as the transfer of Scandinavian characters, Finnish reference numbers and payment dates. As a consequence, it looks like the existing Finnish inter-bank payment system (PMJ) might be shut down at the end of 2011 in line with the Finish SEPA credit transfer migration plan that we referred to earlier.

Other approaches to cracking the reach nut are also being explored. VocaLink and Equens, for instance, have each worked towards offering pan-European ACH propositions via a mix of ACH linkages and partnering with banks/financial institutions.

The pace of national migration to SEPA will clearly have a major influence on the speed with which the anticipated consolidation of the CSM market will happen, as will the extent to which CSMs can ensure technical inter-operability using the varying approaches to achieving 'reach' and scale.

Today though, the degree of harmonisation is not yet sufficient to create total inter-operability for SCT and SDD across Europe, between different categories of CSMs, nor to yet have triggered processor consolidation in a material way.

(7) SEPA for cash update: has the bleeding stopped yet?

To complete our tour of the key SEPA deliverables, let's finish this Title with a very quick revisit to the world of cash – a topic I nearly forgot to return to given all the other excitement generated by recounting the dramas around the design of the SEPA schemes and the related stories concerning cards and infrastructures.

We last looked at the SEPA for cash idea (a counterintuitive concept in so many ways) in Title III, at a point where the EPC's Cash Working Group had just reached the scary conclusion that the cost of cash to society might add up to as much as €50 billion per annum and had come up with nine recommendations for 'things that needed to be done', ranging from developing joint cards and cash strategies to evaluating – with the ECB's help – the case for a Europe-wide cash handling infrastructure.

Well, one significant action since then has been to create the exciting-sounding concept of a Single Euro Cash Area (SECA), followed by the publication of the EPC policy document 'The SECA Framework' in March 2006. Developed in close consultation with the Eurosystem Banknote Committee, banks and other market participants, the idea behind SECA is to create a level playing field for cash ensuring that the basic cash functions undertaken by the NCBs in the Euro area become interchangeable – in other words to create a common level of service and processes.

Consequently, one of the ideas behind SECA is to increase efficiencies in the cash-handling cycle in order to reduce costs to society as a whole. Additionally, the other SECA ambition is to encourage consumers and merchants to migrate from cash to payment cards and other electronic payment types – a key goal of the SEPA initiative.

Beyond coining the SECA concept (as it were), the EPC also developed recommendations aimed at bringing about a common Euro-wide infrastructure for wholesale cash based on a number of key principles – such as the development and adoption of common security requirements for Euro note transportation, and the identification of best practice standards for coin and banknote packaging.

For its part, the ECB/Eurosystem, issuer of Euro banknotes (interestingly, coins remain a national responsibility), published in 2007 its own roadmap entitled 'Measures for More Convergence of NCB Cash Services'.

Finally on our whistle-stop tour of cash developments, we should note that following the publication of a White Paper in May 2009, the market is now awaiting the EC's contribution to the cash debate, in the form of a proposal for a Regulation on cross-border Euro cash transport by road.

As a consequence, hopes are apparently now high (at least among the people who dream about such things) that in the future the principles of the Single Market will apply to the daily business of cross-border cash transport by road.

A final point to mention in the cash context is that the EC has recently published a Recommendation on the scope and effects of the Euro as legal tender (March 2010), which lists a number of points that are rather questionable in the context of the industry's work towards making the use of cash more efficient and increasing incentives for customers and businesses to move from cash to electronic payment methods. Obviously the acceptance of Euro banknotes and coins for payment in retail transactions should be a decision left to market forces and individual security preferences of businesses – the recommendation states the opposite; recommending acceptance of high denomination banknotes in the context of retail transactions again does not appear to be the right thing if we want to discourage money laundering, tax evasion and organised crime; recommending to ban surcharging of Euro cash payments runs counter to the otherwise openly stated objective of getting PSPs to price payment services and instruments in line with costs. Let's see how that story pans out.

Title VII
Postlude: The Future for European Payments and the Emergence of a Global Agenda

Introduction

In this Title, I will examine where we are today with the PSD, SEPA and the overall payments integration agenda for Europe. Even though rules and standards are in place, much still needs to be done to achieve a properly functioning Single Market for Payments.

At the same time, I will also take a look at other parts of the world to see whether the European project has already started (or is now starting to) attract attention elsewhere and whether other upcoming or existing regional integration initiatives are proving successful. The general trend of regional economic and monetary integration in an increasingly globalised world appears to warrant a more enthusiastic approach to payment systems creation (by some) and innovation as well as harmonisation (by others).

(1) PSD: Life after implementation?

In this chapter, we take a look at what life (well, payments at least) is starting to look like in the early post-PSD landscape and whether we are starting to see reality matching up to the very high expectations the PSD's creators had.

Still short of a few countries that as of August 2010 have not yet got their PSD legal acts together (Greece just managed it on the 13th of July and Sweden on the 1st of August!), the more unnerving issues today, however, seem to lie with quite a number of banks in PSD live countries, believe it or not! Practical issues that have surfaced in the market since the PSD went live are in part a reflection of initial adaptation issues but more worryingly could be a foreboding for more longer lasting trends which will need additional time and effort to resolve.

Living with PSD: initial experiences

In the months since November 2009 a number of issues began to materialise as banks and other PSPs have started to put their new processes into action. It is still maybe too early to say for sure which of these actually constitute a lasting trend and which are merely temporary 'teething problems' during a period of adjustment by banks and their customers to the new PSD environment. Additionally, the position has certainly been obscured for the time being by confusion as to how to deal with the late transposition countries. More importantly though, some genuinely differing assumptions on the correct interpretation of PSD provisions have been unearthed in a number of countries since 1 November 2009.

There are worrying indications that several of the issues which started emerging in the first month after the PSD went live still largely remain, suggesting that some banks may have more to do to provide sufficiently clear information and advice to their customers. To ensure full compliance across the entire market, thus allowing all customers to realise and appreciate the full benefits that the PSD offers to them, banks will need to improve their transparency and procedures in line with the PSD's requirements.

For a quick feel for the types of issues that have been experienced thus far, here are some examples (see Table 7.1):

Table 7.1 Examples of practical issues experienced since PSD went live

	Practical issue	**Comments**
(1)	Instances of inconsistent usage of – and handling of – charging options (OUR/SHA/BEN) due to differing interpretations of the PSD's requirements.	This became a practical issue despite the fact that it is clear that the 'sharing principle' and thus the usage of the SHA charge code for payment messages is the default rule for all EEA payments (in terms of currency and geography).
(2)	Instances of significant and/or unexpected deductions/lifting fees applied by beneficiary banks without having clearly agreed those in advance with their customers – leading to a situation where the beneficiary unexpectedly sees a smaller amount on his account than he was expecting.	The dream of SHA can sometimes look like the nightmare of BEN. This leads for example to the sending party – e.g., employers – being asked to compensate for the amounts that have been deducted by the receiving bank. The PSD clearly prohibits deductions unless these have been agreed between receiving bank and its customer.

(*continued*)

Table 7.1 Continued

	Practical issue	Comments
(3)	Examples of more frequent 'non-STP' charges applied by some banks.	For some reason, reference is still being made in the inter-bank space to out-of-date conventions such as the inter-bank convention on payments (ICP) and the 'Convention on a basic standard for euro retail cross-border credit transfers in the countries of the EU', including the definition of 'non-STP' found therein. Some players have also started levying more frequent and larger 'non-STP' charges in response to the PSD.
(4)	Examples of unexpected 'SHA-claims'	Due to the significant revenue loss associated with the removal of OUR transactions and thus the inability of an intermediary and/or beneficiary bank to claim additional funds from the sending bank (and its customer), several banks are suggesting that the claims principle (and therefore the convention of the sending party paying all charges) is in their view now applicable to SHA transactions (some banks even refer to 'BEN PSD' payments in the same context, clearly failing to appreciate that BEN is entirely out of the picture since Nov 2009). This practice results in additional charges to the sending side, which is neither in line with the 'sharing principle of charges' nor with the principle of ensuring pricing transparency to sending customers up front.
(5)	Examples of unexpected 'PSD handling fees'	Due to the PSD rule that prohibits deduction from the full amount by intermediary providers, some of those intermediaries have begun to charge not only the banks they provide a clearing service to, but also the other side. This is of course not a procedure that is established by the PSD and sending or receiving banks cannot be forced to pay for an exclusive routing arrangement agreed between other parties.

(*continued*)

Table 7.1 Continued

	Practical issue	Comments
(6)	Uncertainty as regards the application of several core PSD principles including – but not limited to – the question of what type of transaction constitutes a so-called one-leg transaction.	Can lead to confusion and inconsistent treatment of transactions to the detriment of the customer.
(7)	Decision by some banks in PSD live countries to apply PSD rules only to those cross-border payments where the sending and/ or receiving country is PSD live.	Clearly non-compliant. In practice this leads to situations where for example an intermediary bank, taking this approach, deducts its charge from the transaction, before passing it on to the beneficiary bank in a non PSD-live country. This can also involve situations where the sending and receiving country is PSD live (e.g. if the payment is routed via a third country intermediary, which decides to deduct from the payment).

Whatever the explanation behind such issues, it is already clear that continued dialogue within the banking industry on a European level remains just as important as it was before the PSD went live in order to promote common interpretations of key PSD principles, identify best practices and ensure a positive and consistent end-customer experience.

A problem SHAred?

The issue that has perhaps caused the most confusion since the PSD went live, both in terms of inter-bank discussions, but also with a clear knock-on impact for clients, is one of our all-time favourite topics, the charging principle in the PSD, in other words point (1) in Table 7.1 above.

As noted earlier in this book, the EC's clear view is that the 'sharing principle' is intended to apply under the PSD. Having highlighted what that should mean in practice in Title IV, it is worthwhile at this stage also to recall again why this principle was chosen – beyond the intention of making charges more transparent on either side of the transaction. At the time of drafting the PSD, there was a clear plan and roadmap for SEPA migration with the expectation that markets would have largely migrated by 2010. The terminology of the 'sharing principle' comes directly from the SEPA CT Rulebook and the reason for not stating any specific rules in the PSD around which charge code should be used under the 'sharing principle' is down to the fact that the ISO 20022 XML schema do not use any of the traditional charge codes (OUR, BEN, SHA) – these are only known in the SWIFT MT messaging environment. In fact the SEPA charge code is 'SLEV' with the underlying meaning of shared charges. This means that in the current landscape, where SEPA migration has not yet happened and thus MT messages are still being exchanged for SEPA-eligible transactions, the charge code that best reflects the 'sharing principle' is SHA and should thus be populated as the charge code when sending out a cross-border or domestic credit transfer.

Having solved this part of the mystery, there is another slightly confusing element in the PSD on a related topic, namely the caveat that an alternative charging principle may apply in cases where a currency conversion occurs. This partial u-turn, effectively re-opening the door for the OUR charge code, was included on the assumption that in case of a currency conversion on the sending side FX fees are paid via the OUR charging option – with the sender effectively saying, 'I want a currency conversion as part of the payment and I am happy to pay for it'. This of course doesn't happen in practice as those charges are paid separately as part of the very separate FX conversion procedure (which, by the way, is not a payment service in itself).

At the same time, and of far greater concern, we also observe the OUR option sometimes still being employed even if there is no currency conversion on the sending side by PSPs in a few Member States who claim that the nature of their local transposition means that contractual freedom on this point is still available. You might wonder why this is the case, so here is a short explanation.

With PSD coming into play a number banks have decided to offer a specific variant of the OUR option. Traditionally, the OUR option works as follows. A sending customer decides he is willing to pay all the charges. This will result in a claim sent back by the receiving bank (and intermediary bank if there is one) to the sending bank, which will pass the request for additional fees back to the sending customer. The beneficiary is credited the full amount as the sender paid all charges. Post-PSD however, the sending customer needs to know in advance how much he needs to pay for a transaction. Therefore, in case the sender still wants to pay all charges (even though that is not in line with the 'sharing principle' as previously explained) the OUR option can only be offered in its so-called claim-protect or guaranteed variant. This means that the sending bank will populate the payment message with the charge code 'OUR' (the same as in the traditional case), but any claims for fees by the receiving and intermediary banks will be absorbed by the sending bank on behalf of its customer. On this basis, the up-front charge to the sender is clear but at the same time likely to be more expensive than if the 'SHA' option had been used. This approach has allowed a number of banks to generate significant fee income from the PSD, even though this happened in an arguably rather non-compliant way. At the same time, the problem also partly lies with some intermediary and beneficiary banks, which have continued to behave according to pre-PSD principles by sending charge claims back up the payment chain, even though the PSD requires them to levy charges on their own customers only.

This situation is of course a concern, as a widespread non-compliance to what the PSD mandates does not help market harmonisation. In addition, the use of OUR post-1 November 2009 will not always result in the desired outcome of the payee being credited without any fee being levied by the receiving PSP. As a consequence of the PSD promoting the transparent agreement on charges between providers and customers at each end of the payment, the sending PSP cannot guarantee to its customer what charging arrangements may have been reached between the beneficiary and the beneficiary PSP.

As a further charging-code related complication, the PSD does not (of course) express any view on the appropriate level of inter-bank charging, or how this should be undertaken now that deductions from the full amount, are no longer permissible. This change is causing something of a practical issue in the inter-bank space at the present time, triggering occasionally heated bilateral negotiations. The overall guiding principle that logically ought to apply here is straightforward – namely, that an intermediary bank that, for example, provides indirect access to payment systems such as TARGET2 or EBA STEP2, should surely be charging its indirect participant bank for this service. In other words, where the intermediary is acting for the sending bank, this is the party it should be looking to charge, whereas where it is acting for the beneficiary bank, this is the party it should be looking to charge. Easy to say, but not so easy for the market to immediately adjust to in practice it seems, as we still often observe attempts by these providers to also charge the other side of the payment chain, in situations where this party has not chosen them as a clearing or intermediary provider but is required to use them simply because of the exclusive routing arrangement in place to reach the other side. Frankly, in a SEPA context banks in Europe should start moving to greater usage of direct connectivity or enhanced indirect participant solutions, such that the efficient system is actually used in an efficient way!

Just to round off the picture, the worst that has been observed so far are instances where the use of the SHA charge code has resulted in the look-and-feel of a BEN payment at the other end of the payment chain. What I mean by that is cases where the beneficiary bank, in practice, has been continuing to deduct its 'usual' cross-border payment charge from the full amount before crediting the payment. While with a pre-PSD BEN transaction every party in the payment chain, starting from the sending bank, was free to deduct its charges – totally banned now in Europe with the PSD – the case I am talking about is arguably just a smaller version of BEN, where only the beneficiary bank deducts. However, where this happens without transparency and in the absence of an agreement with the beneficiary customer, this is not permissible anymore. After all, the PSD attempts to make payments more efficient and transparent for users.

Next steps of the PSD Expert Group

So, in the light of all the above, since 1st November 2009, the PSD EG has actually continued to be rather busier than it might have expected to be.

To help resolve the observed inconsistencies and issues as speedily as possible, the PSD EG prepared an Addendum to the existing PSD guidance document, which was launched in early June 2010. In respect of the continuing confusion surrounding the charging option question, the PSD EG has proposed the usage of SHA as a best practice even where there is a currency conversion (thus mirroring the forward-looking approach adopted in the SEPA schemes on this point) and also suggested that it would be appropriate for PSPs to provide a 'health warning' to their payers in any cases where the OUR option is still being offered. In addition, the Addendum provides further clarifications in the context of intermediary charging principles as explained above.

The work undertaken by the PSD EG up to this point has been focused on the specific topic of PSD legal and market compliance and did not include a review of the pre-PSD existing inter-bank principles set out in documents such as the EPC's ICP and Convention on Credit Transfers in Euro. However, whilst these conventions are no longer valid, being based on outdated EU legislation, they have never been formally repealed (apart from in the specific context of the SEPA CT Rulebook) and are still being cited by some banks, for example, in bilateral inter-bank charging discussions. Hence the European banking industry has decided to leverage the knowledge of the PSD EG, which accordingly has recently commenced a review of these pre-existing conventions in the specific context of the PSD and Regulation 924/2009 both now being in force, with a view to making appropriate recommendations.

As an aside, it is interesting to reflect at this point on how long some of the outputs and contributions of the Heathrow Group have managed to live on! As we know from Title III, it was the Heathrow Group which did the initial foundation work which was then built on by the EPC to become the Convention on Credit Transfers in Euro and the ICP convention. As stated above these are only now being reviewed, some eight years later. Additionally, it was only in late 2009 that the industry TARGET2 Working Group conducted a full review of two other Heathrow Group deliverables, which had existed in the market since 1999 – namely, the Conventions on inter-bank compensation and the accompanying liquidity management guidelines – and which had been put in place originally as one of the key measures to prevent chaos in the inter-bank payments market when the Euro was introduced.

Returning to the present though, it is fair to conclude overall that the payment industry still has much to 'clean up' after the implementation of the PSD and the PSD EG still has its work cut out to achieve its mission to help bring order out of chaos.

So, is the PSD starting to achieve its (many) objectives?

The big question of course is whether this landmark piece of legislation really will lead to the envisaged legal harmonisation of the European payments market, and whether (and to what extent) it will be successful in achieving its many, many, objectives that we explored in some depth earlier in this book. As a quick refresher, don't forget that these included: support for SEPA (you may remember the bulk of the benefits cited in the PSD's Impact Assessment hung off this point); increased transparency and protection for customers; greater efficiency in payment processing; increased competition in the payments market from traditional and new providers and much more.

Certainly it is true to say that vast sums have been spent across the banking industry (in particular) on compliance costs, reviewing and reissuing terms and conditions, upgrading technology platforms and of course on law firms, consultants and project management teams (all estimated as several Euro billion at some stage) ... so it is to be hoped that the results will be worth it.

It is of course far too early, only nine + months in at the time of writing, to make a full assessment on this point. The forces of change that the PSD was trying to unleash move slowly (the super-tanker analogy was never more relevant) and it could be a number of years hence before we can really be in a position to look back and pass judgment – probably in the form of another book (now – there's a thought!). However, there are early clues and signs to be found, if you know where to look.

For example, on the new competitors front it is interesting to see what has happened so far in terms of the applications that have been made for PI licences.

From initial statistics provided by 13 Member States (March 2010), it seems that 71 PI licences have already been granted and 79 more are under review. In addition, a further 466 entities have so far been waived in accordance with Article 26 of the PSD – in other words the number of small institutions who don't have to meet the full PI requirements so long as their turnover remains low and they restrict their activities to the Member State within which they were licensed (so no EU-passporting). Surprising to some will be the fact that all of the 'waived' institutions as well as the vast majority of PI license applications made thus far turn out to be in the UK, which of course throughout the PSD political negotiation saga was the country that had argued perhaps the strongest for a reasonably 'light touch' PI regulatory regime. It remains to be seen, therefore, whether other Member States that historically have had no experience of non-banks providing payment services will start becoming more open to the idea – at regulatory as well as payment service user level.

Also on this topic, it will be interesting to see whether large corporations, such as retailers or telcos who might perhaps have been eagerly sizing up the opportunity to enter financial services by starting with payments and a PI licence will begin moving in that direction.

So one to watch with great interest, but the day of the PIs still seems a little way off, at least at this point in time.

But don't forget that – as mentioned above – the biggest benefits from the PSD, in financial terms at least, were seen by the EC as flowing from the support it would provide for SEPA. In the very next chapter of this Title, we will be taking a look at where the SEPA project stands at the moment, and what more is needed to assure its success. However, an interesting issue to reflect on here is the rapidly growing interdependence between the success of the PSD in its entirety and the successful adoption of SEPA.

As commented earlier, it was perhaps a slightly curious approach to justify a legislative intervention of the size and scope of the PSD by pinning the lion's share of the benefits on the positive things that SEPA would bring, when the said legislative intervention in fact contained so very few specific measures that actually directly supported the SEPA project. Hence it is a little ironic that it is now SEPA that needs to ride to the PSD's rescue rather than the other way around. The various 'teething troubles' that we have seen in adjusting to the PSD in the customer-to-bank and bank-to-bank space in the context of the use of appropriate charging options, or with regard to returns and whether they should be applied in full, were all anticipated when the SEPA schemes were laboriously drafted – and hence it is now the mass adoption of the SEPA schemes that represents the neatest solution for rapidly establishing order and consistency with regard to cross-border and domestic Euro payments in Europe.

In a couple of pages, we will examine more closely the question of how to reach full migration to SEPA and what this would mean, but the point to note here is that the fates of the PSD and SEPA continue to be inextricably linked.

What might be included or changed when the PSD is reviewed in 2012?

Many people in the market – some of whom should perhaps know better – are already talking up the prospect of 'PSD II: the sequel' before we have even really begun to digest PSD I. As mentioned above, there are certainly practical aspects that still need sorting out in the market, and the EC too still has some work to do to ensure that the remaining late countries complete their implementations before the end of 2010, as well as to ensure corrective action is taken in a few cases where Member States' implementation on certain points deviates in a material way from the source text of the Directive. In fact, the EC recently issued the first level of infringement procedures against those EU Member States that have either failed to complete the PSD or delivered only partial rather than full implementation.

As we of course know from examining the content of the PSD earlier, the Directive (as with all EU Directives) includes a review clause, in this case with the fateful-sounding date of 2012 (remember the Mayans' prediction), in which a number of the topics that were negotiated out of the legislative text first time around were parked for further discussion – for example, whether to cover one-leg transactions and non-EEA currencies.

Clearly these issues will give rise to more debate and negotiation in due course, but at this point it is really far too soon, in mid-2010, to be taking a firm view on what will need to change when the review is undertaken, or to conclude that a radically altered approach will be needed. What is clear, though, given the multi-billion Euros that have been spent on compliance with the new regime, is that a Better Regulation approach would require in due course a thorough post-event cost-benefit analysis of what has been done so far in order to determine properly the context for any next steps.

I shall return a little later in this narrative to some more reflections on the PSD. First though, we need to turn back to developments concerning our parallel story: SEPA.

(2) Je Ne SEPA?: Achievements so far and next steps

As we reviewed in some detail in Title VI, the harmonisation of financial infrastructures and standards that SEPA is intended to trigger presents tremendous opportunities. At a macro level, in the context of the study conducted at the request of the EC, the replacement of existing national payment systems by SEPA holds a market potential of up to €123 billion in savings and efficiencies, cumulative over six years and benefitting the users of payment services (PSUs). At a practical level, SEPA provides ample opportunity for businesses to implement fully standardised and automated solutions allowing for payables and receivables centralisation and end-to-end straight through processing. SEPA will thus allow the removal of existing obstacles due to different national payment schemes, formats and systems across the market as well as facilitate an overall improvement in cash management and liquidity/cash forecasting capabilities for businesses across Europe.

So much for the theory, as the reality is that the take up of SEPA has proved to be much slower than was hoped for. This slow uptake is a major concern for the banking industry and the regulator community in the EU, but should not really come as a great surprise. Past examples from other major European projects (for example, the Euro changeover) have demonstrated that an end-date of some sort has always been necessary to achieve the required momentum. Certainly this is proving to be the case for SEPA as without an end-date for migration to the SEPA CT and DD schemes the bleak reality is that SEPA is unlikely to ever reach critical mass.

In this chapter, I will examine the challenges involved in finding the solution to achieve full migration to SEPA in a way that all stakeholders will be able to accept, and in a short enough timeframe to allow the benefits of all the investments that have been made – and continue to be made – to at last start to be realised.

The good news is that there are finally positive signs that the current impasse is in the process of being broken, thanks to emerging agreements between EU regulators that the required answer to get SEPA off the ground for good is to be found in EU legal intervention. There is however also some bad news – at least for the time being – as there appears to be still a concern on the EC's side that migration to SEPA schemes could prevent competition and would appear like endorsing a monopoly. In fact the opposite is true. The fact of having one common set of schemes as opposed to different local ones will effectively lower the barrier to entry and thus support further competition in the payments space in Europe.

Let's look at this in detail ...

SEPA migration – the need for an end-date?

The state of SEPA and why something needs to be done now

A few years into the SEPA project it now feels that the setting of an end date, or dates, will be a crucial step if the SEPA project is to have any prospect of delivering fully against its objectives, thereby contributing to the realisation of a key element of the Lisbon Agenda, these days the Europe 2020 strategy. However, it is worth examining the case for an end-date in more detail here, not least as the idea still does not yet have universal acceptance.

The easiest way to address this is perhaps to look at the issue from the other end of the telescope and therefore to consider what would be the likely outcome if no end-date(s) were to be set? The reality is that a number of negative consequences can be clearly foreseen in such a scenario.

Firstly, without an end-date for migration to the SEPA CT and DD schemes, the stark reality is that migration itself is at risk. The small 7.5 per cent[1] of SEPA CT payments in Europe after more than 2.5 years is not going to get us very far very fast. For SDD the initial statistics suggest that around 30 per cent of eligible SEPA banks – the current figure as of July 2010 is 2814 – are participating in the SDD Core scheme and 2547 banks have joined the SDD B2B scheme. SDDs cleared by SEPA-compliant CSMs have reached a mere 0.05 per cent according to ECB statistics by end April 2010. The volumes through the EBA's SEPA DD PE-ACH showed a peak per day, as at June 2010, of only 350 Core

SDD collections (of which 90% were local transactions in Belgium) and 900 B2B scheme transactions (of which 60% were local transactions in Germany). Bilaterally cleared figures, which are not easy to monitor, appear to show more significant volumes of transactions (for example, around mid-2010 it is claimed that one bank already processed 1.5 million SDDs per month on a bilateral basis).

The question to ask then is are these low volumes the result of a failure of the scheme design or of product availability? While there is certainly scope for arguments in favour of both sides, the current situation is a reflection that whatever the level of functionality in a new scheme or product, there will always be a natural inertia factor to overcome and this is indeed true when it comes to migrating domestic volumes to SEPA. The strong likelihood is that without the certainty that an end-date will provide in terms of a planning timetable and a clear reason for action, it is very likely that SCT will perhaps reach 15 per cent of possible eligible volumes within the next 2–5 years and then plateau. The same argument and hypothesis also holds true for SEPA DD – which without the stimulus that an end-date will provide will struggle to gain traction beyond adoption for cross-border transactions and/or by smaller countries/communities who may find it economically and practically more compelling to fully embrace SEPA standards and products.

Secondly, and as a direct consequence, the core benefits from SEPA would never be realised. The independent study carried out for the EC in 2007 painted a number of scenarios based on speed of adoption. The study demonstrated that full migration is necessary to achieve these benefits and that the scenario of reasonably rapid adoption was the most efficient way of realising these benefits.

One of the efficiencies that SEPA will facilitate is the hoped for significant reduction in the number of payment processors (or Clearing and Settlement Mechanisms (CSMs) in SEPA terminology) in the market, in favour of a much smaller number of competing processors, each with major scale benefits. This model will never be realised unless the adoption of an end-date triggers the migration of domestic volumes away from their current legacy schemes and associated processors. While of course it is possible to imagine a future where these legacy schemes and processors co-exist with SEPA for an extended period, this would be a deeply inefficient future involving major duplication of costs and the perpetuation of national processing markets with single processing suppliers and much less opportunity for pan-European competition.

Additionally, achieving the necessary universal 'reach' will always be an issue for the SEPA schemes in the absence of full migration (the classic 'chicken and egg' dilemma). Lack of reach would continue to constitute a significant barrier to mass scheme adoption by corporate and retail clients, again preventing a more healthy competition between PSPs in the market.

At a political level, the consequence would be that the final stage of the Euro integration project – the creation of a competitive and integrated single market for retail payments – would never be completed and the core PSD objective of enhanced competition from traditional and non-traditional PSPs would equally fail to be fully achieved.

The banking industry across the EU has already invested many billion Euros in preparing for SEPA in the understanding that the SEPA vision (which depends on the achievement of full migration) was a shared political vision that would be fully supported and jointly executed by European and national authorities together with the industry. At the same time, banks needed to make changes to ensure compliance with Regulation 2560/2001 (now Regulation 924/2009), which was clearly designed as a regulatory incentive towards the achievement of SEPA, and also more recently had to invest substantial amounts in preparing for the PSD.

Finally, as we know, the EC has long held the view that while delivery of the 'core' SEPA services (SCT, SDD and SEPA for cards) is in itself a desirable goal with major competitive and efficiency benefits, what is equally important is the role that these deliverables have to play as the foundations upon which a range of 'e-SEPA' services such as e-invoicing and e-payments can then be built, unleashing major additional expected benefits. However, there is a very high risk that if SEPA migration is not achieved in a reasonably short timeframe, one of the consequences will be that these additional future looking and innovative services will never come to fruition because the business case may never be sufficiently compelling in a fragmented EU market. In the absence of a broadly rolled-out SEPA there is no practical way of building on this standard basis to offer value added services or new methods of executing payments in the context of 'e and m-SEPA'.

So, non-realisation of full SEPA migration – which is the very likely outcome in the absence of an end-date (and I should say here an end-date that covers the right scope) – would result in the failure of this entire set of regulatory and self-regulatory measures and hence compromise the achievement of EU payments integration.

Assessing common objections to an end date

While the large majority of the market is now in favour of having an end-date, a number of objections have been put forward by some market participants. It is worthwhile briefly exploring a few of these now.

For example, a point that has sometimes been made is the need for SEPA schemes to ensure so-called 'non-deterioration' of current products and services before considering the question of an end date. The problem with this argument is that the 'non-deterioration' principle is too subjective a measure for assessing the true attractiveness of SEPA based products and services. Additionally, if 'non deterioration' is interpreted as meaning 'no change' then this test will never be met, given that it would be neither possible, appropriate nor desirable to replicate all the features of existing local CT or DD schemes within the SEPA schemes. The key tests should rather be: (1) whether the core features built into the current versions of the schemes are sufficiently well designed to allow the migration process to commence; (2) whether there is a demonstrated willingness on the part of the EPC to modify and enhance the scheme features over time to take account of additional stakeholder requirements; and, of course, (3) whether there is a willingness of Member States to support the adoption of new instruments, directly on behalf of the public sector and indirectly by facilitating communication to consumers and SMEs. As expressed in the EC consultation on SEPA migration (summer 2009), non-deterioration is apparently seen in the context of the price/quality ratio of the payment service. Obviously, this ratio will only improve if the market becomes more competitive and that will only happen if PSPs compete on the basis of common ground rules. Otherwise, PSPs can hide behind domestic schemes and standards that make it difficult for PSPs from other countries to compete with them.

It is argued by others that it would be important to wait for a critical mass of volumes to have moved to the SEPA schemes before setting an end-date. The flaw with this argument is of course that the outcome of such an approach will be that full SEPA migration will never happen. Without the catalyst of an end-date it is very likely that the adoption of SEPA standards will never reach a level of much more than the already-mentioned 15 per cent of the possible total volumes (that's a guess, but I think it's a good one).

A further objection sometimes raised is that setting an end-date would remove the pressure on banks to make SEPA-based products and services attractive and competitive. Here, I would argue strongly that the contrary is in fact true. The whole idea about SEPA is that it will help establish a higher level of competition in the market – between banks; between banks and non-bank PSPs; and between infrastructure providers (recall the open access criteria of the SEPA schemes, in line with Article 28 of the PSD!). One consequence of this is that banks and other market players (such as vendors and software providers) will need to build ever more competitive and innovative products and services based on the common standards established by the SEPA schemes if they are to be successful in this new market reality. Of course, in terms of the competition point it should also be noted that the argument that endorsing SEPA schemes would be like endorsing a monopoly is equally flawed, as standards adoption needs to happen at market level. Otherwise, we would not be able to travel by rail or make mobile phone calls. All these things are effectively enabled due to common standards. Once standards are in place and adhered to, competition can flourish.

It also seems obvious that if regulatory intervention would push for competition between payment schemes, as opposed to PSPs (where competition really should be), the opposite will occur. The outcome in this case would be to simply continue and extend today's situation where we have a multitude of domestic Euro payment schemes, which do not and cannot compete with each other, because the schemes are based on different rules and technical standards. Even requiring the implementation of one technical standard based on the ISO 20022 XML is not on its own enough to result in interoperability of schemes because schemes rules would still be different. From a PSU perspective a multitude of schemes would not help him streamline his processes to increase efficiencies. Instead the existing scenario of needing to accommodate multiple domestic payment solutions would continue. And, after all, the market would not be integrated but continue to be fragmented. Hence what is needed is a harmonised standard – the SEPA schemes.

Finally on our quick tour of the most popular objections, it is sometimes argued that it is simply too early to be discussing the need to set an end-date with volumes of SEPA CTs running low and SDD only just launched. On the contrary, these two observations are both powerful arguments as to why the end-date discussion needs to be happening right now and why it needs to reach a conclusion as soon as possible if market confidence is not to be lost in SEPA.

Sounds like we still need an end date then, but what might this mean?

The next question to answer is 'what does the concept of an end-date actually mean?' Would it require a 'Big Bang' changeover? Is it necessary for any requirements to cover PSUs or should they be limited to the inter-bank (or inter-PSP) space? Does it mean that all existing types of non-SEPA Euro CTs and DDs would have to be withdrawn? It is worth spending a few moments briefly exploring some of these questions to try to bring additional clarity to this critically important element of the debate.

Firstly, it is important that an end-date for SEPA migration implies a final cut-off date for full migration to the SEPA schemes. This means that current domestic Euro credit transfer and direct debit schemes and processes will be switched off and replaced by the common SEPA schemes.

It is also sensible to have a single date at EU level but with flexibility for communities that are ready earlier to move more quickly if they wish to do so. In addition, there are a number of practical interim steps that can tangibly and progressively move the European payments industry towards SEPA migration to ensure that things don't come in the form of a 'big bang'.

The initial step, for example, might be to establish the requirement to use IBAN/BIC as the key identifiers for customer accounts at national level. As previously highlighted, Luxembourg and Slovenia are using both these identifiers and have migrated their domestic CT traffic to SEPA, with Finland as well as Spain joining the pack shortly. There are however quite a number of other EU countries that have adopted the IBAN (only!) for domestic transactions: Italy, Greece, Malta, Bulgaria, Romania, Latvia and Lithuania (whilst Polish BBANs are based on the IBAN format). As such these countries are not yet fully using SEPA but have at least taken an important first step in the right direction. Other examples of tangible interim steps have already been initiated by the EC, namely, setting the framework and milestones for the EU public sector to start switching their payments to SEPA CT and SDD.

So what is end-to-end migration then? It is the state that is reached when not only banks have migrated their CT and DD offering from legacy schemes to the SEPA scheme and standard but when all customer types are also ready to use the SEPA-based CT and DD products. Please note (as highlighted earlier) the fact that products are based on the same technical standard does not mean that they are the same – this would imply that all customers will get exactly the same product with exactly the same functionality. On the contrary, SEPA as a standard enables PSPs to allow for a number of optional information elements to be built into their payments solutions and furthermore PSPs will compete on the degree of automation, the frequency and breadth of information provided to customers as well as the integration of SEPA products in the PSP to PSU context. Clearly it is essential as part of this process that PSUs, vendors and infrastructure providers also fully embrace migration to SEPA – it is not sufficient for the migration to be limited to the inter-bank/PSP space. This explains why various market participants have been calling for the end-date to apply equally to all these different stakeholders.

To an extent, however, this particular aspect is a somewhat artificial debate, in the sense that setting – and of course widely publicising and promoting – a migration deadline at inter-bank/PSP level will inevitably mean that, as banks/PSPs move from legacy Euro schemes to SEPA, offering SEPA-scheme-based payment products will become the standard and other stakeholders will naturally be part of the adaptation and adopting process.

Consumers, having by the time the end-date is approaching already adapted to the IBAN, will not perceive major changes in their usage of CT and DD services; rather – and well beyond the requirements of the 'non-deterioration principle' – they will be advantaged by the fact that they will also be able to benefit from paying for goods and services via pan-European Euro direct debits. This in turn will save them cost and time, as the requirement of holding a domestic account to execute DDs will no longer be applicable (in short, cross-border collection capability removes the need to open accounts in other countries within SEPA). And, of course, with more competition in the market the price/quality ratio will improve to the benefit of the user.

Corporate customers will see their payment propositions evolve from where they today use domestic payment solutions for CT and DD executed via local infrastructures to SEPA standardised CTs and DD that are exchanged via SEPA-compliant infrastructures and in line with the SEPA ISO 20022 XML technical standards. They will of course also enjoy similar benefits to those enjoyed by consumers. At the same time there will be various options of a corporate to make use of SEPA-scheme-based products and services depending on the capability and service suite of its PSP. For example, smaller businesses might find it more suitable to access SEPA via multi-bank gateways or service bureaus, while larger corporates and banks/PSPs will establish SEPA connectivity via the corporate's ERP (Enterprise-Resource-Planning) system. All business customers need to ensure that their internal account number databases are adapted to IBANs and BICs and relevant customer communication should facilitate this task. Hence there is a need for an end-date that is set to fit with the natural investment cycle of 2–3 years. It is important to add that for businesses to enjoy the benefits of SEPA, banks are already offering services to convert the XML inter-bank message to at least some of the international ERP message formats, which therefore means that XML implementation by those businesses is not an immediate necessary step. At the same time, the large ERP providers are working on enabling a more streamlined interconnectivity with the SEPA standards of banks. Hence, there is no need to require businesses to also implement SEPA XML standards, but rather a need for more solutions in the PSP and IT vendor space to accommodate business needs. Infrastructure providers as well as IT vendors will only continue to be attractive if their SEPA proposition is in place and viable.

Accordingly, while it is essential that all these stakeholders are fully aware of the indirect implications that an end-date will have for them in terms of its application to the services that they receive and/or provide, the reality is that if, as explained above, inter-bank/PSP SEPA migration is mandated, end-to-end migration will become the natural consequence.

In terms of an outlook on the payment service landscape in a full SEPA migration scenario some existing 'legacy' payment types would still continue to exist to fill country-specific or pan-European niche requirements. Furthermore, systemically important real time payments transacted via RTGS systems such as TARGET2 cannot be replaced by SEPA, as the latter was designed for retail mass payments (including batch processing).

More broadly, it will be necessary at national/community level – but against a set of objective criteria established at European level – to identify those 'exception' cases where it would be in the public interest to maintain an existing niche service rather than including it within the SEPA migration exercise.

An end date set by the market, or through regulation?

This is an easy one to answer. Setting an end date via self-regulation alone sounds like a nice idea, but in reality is insufficient. There is a very clear limit to the extent to which industry alone can mandate something as significant as full migration to SEPA.

Furthermore, while the details of the SEPA schemes have indeed been designed by the market, at its core SEPA is a political vision with its roots in the Lisbon agenda. Therefore, it is only appropriate – as well as necessary – that achieving full migration should be a shared task between industry, the regulatory community and other key market stakeholders – with regulators playing their part through a show of willingness to be 'early adopters' of SEPA products and services (both the EC and ECB are

SCT users already); playing a role in the broad communication program which will be necessary; and showing tangible political commitment by setting an end-date.

So, that's my view.

And now, what does the EU regulatory community think?

The Regulators' evolving position on SEPA migration and end-dates

Despite – or maybe because of – SEPA being a politically inspired self-regulatory project, the EC and ECB were both originally of the view that migration could be achieved naturally as a consequence of market forces expected to be at play. However, the lack of progress on SEPA adoption has prompted a gradual but major re-think by the European authorities. The first positive sign of a new attitude showed itself during the review of Regulation 2560, which as we know, included a new requirement to ensure that those banks that offer domestic Euro DDs today should be compelled to join the SDD Core scheme by 31 October 2010. That was really the moment at which SEPA ceased being a 'self-regulatory' initiative only and moved into the complex and exciting (but occasionally confusing) realm which can best perhaps be described as 'Co-regulation' – the interplay of industry and regulators.

Following a major public consultation that the EC held over the summer of 2009 into the question of whether SEPA needed an end date and the potential role of the regulatory community in agreeing or providing this, the next major breakthrough came when the Economic and Financial Affairs Council (ECOFIN) recorded positive conclusions[2] on 2 December 2009 – recognising that a potential legislative next step in that matter should be investigated. In particular, the Council conclusions considered that 'establishing definitive end-dates for SDD and SCT migration would provide the clarity and the incentive needed by the market, ensuring that the substantial benefits of SEPA are rapidly achieved and that the high costs of running both legacy and SEPA products in parallel can be eliminated'. Additionally, and encouragingly, the conclusions also called on the EC 'in collaboration with the ECB and in close cooperation with all actors concerned, to carry out a thorough assessment of whether legislation is needed to set binding end-dates for SDD and SCT and to come up with a legislative proposal should this assessment confirm the need for binding end dates.' In the context of the highly politically sensitive and understated code that the language of such Conclusions is crafted in, these two sentences were bold indeed.

The EP went even further than this when adopting a Resolution[3] on 10 March 2010 which called on the EC to set 'a clear, appropriate and binding end-date, which should be no later than 31 December 2012, for migrating to SEPA instruments, after which all payments in Euros must be made using the SEPA standards.'

In response to this clear – and highly positive – mandate from the other two EU institutions, the EC, via Commissioner Barnier's DG Markt team is very actively engaged in consulting with Member States and with the industry on exactly what form this legislative intervention should take. At the meeting of the Payment Systems Market Expert Group (PSMEG) on 23 March 2010 the EC tabled a discussion paper titled SEPA Migration End-Date which sought views on the issues of what type of legislative intervention would be appropriate; what the scope and content of any legislative text should take, and finally how to address the question of whether/how to allow the preservation of certain niche existing services at domestic level.

It also emerges from the consultation paper that one of the key questions to get right in any legislation will be the scope (if we remind ourselves of the PSD here, the scope of a legislation, if not sufficiently clear and simple, has the potential to compromise the entire law). For example, should the focus be on (1) the adoption of technical standards (and if so, by whom), (2) the adoption of the SEPA schemes and/or (3) the establishment of 'essential requirements'?

Potential outcome for SEPA: an end-date Regulation?

The most probable outcome at the time of writing is that an EU Regulation will be agreed as the appropriate instrument to use (in line with the view I have consistently been advocating).

On 2 June 2010 the EC published a Working Paper on SEPA migration end-dates and invited all parties involved in the SEPA process to respond to the thoughts set out in the document. In its published high-level response note dated 6 July 2010, the ECB chose to demonstrate again their support for the proposal to impose an end-date, stating very clearly that 'the Eurosystem is of the opinion that there is a clear need for a binding EU regulation that sets an end date for migration to SEPA credit transfers and SEPA direct debits' and further that 'a legally binding instrument is considered as necessary for a successful migration to SEPA as the project would otherwise be under serious risk of failure'.

In the context of the ambitious timeline to bring forward the legislative proposal, one of the critical elements is (as always!) to determine and refine the approach and scope in order to achieve the goal of SEPA migration without triggering unintended consequences. As regards the various elements outlined in the EC's Working Paper, the view which I favour and that seems to be gaining ground with industry and regulators, is that of a carefully targeted approach that sets progressive SEPA-specific measures including key building blocks such as: 'full reach' across the Eurozone for SCT as well as SDD; full adoption of the ISO 20022 XML SEPA standards in the inter-bank space; migration within each Member State from existing SEPA-eligible legacy Euro retail CT/DD schemes to the SEPA equivalents; and the establishment of guiding principles for the retention of niche domestic Euro DD/CT-type services at Member State level. (Note: At the time of writing there have been recent moves – which seem to be succeeding – to have the German ELV system (Elektronisches Lastschriftverfahren) excluded from the scope of SEPA migration, on the basis that ELV transactions are initiated by card. A potentially concerning development if you are a fan of full migration, given ELV is far from a niche system, and that whilst a card is used as the initiation channel, the underlying processing is via the local direct debit scheme – a clear candidate for SEPA migration. Whilst in principle the objective should be to migrate these transactions to SEPA, a scheme variant might need to be developed to accommodate the shorter collection cycle – as might also be needed to accomodate urgent payments under the SCT scheme.)

The point really to my mind is that a significant degree of harmonisation at the technical and scheme level is necessary to create the single payments market and unlock competition, and hence that the forthcoming legislative intervention will need to promote clearly the movement from legacy domestic Euro retail CT/DD schemes to the SEPA schemes, which means that the corresponding legacy schemes at domestic level will need to be switched off. It is worthwhile reminding the reader here that the majority of banks adhering to the SCT scheme since 2008 are not yet truly ISO 20022 XML compliant but are rather using message standard converters to be able to participate in the scheme (at inter-bank/PSP level), which of course means that a full SEPA solution with all its additional benefits that stem from the ability to provide enriched information in the payment message is not yet offered to the customers of these banks. Therefore, the argument of parallel investments and costs (in SEPA and legacy) so far largely refers to the smaller group of multi-country and larger domestic banks that have actually already become SEPA compliant in its true sense. The question as to how to practically manage the implementation of a new standard in the market as well as the continuing evolution of this standard, in the absence of a viable enforcement mechanism, is still an open one.

The very latest development in the SEPA migration saga is that a draft proposal for an 'EU Regulation for setting essential requirements for credit transfers and direct debits in euro' has been leaked into the market (during July 2010). In its current form, the proposal unfortunately does not opt for clearly mandating a migration to SEPA schemes but instead lays down broad rules that should be followed in the context of all Euro credit transfers and direct debits (significant scope creep – maybe even as far as TARGET2!) with the underlying expectation of creating competition between payment schemes, in a way which could have the unintended consequence of limiting competition where it should really be taking place – i.e. between PSPs and also between infrastructure providers. The proposal does not provide for any deadlines for phasing out legacy Euro payment schemes and therefore gives no outlook as to when cost savings for users resulting from the consolidation of cash management operations would eventually kick in. While cross-border reach for Euro credit transfers and direct debits is mandated (a key requirement!), the EC at the same time envisages a situation where new competing credit transfer or direct debit schemes emerge in line with the list of essential requirements and standards that are provided in the annex to the regulatory draft proposal. This approach fails to recognise that competition is dependent on standardisation (as previously explained) and that multiple payment schemes would not help customers with their streamlining of payment processes as schemes cannot in practice be made interoperable. The interoperability is in fact at play in the area of payment processing – the infrastructure space. SEPA, because it is a standard, has by its very nature already introduced competition in this space (split of scheme and infrastructure, remember?).

And finally, if the EU regulator were to decree a detailed set of 'essential requirements', he would effectively be taking on responsibility for the further development of all Euro payment schemes that fall under the proposed definition, by driving their evolution. This would be completely impractical, risking to stifle innovation as well as competition between PSPs.

So, lots more potentially tricky debates to follow ... fingers crossed.

SEPA Governance and stakeholder engagement – between a rock and a hard place?

There is clear evidence from the market that the current SCT and SDD scheme versions already meet the majority of core customer needs, and also through the ongoing EPC scheme enhancement process there is proof of industry's willingness to evolve the schemes where there is a clear customer benefit for doing so.

However, one of the biggest challenges for the EPC since its inception – and one that is in very sharp focus now in the context of the end-date discussion – is the one of ensuring the appropriate level of wider stakeholder engagement in the scheme-development process.

As a recent case study of the kind of misunderstandings and disagreements that have been prone to break out occasionally – despite the existence of the Customer Stakeholder Forum set up by the EPC – there has been something of a public row between the EPC and the Bureau Européen des Unions de Consommateurs (BEUC), the European consumers' association, concerning the level to which the SDD Core Scheme provides the necessary level of consumer protection. At its root, the disagreement goes back to the EPC's decision of adopting the CMF rather than the DMF as the basis for the SDD scheme, for reasons that we went into in some detail in Title VI. However, there are elements of the BEUC community who have held the perception that the CMF approach, despite being used today by citizens in many EU countries is inferior in its level of consumer protection when it comes to handling unauthorised transactions. The EPC meanwhile has steadfastly maintained that the SDD scheme is fully aligned with consumer rights as defined in the PSD and indeed goes further by granting consumers a 'no-questions-asked' refund right during the eight weeks following the debiting of a consumer's account; during this time any funds collected via the SDD Core Scheme will be credited back to the consumer's account upon request. In contrast the PSD, we may recall from Title IV, only grants a refund for authorised transactions if the amount at the time of debit was unknown to the consumer and at the same time turns out to be unexpectedly high in the context of the person's normal spending pattern.

In addition, the EPC has argued that PSPs servicing billers who collect DDs must ensure that only trustworthy billers are able to collect payments via SDD. Also, to help in meeting the preferences of consumers living in countries currently using an alternative direct debit model, the SDD includes the option to create mandates through the use of electronic channels – that is, the e-mandate option we looked at earlier.

As a way of – hopefully – defusing this rather damaging debate, the EPC Plenary agreed at its meeting in March 2010 to also deliver an optional 'New Mandate Check' functionality to be included in the next release of the SDD Scheme Rulebooks for end 2011. The NMC functionality provides an extended timeline for the optional verification of mandate information by the debtor bank, which will help to further reduce incidences of unauthorised debits. The NMC could also serve as basis for individual banks or banking communities to develop AOSs by building on this functionality.

It was politically very important for the EPC to progress this small functional enhancement, as it is seen as a key measure to make stakeholders more comfortable with the SDD scheme. Hopefully it will succeed in this aim!

Improved SEPA governance, in particular at EU level, was one of the priorities identified in the EC SEPA Roadmap adopted in September 2009, and was picked up again by the ECOFIN Council of last December as a result of which they invited the EC and the ECB to establish, before mid-2010, an additional SEPA governance and monitoring structure at EU level. As a consequence, and partly with a view to trying to avoid future disagreements between market stakeholders of the sort described above, the EC and ECB recently established the 'SEPA Council' – a new high level governance forum chaired jointly by the EC and the ECB which brings together a small number of representatives from the payments industry and the user community to discuss the future direction for SEPA at a policy level.

The SEPA Council, now up and running, is charged with objectives such as promotion of the realisation of the SEPA vision; provision of a strategic direction for EU retail payments in Euro; and monitoring and supporting the SEPA migration process. The first meeting took place in early June 2010 and a positive formal declaration was issued publicly by the group on 14 June. This declaration included the rather timely message that the Members of the Council 'stressed their strong support for the establishment of end-date(s) for migration to SEPA Credit Transfers and SEPA Direct Debits by means of legislation at EU level and welcome the intention of the European Commission to come forward with a legislative proposal in close cooperation with the European Central Bank'. The declaration also called for other supportive measures, such as 'targeted communication efforts by the national authorities, the banking industry and the national SEPA Coordination Committees to improve the general perception of the project and to facilitate user-friendly market migration'.

Let's see how that will work out if the EC ends up taking on the role of defining the 'essential requirements' for competing Euro schemes going forward ...

SEPA – suffering from the financial crisis?

When looking at such a large-scale initiative as SEPA, we obviously cannot fail to mention the financial crisis and how this might be affecting the SEPA timetable as well as the priority being given to the project.

We all remember – only too well – the slow but steady unfolding of the financial crisis that started in 2007 and was escalated in dramatic style with the failure of Lehman Brothers, triggering an avalanche of market reactions that ultimately led to a period of general distrust of the financial services industry at large by politicians and customers. Complaints about inappropriate and/or inefficient regulation of the industry are now motivating an energetic, albeit concerning, degree of regulatory activism and public opinion is at an all-time low.

These developments have of course had implications for the speed of SEPA compliance and adoption in banks across Europe, with the main risk being that the general trend of increased government involvement and associated crisis-reaction acts as a catalyst of continued national fragmentation, rather than SEPA integration. This trend can also be observed in the infrastructure space as we see CSMs being built at national level where previously none existed (for example, in Austria). This of course runs counter to the expectation of further CSM consolidation and centralisation with the emerging integrated European payments market.

Next to this political dimension, the growing cost for banks triggered by ever-rising levels of compliance requirements – whether it is capital, liquidity or more consumer protection – is doing its best to divert investment Euros from SEPA and other innovative solutions. The desire to innovate and improve is being overshadowed by the imperative to comply. While, even before the crisis, up to 50 per cent of a typical bank's annual project budgets could go into compliance, we are now looking at potentially much higher levels and unless you have defined SEPA as a compliance project (which some luckily have done!) there is a risk that you will not get very far with it now.

So how can we turn this around? Times like these require more than ever the building of trust with your customer, and SEPA can in fact be one means of supporting you in that challenge. After all, providing a harmonised efficient and cheaper service will certainly find some appeal with bank customers. Looking at the other side of the coin, banks pressured to cut costs and look at more efficient processing solutions could suddenly recognise the potential of SEPA as the Holy Grail enabler for optimised back-office processing with lower costs, higher efficiencies and broader geographic reach. SEPA presents an opportunity to take a fresh look at a major part of the bank's value chain. So, seen through that lens, the impact of the financial crisis is that decisions on SEPA in fact need to be made faster rather than slower.

Another interesting angle to consider is related to the degree of fallout from the financial crisis. Looking at Europe, the consolidation of banks and ACHs, which is expected to see a major push as a result of SEPA, has already been accelerated by the crisis, at least with regard to banks. Among those still standing, between one and four of the top banks in most EU Member States have required some degree of government funding to withstand the storm.

Those that have not been hit too hard and that also have taken a strategic view on SEPA have the potential to become the leaders of the next round, leaving the weaker parts of the market that have just started to invest (or not at all just yet) looking a little exposed. So at least we've now got some interesting dynamics back into the market and the coming months and years will see how players respond to their respective situations. This could include collaboration, partnership and even outsourcing, depending on the core business focus – meaning that sharing the burden will become a potential solution for some (work with a bank/PSP that is SEPA-ready). What is certain is that the SEPA train cannot – and should not – be derailed and that any developments will surely ultimately find their way in the right direction.

The other conclusion, as illustrated earlier, is of course that regulatory mandated SEPA migration and a clear end-date for legacy instruments, standards and systems is increasingly essential to give sufficient momentum to the whole endeavour (subject to the right outcome of course!).

SEPA – the next steps into E&M

At the current time it is true that for most market participants the full realisation of SEPA still feels like something that belongs in a galaxy far far away. So the thought of innovative Internet and mobile-based SEPA services is perhaps even more fantastical to their ears. The big question we need to answer here, however, is to what extent could the SEPA initiative not only lead to a harmonisation of basic domestic CT and DD processes across Europe but also pave the way for the 'e-age' by introducing paperless channels for the end-to-end process.

Looking back at the EPC's activities since its inception in 2002, one of the many working groups and task forces set up was to look at e&m-payments. Having been closely involved with the e&m-payments task force since its beginning, I can confirm that the work undertaken in this space was always full of grand ambitions but would regularly be de-prioritised when it came to strategic EPC Plenary decisions (meaning perhaps that it was never really part of the core strategy in the first place).

With this in mind, let us now examine what this famous e&m SEPA actually stands for, how the industry in Europe is getting on with it (as a clue, don't forget that many players have as yet still to come to grips with the basic SEPA ISO XML implementation), how EU authorities view the progress so far and what we all stand to gain if e&m SEPA was to become the next reality in European payments.

The eSEPA story

Having tracked the progress of the e&m SEPA project since 2002, the 2010 status – even though it promises much – still lacks rather much by way of concrete fulfilment. The idea of eSEPA is to create a framework that will support e-commerce by providing guaranteed online payments to web-retailers in a way that reuses the SCT as underlying processing standard in the bank-to-bank (or PSP-to-PSP) space. In a nutshell, a customer should be able to shop online and as an alternative to paying for an airline ticket (as an example), by credit or debit card, should have the ability to trigger an online payment directly from her/his current account – thus avoiding any card related charges. To make this work, a process is required whereby when this option is chosen, the customer is redirected in a seamless way from the web-merchant's Internet site to the online banking portal of her own bank. Following completion of the relevant security identification and authorisation procedures, the customer can then initiate a payment to the web-merchant via a pre-populated SCT online form. This solution would thus be an invoicing and payment solution in one, levering the eSynergies of such a process.

The EPC has gone down the route of the framework approach – as is very familiar to us already in a cards context – leaving the long-term fate of eSEPA to be determined by market forces. One of the reasons for this decision can surely be put down to the fact that in Europe today we have three existing national e-payment schemes, IDEAL from the Netherlands, Giropay from Germany and EPS (e-payment standard) from Austria. The size of the task that would have been involved in building a brand new scheme, not least having to negotiate between these three countries and with the rest of Europe as to which elements would have constituted 'best of breed', was maybe a little too daunting to those coming fresh from the challenges of doing just this during the creation of the SCT and SDD schemes. Therefore, the EPC is currently finalising the eSEPA framework and a community consultation has already been completed. At the same time two e-payment messages covering the e-payment proposal and guarantee elements have been reviewed by SWIFT and Implementation Guidelines are now being prepared. It is intended that the framework will define minimum criteria covering legal as well as security related aspects that must all be fulfilled by any national e-payment scheme looking to become eSEPA compliant. The key requirement for any scheme enrolling in the eSEPA framework is to become technically and commercially interoperable with all other eSEPA participating schemes. It is believed that a specific SEPA logo for the participating e-payment schemes will also help to create a recognition effect with users.

The ECB is not yet entirely convinced that a framework represents the best solution (a similar tune to the cards discussions) and has highlighted that a scheme-based approach might bring eSEPA more speedily and broadly to the market. Certainly, it is easy to see that having a central scheme owner – a role played by the EPC for SCT and SDD already – would support implementation and use of the scheme. By helping stimulate debate on this topic, and more generally by being strongly in favour of the eSEPA agenda, the ECB is also helping the banking industry to realise that if they fail to engage in harmonised next-generation payments initiatives such as the eSEPA initiative they will miss out on future market share as other providers – such as non-bank PIs – will take their big chance and fill the vacuum. It should surely therefore be an obvious strategy for banks to get eSEPA in place as soon as possible, but based on past history within the banking industry, external prompting is still likely to be needed to really get things moving.

Some would go so far as to argue that e-payments will become the future for payments. If interpreted in the sense of moving from paper to electronic payment execution this is indeed the place to go and banks need to realise that they cannot escape this evolution. Building SEPA standards on top of the old environment and slightly re-engineering the infrastructure space by moving to the SEPA ISO XML is – while important – only an interim stage, prior to the next big evolutionary step which would see a radical removal of all old systems followed by the introduction of a completely new infrastructure based directly on internet real-time technology. Examples of this can already be found in Finland where the airline e-ticketing system is built on Internet technology for the real-time e-world.

In a future vision an 'e-all-around' scenario would encompass that an e-order would automatically generate an e-order confirmation, an e-invoice and an e-payment, with all participant records being updated automatically, including updating of the receivables and payables databases of the respective PSUs. eSEPA could thus be used as a platform for much more than just providing e-standards to replace current paper standards by going beyond and employing e-synergies. At the same time it is a given that the overall success of SEPA will depend crucially on the eventual success of eSEPA – if the latter fails, the whole project risks failure, with new non-bank providers exploring successful e-alternatives.

E-mandates in SEPA Direct Debits

In our idealised 'e-world', the SDD scheme would of course have included the e-mandate as a mandatory means of setting up mandates between debtors and creditors. The e-mandate solution, as highlighted in Title VI, remains only an option in the SDD schemes at this point, really for the same reasons that eSEPA is not yet a standard offering. Ultimately though, SDD without e-mandates will not fly in the e-world and increasingly customers can be expected to demand the electronic option – whether to save more trees, or as part of the increasingly popular 'eRevolution' (or both).

So what might it be that is holding the banks back?

The whole e-story is often perceived by many banks as a major and rather threatening IT project, requiring everything that had been previously documented on paper including all associated procedures, now to be transformed into an electronic dematerialised representation. If we look at XML, it is true that the old way of processing will need to change. As mentioned in Title VI the use of the XML syntax enables different systems to communicate with each other, which opens the door for more complex and speedy processing. Against the background of the general move towards a real-time environment, which we already enjoy with email and mobile phones (noting by the way that keeping a telephone bill balance is much the same technically as keeping a payment account balance), there will be a need to reengineer all kinds of business processes including payments in order to achieve an end-to-end real-time processing across the network.

Clearly all this will not come cheaply. On the other hand, it could be argued that banks without e-services will of course by definition be without e-customers and e-revenues. E-services will create e-revenues, but in a competitive environment in line with the cost-level of e-production.

Overall, the rules for the future e-banking-markets are clear and the 'delaying-game' being played by some (for a mix of good and bad reasons) will need to end, hopefully quite soon.

E-invoicing and SEPA

Believe it or not, around 32 billion invoices are generated annually in Europe. When you stop and think about it, the humble invoice plays a mission critical role in linking the physical supply chain – the delivery of goods – with the financial supply chain – the process of financing and payment. An invoice also supports the collection of VAT, a key component of government revenues.

The exciting news therefore is that e-invoicing is something that is already happening! This initiative, essentially the replacement of paper invoices by electronic messages, is being driven by a 'desire to improve efficiency' (translation: reduce costs please!) from enterprises of all sizes, including public administrations. The adoption of e-invoicing throughout society is very enthusiastically supported as a public policy priority by the EC, featuring in the Europe 2020 Strategy, and across many Member States of the EU. Aside from efficiency and cost benefits, many have pointed to the green benefits. Indeed, the Department of Environmental Strategies Research at the Royal Institute of Technology in Sweden has estimated that replacing paper with electronic invoices would lead to carbon reductions corresponding to 39,000 to 41,000 tons of CO2-equivalents per annum ... in Sweden alone. Extrapolation across Europe would suggest an annual carbon reduction potential of a good 1 million tons of CO2-equivalents!

Several initiatives can be observed today in the context of e-invoicing. The EC has provided some supporting legislation to facilitate it and is currently proposing an improved legislative framework for VAT, which will further simplify and encourage e-invoicing. The EC has also set up an Expert Group to analyse the way forward and propose a Framework that defines a path for further promotion. Its report was published in November 2009.

Additionally, EU governments are supporting public procurement through e-channels from catalogue to invoice. Private sector IT service providers and banks are rolling out services and solutions and some would argue that there are almost too many such providers. All parties are developing standards and common agreements.

Of our 32 billion annual invoices, about half are B2B (business to business). Growth rates for e-invoicing are between approximately 25 per cent per annum for B2C (business to consumer) and 50 per cent for B2B. Before we get too excited about these growth rates, we need to realise that they are coming from a low base, as currently the proportion of invoices that are electronic is less than 10 per cent of the total issued. So far, the use of e-invoices has been dominated by large enterprises, typically on their accounts payable side where they require their suppliers to submit an electronic invoice, often following an electronic purchase order to the supplier. In the B2C space, many large billers are providing their consumer customers with e-invoices either via a portal or through a bank.

The SME (small and medium-sized enterprises) market is a huge area of opportunity as penetration here is quite low, except for the volumes required by their larger customers. SMEs will only be attracted into the practice of e-invoicing if there is a compelling business case, and ease of use through minimal IT effort. Current steps taken to simplify the legal environment around VAT, to improve standards and interoperability, and to provide attractive services and solutions should encourage much higher levels of adoption in the years to come. The UN/CEFACT cross-industry standard is now being proposed as a common data model.

While e-invoicing can be provided with or without banks (the latter point not necessarily being widely appreciated) banks do nevertheless have a key role to play. Given that a payment usually occurs after an invoice is submitted, the dematerialisation happening in the invoice and supply chain space for banks represents both a threat and an opportunity. The threat is that other processes and actors may impinge on the value-added opportunity in payments. The opportunity is the chance to generate new top-line revenue from delivering invoices, providing archiving services to offering new bundles of services through electronic and Internet banking. That is not all: there is also the opportunity to provide supply chain finance based on the rich information flows as well as to generate much better risk management data about bank customers.

For SMEs today, e-invoicing can be complicated by the need to connect to a variety of enterprise platforms based on a three-corner model. The opportunity for a bank, therefore, perhaps with the support of a service provider, would be to provide SMEs with an 'aggregator' or one-stop connection to the eco-system. Indeed banks have an unrivalled installed base of SMEs to whom they could offer such a value proposition and act as a catalyst for filling the current gap in the market. However, other models exist and the banking industry would need to be proactive (more so than usual perhaps) to seize this opportunity.

In B2C too banks have a great asset in the form of Internet banking through which access to invoices can be provided, thus avoiding the need for a consumer to log on to multiple web-sites provided by utilities etc, where e-invoices are made available. Many banks already offer this service, for example in the Nordic countries and Belgium.

Banks are used to offering a four corner model for payments and a similar technique can be used for e-invoicing, with each bank or service provider serving its own customer through its own e-channels and then using a common infrastructure of network and standards to create interoperability. As such, banks have the possibility to explore synergies and e-invoicing can be a future revenue generator.

Some forward-thinking banks already clearly understand the future possibilities of e-invoicing while others are still focused on looking in their 'paper-world mirror'. Overall though, a truly successful eSEPA would require e-invoices to gain real momentum. In future, customers will strongly demand e-invoice services and somebody will fulfil their request.

SEPA and the growth of e-invoicing are similar because they hold out the prospect of greater harmonisation and efficiency on a pan-European scale. E-invoicing is a huge multifaceted development primarily driven by corporate entities and public administrations. It is not driven by banks, but they can help in the ways described above. SEPA and e-invoicing can and will reinforce each other as more and more business processes are de-materialised and new technology standards are adopted.

This point is fully appreciated by the EC (as mentioned earlier) who organised a major pan-European Conference which took place on 27th and 28th April 2010 under the auspices of the Spanish Presidency of the EU. There the recommendations and findings identified in the Expert Group's report were debated with a particular focus on SMEs and e-invoicing, interoperability, standards and the legal framework. When you think about it, all rather reminiscent of the famous EC Round Table in November 2000 on 'Establishing a Single Payment Area: State of Play and Next Steps' that we learnt about in Title III ... and we mustn't forget what that was to lead to!

What's the plan with mSEPA?

Given that the title of the relevant EPC task force in this area spanned 'm' and well as 'e' (and of course the rapidly-increasing use of the mobile phone for banking applications), any reader could now be forgiven for expecting that the progress of m or mobile-payments in a SEPA context must surely be at least at the same level as 'e' – that is, being on the verge of presenting an m-payment framework, a scheme, or something along those lines. On the contrary, the reality isn't quite that rosy yet and that's the case for many reasons, including some fair justifications. To explore briefly where we are with m-payments let us first of all gain an understanding of what is meant by m-payments in SEPA.

The EPC's specific focus in this area has always been on the mobile phone as a channel for the initiation and receipt of credit transfers, direct debits and card payments in Euro. This means that operating an m-payment service in SEPA as a bank/PSP will require being able to support SCT, SDD or SEPA cards payments first – as the underlying processing standard – and then as the second layer the bank/PSP will need to enable customers to access these payment services via a mobile phone, rather than only via Internet banking or in-branch over-the-counter banking. The detailed efforts currently employed in this space focus on mobile proximity card payments, which of course in some cases are already provided by individual players or three party arrangements. The idea though is to increase the spread of those solutions so that every retail customer – from Portugal to Estonia – will benefit from the ability of contactless mobile payments. Of course, the big dependency here is the willingness of merchants. Public authorities on the other hand often play a key enabling role in this space, for example when looking at contactless public transport.

Many happy years have been spent by the EPC's m-payments task force in analysing the market and entering into cooperation agreements with mobile and standards organisations and associations such as GSMA, MobeyForum, EMVCo, AEPM (Payez Mobile) and so on. To sum up the proposed direction being taken in relation to m-payments, the EPC adopted a Mobile Payments Roadmap (we like Roadmaps!) in 2009, which sets out three core objectives: SEPA card proximity payments (excluding person to person payments – P2P), SEPA card mobile remote payments (covering P2P, person to business (P2B) and B2B) and SEPA credit transfer mobile remote payments (for all use cases). In addition, thanks to the cooperation with GSMA, project work is ongoing to develop contactless Near Field Communication (NFC) based payments using the mobile. Again, it is clear that this is all about identifying and implementing harmonised standards, which eventually will facilitate competition as well as responding to users' needs.

The ECB is now understandably asking for sight of some tangible progress that would actually see the launch of customer solutions covering proximity m-payment solutions that are not only based on card payments but also re-use SCT and SDD as well as pre-paid payment solutions. The EPC is of course only a facilitator for banks to provide such solutions as it aims to create the harmonised inter-bank standards and rules to enable these types of services. On the one hand, therefore, the delivery of a harmonised standards framework for sending and receiving mobile payments and direct debits/card payments in SEPA is an urgent requirement to get the project off the ground. Ultimately though, the degree of success will of course depend on individual banks' business objectives and the commercial deployment of these services. Other factors will nevertheless influence the m-payments proposition to become a new synergy driver – for example, in future everyone (most probably) will have a smart phone as these gradually become more cost-efficient to provide than limited-service phones. These smart phones will be like mobile mini-PCs, giving banks additional possibilities to provide more services and explore synergies arising from mobile customers.

In that kind of market you have to go for long-term solutions based on small margins but large volumes. Every new synergy-level will in one way or another reduce the number of legacy service providers – which is what SEPA is also about!

In July 2010 the EPC published a White Paper on Mobile Payments, focusing on mobile contactless card payments and also making a little excursion into mobile remote payments. It will be interesting to see further developments that will leverage efficient SCT and SDD schemes, rather than staying only with cards.

So what of the future for banks and e&mSEPA? Why are banking developments in this space so slow? You can see e-developments in all other industries and even in the public sector space, but there seems to be something of a standstill in banking. Do the banks not see the need for development? Or conversely is there a 'perfect storm' approaching with what we are experiencing now being the calmness before it breaks out? Banks seem to somehow lack incentives for innovative developments and appear to require a lot of extra resources when they do innovate. Still, here we speak about innovation in a collaborative space, which is of course different from the multiple innovations that do happen in the context of three party/own initiative solutions. However, to get SEPA e&m off the ground, more momentum at industry-wide level is needed. Therefore my conclusion is that we will need some kind of very basic incentive change for banks and SEPA if we are ever going to see full realisation of the future e&mSEPA.

(3) Completing the picture: the world is watching

In the course of my excavations in preparation for this book, I rapidly reached the conclusion that a study on payments harmonisation that looked at Europe alone, without reference to what some other countries and communities are doing, would be rather incomplete. After all, Europe is neither the centre of the earth, nor the only region that is on the path of integration. Accordingly, I broadened the net of my research to see what else I could catch as examples of the interesting new species that is regional integration, specifically looking at the monetary and payment systems part of it. In doing so, I have made two intriguing observations.

The first is that the European experience is being closely watched by onlookers from outside (rather as one might monitor an exciting laboratory experiment). After all the European banking industry is a pioneer for the implementation of the ISO 20022 XML message standard. With the launch of the SCT and SDD schemes, European banks are the first in the world to deploy this new global data format for mass payment transactions in Euro across a large market (I can't seem to stop repeating this). This innovation is likely to have an impact far beyond Europe, as corporates and banks in Asia, the Americas, the Middle East and Africa are already beginning to realise the global implications of 32 countries moving jointly towards this international standard.

The second observation is that various elements of the European payments endeavour are not as unique as maybe those of us who are living in it might previously have thought.

In the course of this chapter, I will undertake an exploration into both of these observations. But, just before doing so, it is relevant to remind ourselves of the key ingredients that have gone into baking the EU payments integration cake, in order that we can better identify how these elements are being used elsewhere, either individually or in combination.

The following table (Table 7.2) shows the four key forces of change that have worked together to create the now familiar tale of EU payments integration and harmonisation.

Table 7.2 EU payments harmonisation: the four forces of change

	Forces of change	**Comments**
(1)	Single Market	The European payments harmonisation project is based on the overall objective of creating a fully integrated Single Market in Europe.
(2)	Standards	The SEPA project chose to adopt common and innovative financial message standards with ISO 20022 XML
(3)	Regional payment solutions	Integration is being realised with a shift from multiple domestic schemes and standards to a single set of regional schemes and standards, ensuring technical interoperability of infrastructures and supporting overall competition – SEPA.
(4)	Legal harmonisation	The existence and deployment of politically inspired legal interventions designed to stimulate the achievement of policy goals such as enhanced competition, consumer protection and payment safety and efficiency – as with the PSD, Regulation 924, AML Directive, Settlement Finality Directive, Regulation 1781/2006 etc.

In the remainder of this chapter, I will highlight some key examples (an exhaustive list would require a book in its own right!) that show these forces for change at work, individually and/or in combination, in other geographies or markets. As we will observe, it turns out that the goal of creating a Single Market with the associated freedoms of free circulation of people, services and capital is not unique to the EU. Furthermore, there are other groups of countries that have the ambition to embrace payment systems integration, the creation of a common currency zone similar to the Eurozone, or both. There are cases where regulatory initiatives in Europe (for example, PSD, Settlement Finality Directive etc.) are viewed as potential legislative best practice to consider as part of regional integration projects. Additionally, in the standards environment we can see examples of an ever-increasing usage of ISO 20022 XML in financial services messaging.

The integration of EU securities markets – another Single Market adventure

Before we start our exploration of other geographies, let's start with an example right under our nose in Europe where key aspects of the thinking behind the EU payments harmonisation initiative have found their way into another domain – namely the EU securities market.

I refer here to the so-called TARGET2 for Securities or T2S initiative. The inspiration, main driver and executor of this initiative is the ECB, which plans to offer centralised multi-currency securities settlement across the European markets (T2S will therefore be the younger brother – or sister? – of TARGET2). Such a capability would represent a significant step further towards the overall Single Market integration project as well as provide significant efficiencies and cost savings for market participants.

In the T2S project we see key forces of change in action, similar to the SEPA initiative as T2S is a Single Market initiative. Furthermore, T2S plans to adopt the ISO 20022 XML standards and formats. And finally, T2S will provide a regional, centralised solution for securities settlement.

Looking more closely at the standards element, the inter-bank messaging standards used for the cash system TARGET2 are not yet ISO XML standards. Instead, TARGET2 uses the 'old' MT formats; e.g., the customer (MT 103/103 +) and inter-bank transaction (MT 202/202COV and MT 204) messages. As well as being an interesting development in its own right, the decision to adopt ISO XML for T2S could perhaps act as a trigger for TARGET2 to also migrate to these standards at some point. In fact, noting for the benefit of the precise reader, TARGET2 already has an XML component in the sense that settlement information concerning the in-built Information and Control Module (ICM) is exchanged in XML syntax. A potential future step for TARGET2 to fully embrace the ISO 20022 XML would be dependent on relevant XML-based messages for this system being in place and for banks to agree to move – unless of course such a change would be mandated by the ECB or the EC! It is of course true that the TARGET system for cash was never designed as a retail payment system (which is SEPA's destiny) but as a high-value payments platform to be used for the purpose of systemically large customer and inter-bank payments. The question, however, remains as to whether in the long run a move to ISO 20022 XML in the high value payments environment would be a good thing or not – it would certainly allow for additional harmonisation of standards.

The choice of ISO XML for T2S was an easy one as the whole system is being built from scratch. TARGET2 on the other hand has a lot of history and legacy, with messages and formats having been embedded in banks', investment houses' and other financial institutions' internal systems. Therefore, any change over to new message types and formats will take time and require a proper business case across all relevant sectors.

So let's look briefly at what T2S is and how the intended efficiencies are expected to manifest once the platform is live – noting that the live date has recently been moved from 2013 to September 2014 due to the complexity of the task.

In essence, T2S is a single IT platform that will be able to deliver securities settlement in a DvP (Delivery versus Payment) mode in Central Bank Money (CBM), all operating in a borderless way across Europe. As such, the immediate effect of T2S will be to create a single pool of securities, improving choice for investors. The ECB's idea is that having all securities settled via a harmonised platform will remove the fragmentation and lack of competition that is still characterising the European securities market to a certain degree. Just as in the past, market participants will still be able to connect via their custodian or directly through a Central Securities Depository (CSD), but beyond that T2S will also enable direct access. All CSDs and direct market participants will hold both their securities and their cash accounts on the T2S platform, therefore also leveraging the existing TARGET2 RTGS cash system. This is possible due to the interconnectivity between TARGET2 and T2S which will ensure the smooth settlement in CBM. The project is currently in the development phase and so far 29 CSDs have agreed to join T2S, including three Scandinavian CSDs from Norway, Sweden and Denmark, which also means that settlement will be possible in the three Scandinavian domestic currencies as well as the

Euro – and potentially also in Sterling if the Bank of England can be persuaded to join. Effectively, all Member State currencies if non-Euro can settle as long as the respective central bank puts up the collateral in the system.

Due to the constructive way in which the ECB had been engaging with the wider market during the design phase, a number of key components have been jointly prepared, such as the User Requirements Document, General Specifications, General Functional Specifications and General Technical Design.

Pan-European settlement capability is of course not something that is entirely new to the European securities landscape. ICSDs, or International Central Securities Depositories, such as Euroclear or Clearstream Deutsche Börse have played an important role for some time by integrating parts of the European settlement space. However, the ECB's proposal goes much further by offering centralised settlement for all markets, with the objective to lower settlement fees for all participants and enable the reduction of back office costs due to the streamlining of interfaces – so no need to connect to multiple national interfaces anymore.

CSDs (and the ICSDs) will have the opportunity to outsource their settlement services to the ECB (but are not forced to do so) and in turn benefit from the to-be-built (and planned to be state of the art) settlement system, save money on costly and complex IT projects in connection to settlement infrastructures, as well as be able to leverage economies of scale from the single settlement pool in addition to potentially broadening their market footprint as well as to enter new business areas such as asset servicing.

Finally, a very significant benefit is expected to arise for all participants due to the fact that aggregate liquidity requirements will fall as a consequence of all users' liquidity/collateral being pooled on the T2S platform, hence removing the requirement to hold domestic liquidity/collateral in all those national CSDs a member is connected to. The advantage is that users can limit themselves to 1 CSD account (or direct account with T2S) that can be used to settle any securities transaction in Europe. In addition, the ECB expects the T2S project to contribute positively to overall financial stability by reducing settlement risk in cross-border transactions.

So overall then, an interesting example of the 'forces of change' that we identified earlier as collectively remoulding of the EU payments landscape at work – the adoption of ISO 20022 XML and the desire for regional technical infrastructures with the integration of securities settlement in Europe under the overall Single Market objective.

Let us now turn our attention outside of the EU, to explore an interesting (but non-exhaustive) list of cases where the EU example is inspiring – and at the same time being inspired by – events unfolding in other regions of the world.

Common and Single Markets – not just an EU phenomenon

The sources that have been drawn on to create the rich tapestry that is payments harmonisation in the EU have critically included an underlying political vision for a Single Market supported by a harmonised legal environment. It is therefore very interesting to note that, particularly since the 1990s, economic and political integration have clearly become more appealing to some other regions across the globe. Keeping in mind that Europe was the first zone to formalise a Single Market, some regions have started by setting out ambitious plans and timelines, while others are delivering regional integration as we speak (read!). Recalling what we uncovered in Title II, regional integration usually starts with the building of Preferential Trading Areas that evolve into Free Trade Areas. As the next step customs unions develop and with further harmonisation of product regulations and standards – as well as the free movement of capital, goods and labour a Common Market is built. In Europe, we have taken this concept to the next level by creating a Monetary Union to underpin economic integration and by making significant steps towards political integration as well as cross-regional legal harmonisation.

Today we have a small, but still very interesting, list of Single Markets that cover regions in the Caribbean, the Andes, Central America, Russia/Belarus, West Africa and Central Africa next to – of course – the European Economic Area (EU + Norway, Iceland and Liechtenstein). In addition, certain parts of Asia, such as those involved in the ASEAN initiative, plus parts of the Middle East with the Gulf Cooperation Council (GCC) are considering or actively working on key aspects of economic and monetary integration.

In the next part of this chapter, I will briefly explore a selection of interesting examples that we can see today, with a focus on Africa, the Middle East and Asia. In doing so, I will analyse cases where the forces of change seen in our European example are at play, for example in the context of large scale payment system integration, adoption of ISO 20022 XML, creation of monetary unions or legal measures to underpin these developments.

Let us start the global tour with a swift move to a neighbouring major continent.

SEPA out of Africa?

Looking back at the last few decades, in spite of many technological advances the African continent has suffered badly from a dangerous cocktail of political instability, dictatorship and war. This has lead at times to the destruction of much of the continent's core infrastructure, such as roads, railway systems, electrical supply and even telecommunications. Accordingly the daunting task that now needs to be faced is to put together a plan to recover what has been lost and create a sustainable economic environment that will lead to long-term economic growth. With this in mind, governments and central banks across the continent, with assistance from the World Bank and other International Aid Agencies, are now focusing their attention on this major challenge.

So what has any of this got to do with payment systems or common currency zones? Even though the challenge that absence or low levels of physical infrastructure pose, Africa has been successful in using mobile banking solutions to bridge these gaps. But there is more going on here. From an economic and financial development perspective, there are actually a number of regional initiatives underway designed to increase the free flow of goods, services and people, including the development of 'free trade zones', 'customs unions' and 'common currency areas'.

The opportunities and challenges vary greatly from country to country, not least given the differing modes of payment in use – with the current predominance of cash and cheques in most countries outside of South Africa. With the exception of South Africa, the state of development of the payments infrastructure is generally relatively poor, and from a regulatory perspective we look at a combination of both liberal and highly regulated markets.

Africa, not exactly the smallest of continents, stands out in terms of the sheer diversity of the pockets of developments now taking place across its many constituent countries. In Africa today, we have no less that 18 Regional Economic Communities (RECs), each with similar goals of fostering cooperation and a degree of economic integration. Two full-fledged currency unions are already in place, each of which has a single clearing house. Another common monetary area is in the process of further development and six more are in the prospect stage of evolution.

With that context firmly in mind, let's take a look at the financial and payment system developments across some of these regional cooperation initiatives. The main regional cooperative initiatives are as shown in the below list (see Table 7.3).

Table 7.3 List of African regional cooperations

- CMA – Common Monetary Area
- SADC – Southern African Development Community
- EAC – East African Community
- COMESA – Common Market for East and Southern Africa
- ECOWAS – Economic Community of West African States
  - WAMZ – West African Monetary Zone
  - UEMOA/WAEMU – West African Economic and Monetary Union
- ECCAS – Economic Community of Central African States
  - CEMAC/EMCCA – Economic and Monetary Community of Central Africa
- MENA – Middle East and North Africa

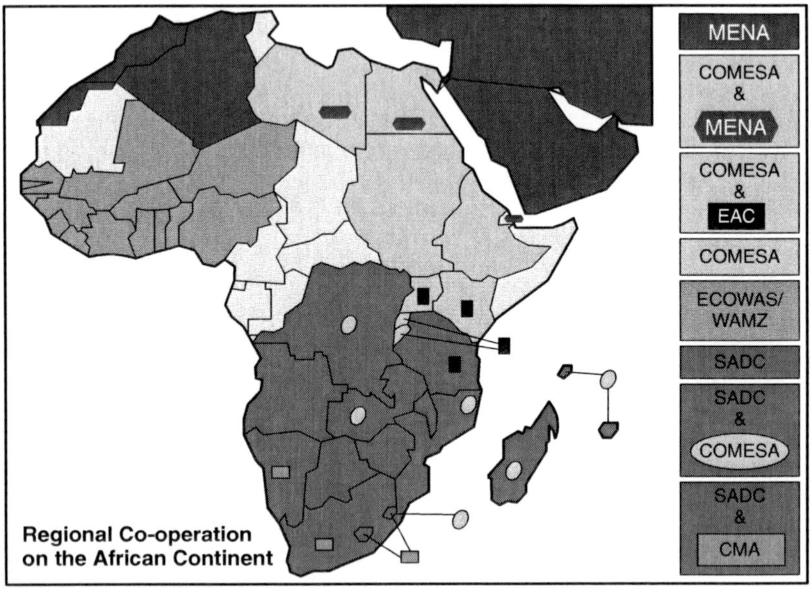

Figure 7.1 Regional cooperation on the African continent

In addition, the map above (see Figure 7.1) graphically depicts some of these regional groupings.

These regional cooperations, despite being of course set up in a way that is designed to support and sustain inter-African trade, are also at the same time very focused on developing two key international trade corridors, namely, Africa/China and Africa/India. The growth in trade across these corridors has increased exponentially and is close to reaching 40 per cent of total African trade, significantly changing the traditional economics of this continent. It should also be noted that the largest growth in worker remittances over the past five years has been between Africa and these two geographies. Accordingly, and hardly surprisingly, there is a strong focus on the need to get the necessary structures and systems in place to improve the financial transaction process within Africa and between Africa and China/India.

The table on the next page (see Table 7.4) lists the countries that are members of this selection of regional groupings and also illustrates the important point that there are a number of countries that are members of more than one regional grouping.

With such a plethora of regional cooperations is it then obviously the case that things are moving rapidly on the African continent on the payments integration front? To answer this question, let's take a look at the goals and visions of the respective regional bodies and see how far cooperation has delivered tangible benefits in terms of integration, economic growth and overall promotion of free circulation of goods, services, capital and people.

Regional Cooperations in the South and East of Africa

CMA – Common Monetary Area

This rather small – and thus more flexible – grouping has been working on creating a monetary area since 1986 and has achieved significant results. While no separate single currency (similar to the Euro) has been introduced in this region as of yet, all currencies are trading on par and the ZAR (South African Rand) is accepted as legal tender in all countries. Lesotho and Swaziland, due to their small size and their historical status as provinces of South Africa, currently operate as branches of South African parent banks with little or no inter-bank interoperability at local level. Formally the CMA was replaced by the present Multilateral Monetary Area (MMA) in 1992 when Namibia officially joined the monetary union.

South Africa and Namibia have developed national clearing and settlement systems and banks are directly connected to these systems.

From a regional governance perspective the central bank payments oversight committee (CMA CPOC) is currently seeking to implement a CMA low-value cross-border clearing and settlement model and will focus on driving the standards and principles for the cross-border clearing within the CMA region. In that context the ISO 20022 XML SEPA standards are considered as the best option to employ (Please note!).

Table 7.4 Membership of the African regional cooperation groupings

CMA – 1986	SADC – 1996	EAC – 2007	COMESA – 1978	ECOWAS – 1975	MENA
Lesotho	Angola	Burundi	Burundi	The Gambia	Algeria
Namibia	Botswana	Kenya	Comoros	Ghana	Bahrain
South Africa	DRC	Rwanda	DRC	Guinea	Djibouti
Swaziland	Lesotho	Tanzania	Djibouti	Nigeria	Egypt
	Madagascar	Uganda	Egypt	Sierra Leone	Iran
	Malawi		Eritrea	Benin	Iraq
	Mauritius		Ethiopia	Burkina Faso	Israel
	Mozambique		Kenya	Cape Verde	Jordan
	Namibia		Libya	Côte d'Ivoire	Kuwait
	Seychelles		Madagascar	Gambia	Lebanon
	South Africa		Malawi	Ghana	Libya
	Swaziland		Mauritius	Guinea Bissau	Malta
	Tanzania		Rwanda	Guinea (suspended)	Morocco
	Zambia		Seychelles	Liberia	Oman
	Zimbabwe		Sudan	Mali	Qatar
			Swaziland	Niger (suspended)	Saudi Arabia
			Uganda	Nigeria	Syria
			Zambia	Senegal	Tunisia
			Zimbabwe	Sierra Leone	United Arab Emirates
				Togo	West Bank & Gaza
					Yemen

Still, these plans are not simple to put into action given that both South Africa and Namibia are keen to maintain and expand their respective national clearing systems. The current challenge for Namibia is how to retain its independence while promoting interoperability with South Africa, allowing for efficient cross-border payments. Also, the fact that South Africa does not accept the Namibian Dollar (N$) at domestic level (even though the reverse is true), again creates reason for Namibia's Governor to remain a little cautious as to how the regional integration is taken forward.

So, conclusion: very interesting developments and one to watch closely in the future.

SADC – South African Development Community

The 14 countries that have comprised the SADC region since 1996 have already achieved parts of their key convergence targets – a free trade area and a customs union. In fact the SACU – the South African Customs Union – is the oldest still existing customs union in the world and was founded in 1910.[4] Now a single central bank and a SADC currency are in plan to become reality by 2018.

A project to modernise the payments infrastructure was established in 1996 to support systems harmonisation and development in a multitude of ways, for example to assist member countries to define a domestic payment strategy and development plan; to facilitate regional integration, coordination and cooperation in finance and investment; to create a favourable investment climate to attract Foreign Direct Investment (FDI); to achieve and maintain macroeconomic convergence; to establish a framework for cooperation and coordination between central banks on payment, clearing and settlement systems; and to define a coordinated regional approach to cross-border payments.

The SADC region – which, looking at the above list of objectives clearly wants in some ways to become the next Euro-like zone – is challenged by the fact that a number of its member countries are really not at the same level, whether in economic development terms, political stability or simply when looking at physical infrastructures. For example, the Democratic Republic of Congo (DRC) is still in the early investigative stages of implementing an RTGS system, which is in strong contrast to South Africa, which has a modern National Payment System and participates in the Continuous Linked Settlement (CLS).[5] Given this constraint, some observers are suggesting that the way to get things moving is with a sub-group of pilot countries, in order to be able to demonstrate tangible results before too long.

An ambitious SADC road map was elaborated and presented in July 2010, determining the different steps that need to be taken to achieve substantial infrastructure integration by 2018 and beyond. The plan defines six key pillars of development, ranging from the definition of an appropriate legal framework for payments (PSD springs to mind here), to the creation of clearing and settlement infrastructures for securities as well as cash transactions. The ambition is to be able to specify the requirements for a legal framework, a regional card-based payment system (see SEPA SCF), a centralised securities settlement system (T2S!), a low-value payments framework (think SEPA!) and an RTGS (and TARGET2) by June 2014. The roll-out of legal rules as well as the technical systems and infrastructures to be employed by those countries able to participate in the first implementation wave is expected for mid-2018. The core principles of the BIS for Systemically Important Payment Systems will play an important role in the SADC integration project and the experience of other single currency unions, such as the Eurozone, will be considered in the context of creating a harmonised retail payment system as well as the underpinning legal framework that will be needed (several European developments will be relevant here).

2010 is expected to be an important year to lay the foundations as well as to bring new perspectives on how to achieve economic and monetary integration in this region.

EAC – East African Community

The EAC, an intergovernmental organisation comprising the five east African countries Burundi, Kenya, Rwanda, Tanzania and Uganda, has a number of ambitious objectives, including the elimination of restrictions on free movement of capital; ensuring convertibility of currencies; promoting investments in capital markets leading to an integrated financial system as well as the coordination and harmonisation of their economic, monetary and financial policies with the help of legal measures issued by the EAC Council and the harmonisation of travel, labour, residential, social, trade, intellectual property rights and environmental policies across the EAC region.

The EAC community has already defined common macro-economic policies and is progressing its harmonisation of laws, starting with banking, payments, contract, insolvency, cheque and electronic information. In 2010, the EAC launched its own common market for goods, labour and capital within the region and a monetary union as well as the creation of a single Central Bank is planned to be achieved by 2012. A single currency, which could potentially be called the EAC Shilling, is also envisaged to be launched in 2012 and a full political federation is envisaged for 2015 (all pretty ambitious!).

Central Banks within EAC are currently working on a single payment system for the region that will facilitate cross-border transactions. While discussions are ongoing to find out how their RTGS system should work, what type of collateral would be required and what participation criteria would need to be defined as entry requirements, the system could be implemented as early as December 2010. Indeed harmonisation of necessary legal frameworks and monetary regulations is also required to be in place before this would go live. Pending the introduction of a single currency, the system will be supported by a multi-currency RTGS platform with National Central Banks in the five member countries of the community expected to open and operate reciprocal accounts for partner states' currencies by December 2010. Foundations have been laid to make local bills accepted throughout the region before January 2011 and national Central Banks intend to publish cross-rates for partner states' currencies also with effect from December 2010. Public awareness about EAC currency convertibility will be raised through sensitisation programmes. It is also expected that by December this year, all the five central banks create a mechanism to ensure that commercial banks and bureaus quote EAC cross-rates as well as to set up the necessary infrastructure for data exchange needed to implement the East Africa Payment system.

If these timelines are followed, the single currency objective for 2012 could be a realistic one. However, it is also clear that the planned multi-currency RTGS system will be a rather sub-optimal solution compared to a single-currency system. One potential learning from the European experience on this topic is that a pan-European RTGS system was only developed once the single currency was in place, given the practical complications and higher funding requirements which would have been involved in attempting to do so earlier.

COMESA – Common Market for East and Southern Africa

This regional grouping already achieved a free trade area in October 2000, with its 11 members not only having eliminated customs tariffs but also having worked on eliminating quantitative restrictions and other non-tariff barriers. Further initiatives exist to promote cross border initiatives, form a common industrial policy and introduce a monetary harmonisation programme.

COMESA's secretariat is located in Zambia and its achievements to date include (among other things) a wider, harmonised and more competitive market; greater industrial productivity and competitiveness; increased agricultural production and food security; a more rational exploitation of natural resources; greater harmonisation in monetary, banking and financial policies and laws; and the harmonisation of macro-economic and monetary policies throughout the region.

Due though to the not insignificant size of this regional grouping, the level of economic and social development of participating Member States still varies significantly, meaning that a payment system and monetary integration à la Eurozone and EU Single Market will continue to be a future dream rather than a feasible project that could be achieved in the short term.

Western and Central African Regional Cooperations

ECOWAS – Economic Community of West African States

The Economic Community of West African States (ECOWAS) was launched in 1975 with the objective of integrating the economies of its – at the time 15 – Member States. Already in those days ECOWAS had the clear objective of creating an economic and monetary union as well as to ensure that the region would operate as a single trading block (not too far off the Single Market logic).

However, 35 years later and despite the creation of a free trade area, little further tangible progress has been made and the ECOWAS Treaty (the Treaty of Lagos) had to be revised in 1993 to loosen collaboration between members. The ECOWAS has two main institutions that are responsible for the implementation of regional policies: the ECOWAS Secretariat and the ECOWAS Fund for Cooperation, Compensation and Development. The latter transformed into the ECOWAS Bank for Investment and Development in 2001. Still, ECOWAS has two very active sub groupings of countries that are working on further regional integration: the WAMZ and the UEMOA.

WAMZ – West African Monetary Zone

The West African Monetary Zone (WAMZ) was founded in 2000 and includes the following member courtiers: the Gambia, Ghana, Guinea, Nigeria, and Sierra Leone. The main focus of the WAMZ is the harmonisation of Member State economies and the creation of a stable currency that could rival the CFS franc, which is used by all other former French colonies in West and Central Africa (except for Mauritania and Guinea). Against that background the WAMZ is discussing the establishment of a monetary union (the name is something of a giveaway) with a common central bank and a single currency to replace the 5 existing currencies – so very much along the lines of the Euro single currency project, albeit on a rather smaller scale. They have even decided where the 'to be founded' West African Central Bank (WACB) headquarters will be located: in Accra (Ghana). A slight challenge is that all of this is supposed to be in place by 2010!

The West African Monetary Institute (WAMI) – rather similar to the ECB forerunner the EMI (European Monetary Institute) – was set up in 2001 to facilitate the creation of the common Central Bank and the introduction of a common currency. The WAMI is therefore currently preparing the creation of the WACB and will monitor and assess compliance of participating countries with established convergence criteria. The WAMI will adopt the objective of price stability, coordinate monetary policies and ensure the physical issuance of the common currency once launched. However, several of the WAMZ countries suffer from weak currencies and regular budget deficits, which are for the time being counterbalanced by the fact that their local central banks print money to fill the gaps, resulting in further weakening of their currencies.

A meeting of the WAMZ was held in Accra in May 2010, which brought more clarity to the next steps in this project. Under the revised plans, WAMZ expects to launch the common currency, named the 'Eco' (sounds a bit like the 'Ecu'!) by 2015 (so not 2010). There is currently no timeline for the establishment of the WACB, however, it is expected that the introduction of an RTGS platform in the region would promote its launch. The ultimate objective is to promote the Eco as the future common currency for all West and Central African states.

On payment standards, the WAMI has provided some practical commentary on the proposed clearing/payment systems:

- The WACB hub will link national RTGS systems of the member countries.
- SWIFT will play a central role in addressing the regional connectivity to the RTGS systems by member countries.
- The WAMZ RTGS system will progress from a platform of system of systems to a unitary single shared platform (similar to the evolution from TARGET to TARGET2)
- The payment system components being developed in the member countries will be multicurrency systems and initially operate in their current national currencies.
- The systems will switch to operate in Eco, upon its introduction.
- The WACB will be the owner and operator of the RTGS system that will interlink the member countries' national central banks.

Still, the plans for a harmonised low-value clearing in SEPA-style are left for future discussions. After all, Europe also started with building a common high-value clearing solution and only after ten years is starting to move on to integrated low-value payments with SEPA.

UEMOA – Union économique et monétaire ouest-africaine

The UEMOA (EN: *West African Economic and Monetary Union* – not to be confused with the WAMZ), was created in January 1994 by the Heads of State and Government of its Member countries Benin, Burkina Faso, Cote d'Ivoire, Guinea-Bissau, Mali, Niger, Senegal, and Togo.

This region has achieved completion of a customs and monetary union and its key objectives going forward include (1) the further convergence of macroeconomic policy, (2) creation of a Common Market, (3) coordination of sectoral policies, (4) hamonisation of fiscal policies and (5) increasing competitiveness across the open market with help of further harmonisation of the legal environment (very much like Europe!).

Clearing (in one form or another) has always existed at regional level (in addition to domestic clearing). The regional RTGS has been live since June 2004 while the regional ACH went live in February 2008. In UEMOA the standard used for high-value payments is MT and a local format (ICOM) is used for low value payments (the SEPA ISO standards could be of interest here in terms of future systems upgrades).

UEMOA has achieved significant steps in its payment systems reform, which was initiated by the regions' central bank – the Central Bank of West African States (BCEAO). With the aim to introduce a move from cash to electronic payments as well as to improve regional legislation on payments, UEMOA has successfully pushed the region to deliver RTGS and ACH systems as well as to develop regional inter-bank card-based systems that use EMV security standards (similar to the SCF!) and a legal framework for payment system safety and efficiency.

The UEMOA region is certainly one of Africa's regions that has achieved the most significant level of integration.

For both groupings – WAMZ and UEMOA – borders in terms of payments processing have been fully removed and a Single Market for Payments is therefore in place in these regions! A monetary and currency union together with a standardised payment platform and a single clearing system for their member countries is a reality. Similar to the practical objective of SEPA, payments and receivables can be cleared regionally via the ACH and there is also a regional RTGS (similar to TARGET2) spanning all member countries. There are no legal barriers to the movement of funds and central bank reporting within these zones is absent (a lesson to learn for Europe here!).

But, the usage of ISO 20022 XML is still something to promote in the context of taking their regional payments system to the next level ...

ECCAS and CEMAC – economic communities and monetary unions in Central Africa

ECCAS, another French abbreviation – *Communauté Économique des États d'Afrique Centrale* – stands for the Economic and Monetary Community of Central Africa and is composed of 11 Member States: Angola, Burundi, Cameroon, Central African Republic, Chad, Democratic Republic of Congo, Equatorial Guinea, Gabon, Republic of the Congo, Rwanda and Sao Tomé & Principe. ECCAS was born out of the Central African Customs and Economic Union that existed since the early 1980s and began its work in 1985. The main objectives of ECCAS include regional collective autonomy, increase of living standards, economic stability and ultimately the creation of a Central African Common Market.

A particular sub-region of ECCAS is the so-called CEMAC, or Economic and Monetary Community of Central Africa (in French: *Communauté Économique et Monétaire de l'Afrique Centrale*), a grouping of six countries – Cameroon, Central African Republic, Chad, Democratic Republic of the Congo, Equatorial Guinea and Gabon – that has already successfully implemented a monetary union.

Similar to the European Single Market, this region has the objective of achieving an African Common Market, promoting economic and social cooperation. Member countries do share common regulatory, financial and legal structures and maintain common external tariffs on imports from countries outside this region. Capital movements in the region are fully liberalised but trade tariffs within CEMAC have only been fully abolished in theory.

CEMAC members also share the same currency, the Franc CFA as well as the same Central Bank. The CFA Franc is strong and stable due to the fact that its exchange rate is tied to that of the Euro and guaranteed by the French Treasury (former colonial links are at play). (NB: the French themselves had to give up their Franc in Europe in exchange for the Euro!) Clearing has always existed at regional level (in addition to domestic clearing). The ACH model was in place in 2008 at domestic level and a regional ACH (similar to the SEPA PE-ACH concept) was delivered in 2009. The high value clearing messages and formats in place are based on MT standards (just like the European

TARGET2 system operates today), while low value clearing is executed with a local format (again, a case could be made to migrate to the ISO 20022 XML in the longer run).

An example of payment system developments in North Africa

Egypt, the first SEPA-replicant!

Believe it or not but the most up to date news indicates that the Egyptian market is introducing a local ACH system to allow for exchange of automated low value mass payments. Egypt currently has an RTGS System in place but for commercial and retail payments the commonly used payment instrument is the rather costly cheque. An ACH will enable electronic retail and commercial payments and the Central Bank of Egypt envisages building credit as well as direct debit functionalities into the system. But the most interesting part here is that Egypt has copied the SEPA rulebooks! The current implementation guidelines proposed for the inter-bank space in Egypt are based on the actual SEPA CT rulebook and the usage of the IS0 20022 XML for the exchange of inter-bank financial messages, with the technical inter-bank implementation guidelines being replicated for Egyptian implementation. The SEPA-replicant ACH was soft launched in June this year and expectations are that by end 2010/early 2011 the market will have fully embedded this new payments process for credit transfers. Direct debit functionality is planned in a second phase. Additional details, for example whether the Egyptian market envisages to introduce the IBAN to be consistent with SEPA going forward still need to be clarified.

An exciting example of SEPA being employed as a domestic best practice with the potential to spread to other neighbouring countries in the future! SEPA is clearly evolving into the Single Eurovision Payments Area!

Moving forward with the African Integration Project

So, as you can see, the African continent is an exciting and vibrant place for growth and change and is clearly gearing up to become a much more significant participant in the global payments village.

It is also very apparent that a number of the regional initiatives in Africa have more than a passing resemblance to what we have been experiencing in the EU – with clear live examples in fact of all four of the key change drivers that we've seen in the EU being played out in different combinations.

Seeing what is already in motion, within each regional grouping and in individual countries, it is hugely important that banking associations and central banks play a leading role in the creation of regional payment as well as clearing and settlement systems, just as they have done (and are still doing!) in Europe. It is equally important that leaders in this field within the African continent continue to engage with their international counterparts, particularly in the EU, in order to exchange ideas and feedback on their respective experiences – both good and bad!

For example, looking at the developments undertaken by Europe with the introduction of the single currency, high value and low value payment systems with TARGET and SEPA, the conclusion that might well be drawn is that without an integrated payments clearing and settlement system, substantial regional integration is not possible (or at best is hugely more problematic to achieve). Successful financial trading clearly depends to a large extend on having safe, secure and efficient payment systems. In order to create these a number of principles could be suggested to form the basis of how the regional payment system projects should be structured. These could include points such as: a clear, common definition of a 'payment service' (now that rings a bell!); solutions to be principle driven and relevant for the country and/or region but with a strong focus on interoperability at national and cross border level; use of existing global interoperable standards – such as our

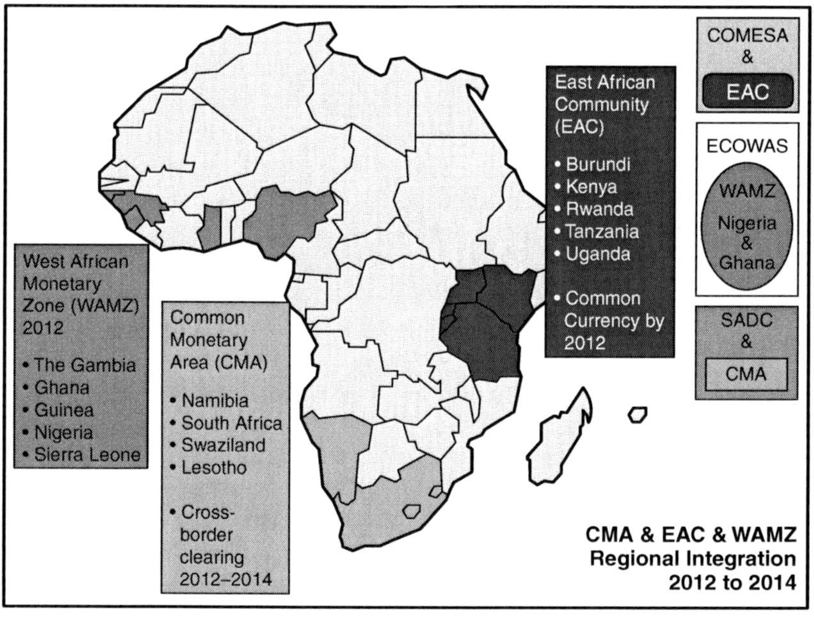

Figure 7.2 Illustration of African regional integration plans 2012–14

friend ISO 20022 XML – instead of a proprietary standards approach; and an appropriate and relevant regulatory oversight framework for banks and non-banks providing financial services domestically and cross-border (also sounds a bit familiar!).

Hopefully, the application of principles such as these will help form a solid foundation to the development of a business case that in turn will ensure the long-term sustainability of the regional payment systems in Africa. The picture above (see Figure 7.2) captures the vision.

In conclusion, Africa's regions are on the path to economic and monetary integration. The regional economic communities described above all form part of the broader African Economic Community, which promotes the overall economic development of the African continent. While the development of such a diverse mix of countries and economies is not going to move forward at a harmonised pace, certain regions have already achieved significant results towards the ultimate goal of economic and monetary union. The coming years will bring more progress, in particular for those regions that are now gearing up for the next steps towards market and infrastructure integration. Stay tuned!

Integration forces at work in the gulf region with the Gulf Cooperation Council

Extreme growth in recent years has been one of the key triggers for a number of countries in this region to closely examine the idea of economic and even monetary union. For example the Gulf Cooperation Council (GCC) composed of Bahrain, Kuwait, Oman, Qatar, Saudi Arabia and the United Arab Emirates (UAE) was founded in 1981. Since then, significant efforts have been made to develop a Common Market, which finally saw the light in January 2008, formalising the customs union that had been in place since 2003, but had not initially proved terribly effective in practice.

The features of the GCC Common Market have in many ways clearly been inspired by the example of the EU and its four freedoms, and rather similar to the EC in Europe, the GCC has a Secretariat, which is located in Riyadh (Saudi Arabia). The GCC agreement provides equal rights to all citizens of the GCC in areas such as employment, social security, education, healthcare, trading in stock markets, setting up companies and buying/selling properties. However, the really hard part – the development of common legislative frameworks and specific regulations on all these topics – was still a long way from completion in 2008 and the classic EU-style challenges of delayed legal transposition, enforcement and a lack of adequate supervision were already apparent in the GCC. While capital mobility is proving relatively easy to achieve, the freedom of financial services, including the right of providers in one member country to be able to open branches in another, is proving to be a more difficult challenge in practice.

In March 2009, a bold step was taken when an announcement was made that the GCC now intends to create a monetary union – the first in the Middle East – by 2010 (again a rather ambitious deadline). The plan essentially looked at creating a common currency for the area and potentially pegging it against the US Dollar or another global currency such as the Euro. Five of the six GCC currencies had already up to that point been pegged to the Dollar for some time. Oman, however decided to stay outside the plans for creating a currency zone – playing a similar role to the UK when it decided to reserve its right not be part of the Eurozone project.

By December 2009, the creation of a Monetary Council was announced and its first meeting took place at the end of March 2010. Due to the fact that the location of the Gulf Monetary Council (GMC) was decided to be in Saudi Arabia, the largest economy of the region as well as the seat of the GCC Secretariat, the UAE decided to withdraw on political grounds. On top of that, the first GMC meeting saw the central bank governor from Saudi Arabia named as chair, with the central bank governor of Bahrain appointed as vice chair (again a thorn in the eye of the UAE).

It is indeed a shame that the UAE is not part of the project right now as the Dubai International Financial Centre (DIFC) has plans to develop state of the art processing systems that will allow financial markets to link across the region – an offshore Euro and US Dollar RTGS system inspired by the Hong Kong RTGS solution – more on this later. A key first step in this direction was made in summer 2009 with the enactment of a Payment System Settlement Finality Law (we have one of those in the EU, too!), marking an important development for the region.

As the ambitious plans of the GCC are mainly focussed on economic growth, a current lack of political consensus and cooperation is slowing down the objective of a single GCC currency and monetary union. 2010 is no longer feasible and a new more realistic deadline will be required soon in order to restore the credibility of this project. Further open questions include by when all GCC countries will have to have ratified the plan for the currency union and whether the new currency will indeed be linked initially to the Dollar followed by a free float that would certainly benefit the area's control over monetary policy. At the same time, monetary policy has first to start converging in this region and a common payment and settlement system will need to be built. Here, a lot of lessons can be learnt from Europe's RTGS and low value systems and a case for adopting the global ISO 20022 XML in the low or even high value space could be made.

Overall, the slow pace with which a Common Market and a Monetary Union can be decided and put into action should not be a deterrent to the GCC's motivation. After all, the EU experience shows that bumps and pot-holes are only to be expected on the road to payments harmonisation.

Around Asia: signs of economic and monetary integration?

Across the Asian continent there are a considerable number of interesting examples of initiatives and cooperations that are relevant to our theme. To give you a few indications of how things are moving in the region, for example the Association of Southeast Asian Nations – in short ASEAN – has been working towards the objective of creating an area of peace, freedom and economic growth across the ten participating member countries since 1967. Regional economic and monetary integration are an ambition, although tangible steps in that direction are still to come. Developments in Hong Kong and Japan are focussing on advancing market efficiencies and reach in the transaction space and India has high ambitions for the next few years in terms of significant payment systems upgrades and integration.

Japan and Hong Kong – step-by-step adoption of new standards

This part of Asia shows a lot of dynamic developments, ranging from systems upgrades to cross-border standards sharing, including again some examples of adoption of the global ISO 20022 XML standards.

Big in Japan: Zengin and JASDEC

Although Japan might be a relatively new – however enthusiastic – player in the ISO 20022 XML community, it has a long history in the electronic payments arena. The Zengin System, a Japanese system equivalent to CHIPS (US) or Euro1 (Europe) started operation in 1973, four years before SWIFTNet was launched.

The Zengin system is planning to change over to the ISO 20022 XML by November 2011, when the current system is at the end of its life cycle. The new Zengin – version number 6 – will add XML to its existing formats, which will also enable extending the current remittance data set of 20 characters to 140 (though more would be possible of course!). In order to allow for gradual migration the Zengin Centre will continue to accept non-XML formats and where relevant format conversion will be performed.

But the use of the ISO 20022 XML is far from the only thing planned in Japan. Interestingly, Japanese banks have already begun to create a business case out of the European SEPA initiative in order to benefit their own consumer and business customers. To enable their users to benefit from SEPA, either in the context of Japanese tourists travelling to Europe and making payments in the SEPA region, or for Japanese doing business in Europe, the international players among Japanese financial institutions plan to offer their Japan-based customers the opportunity to open a non-resident bank account in Europe and to handle all related payments business via SEPA credit transfer and SEPA direct debit across the 32 SEPA countries.

The group of Japanese that their banks particularly have in mind is what is known as the Dankai generation, who hold the majority of Japanese private sector assets, to the tune of some 1.500 trillion yen or 11 trillion Euro (this sum roughly represents the GDP of the 27 EU countries). The Dankai are expected to continue being active in business after retirement from the work force and are known to be IT-savvy and likely to travel abroad in the years to come. For these clients, Japanese banks will, for example, look to issue credit and debit cards compliant with the SEPA Cards Framework (SCF) linked to the non-resident accounts of their Japanese customers.

In light of the above, the Japanese banking community expects SEPA – once fully implemented – to have a direct impact beyond Europe: the harmonisation of the Euro payment market will deliver the infrastructure needed to boost inter-regional trade on a global level.

Looking at the domestic Japanese securities world, the Japanese Securities Depository Centre (JASDEC) had already defined its goal of incorporating Japanese market practices and regulations into the ISO 15022 and ISO 20022 messaging formats in 2007 when signing a Memorandum of Understanding (MOU) with SWIFT. This will help ensure Japan's needs are included in the development of global financial messaging standards. The first steps of this standardisation project were taken when JASDEC adopted the ISO 15022 standard for the matching facility, but there are gaps between the pure ISO 15022 standard and JASDEC's version. With SWIFT's help under the MOU, JASDEC hopes to eliminate these gaps and eventually migrate to the more advanced ISO 20022 XML messaging standard.

While the timeline for JASDEC is ambitious and in line with that for the Zengin – migration to ISO 20022 XML by 2011 – the eventual adoption of global standards and global connectivity will be crucial to JASDEC's future plans to become a leading CSD not only in Asia but possibly also at global level. There is a clear message here to those that have yet to jump on the ISO XML train!

Finally, a couple of other interesting developments to take note of briefly in the context of the Japanese payments market, this time from the public sector. From a high-value payment systems perspective, the Bank of Japan (Japan's central bank) is preparing for the establishment of a new version of BOJ-NET (the Japanese RTGS system) with a target migration date of 2015. It is currently carefully monitoring developments in the private sector in determining the requirements for this upgraded system (maybe ISO XML?). Additionally, the Japanese 'Payment Services Act' (now that has a familiar sound to it) was passed last June (2009). Interestingly, this included provisions designed to encourage non-banks to offer payment services and, in conjunction with the availability of new technologies, is intended to further expand the payment business in Japan for retail payments as well as corporate cash management (very much a PSD-inspired measure).

Hong Kong

It will be recalled that one of our four key forces of change that have been working in combination to create the tale of EU payments integration has been the desire to create regional payment systems and infrastructures linking together more than one country. Interestingly in this context, it is worth taking a quick look at China's province Hong Kong, which has gone through major payment systems re-engineering with the recent upgrade (2009) of its Clearing House Automated Transfer System (CHATS) into what is now considered as one of the world's state of the art systems in that space. The system links Hong Kong to mainland China's Guangdong Province and Shenzhen city and provides cross-border HKD and USD RTGS payment services to banks in Hong Kong and the mainland, thereby improving the efficiency for cross-border flow of funds and settlement efficiency. Due to its multi-currency nature and same time-zone settlement, other markets in Asia are also benefiting from this multi-dimensional payment and settlement system, which furthermore has integrated a custodian system. A key step in this system overhaul was the move from a local platform to the global SWIFTNet, which now facilitates streamlined access to the RTGS system by financial institutions that were already used to using SWIFT for international payments.

The progressive establishment of cross-border links with the clearing and settlement systems of other Asian countries is helping Hong Kong develop into a payment and settlement hub for the region.

Two of the more recent examples include the linkage of USD CHATS with RENTAS (a real time electronic transfer of funds and securities system in Malaysia) and a new cross-border Payment-versus-Payment (PvP) link between Hong Kong's USD RTGS system and Indonesia's Rupiah RTGS system which was implemented as recently as the 25th January 2010.

At the same time, Hong Kong and China are considering developing modern retail payment solutions by creating a common cross-border e-money card and an eftpos (electronic funds transfer at point of sale) framework for small value payments in the region comprising Hong Kong, Macau and the Guangdong Province in Mainland China. A number of practical and legal developments seen already in Europe (another potential link to one of our four EU forces of change) may prove to be helpful in planning out these capabilities. For example the e-Money Directive could be a source of inspiration for the legal basis for issuers of e-money and the SCF might also be of interest for example with regard to the security standards to employ EMV in the cards space.

Inside India – on the road to new payment systems

India is an exciting place when it comes to payment services. With around 1.2 billion people, 600 million mobile phones, less than 200 million debit/credit cards and 76 per cent of its population below the age of 35, innovative developments in payments are a must. While estimates in 2006 indicated that around 90 per cent of consumer spending in India was on a cash basis,[6] this is changing rapidly with a young generation expecting services to be provided via mobile.

In response to this and with view to reaching significant efficiency gains of potentially billions of USD the Reserve Bank of India has set out a list of ambitious goals for the period of 2009–12. A specific body, the National Payments Corporation of India (NPCI), has been set up to deliver a state-of-the-art central payment system infrastructure for all banks, financial institutions and intermediaries.

At this point in time, India has one RTGS, which uses the Structured Financial Messaging Standard (SFMS), a proprietary standard akin to SWIFT messages. The volumes in the Indian RTGS have grown over time due to national regulations which have mandated all inter-bank transactions to be settled through this system, ensuring safety for systemically important payments. In addition to these gross transactions the RTGS also settles the multilateral net settlement batches that originate from the other settlement systems in India (that is, batches from the National Electronic Funds Transfer System, Cheque Clearing batches and certain batches coming from the Clearing Corporation of India). As per the Vision Document on Payments 2009–12,[7] the detailed deliverables in that context include the implementation of a new and more feature-rich RTGS system, which will leverage new technologies and provide for scalability of volumes.

To give some more background, in addition to the above mentioned RTGS India operates the National Electronic Funds Transfer System (NEFT), which also uses the SFMS. This system processes low value retail payments and operates on a batch settlement with multiple batches that are settled intra-day (a potential SEPA candidate then!).

Furthermore, India operates the Electronic Clearing System (ECS) for debit and credit, which allows utility companies to do bulk collections (debits) as well as bulk distribution of funds, for example, payment of dividends to shareholders (and yet another potential SEPA candiate!).

India is also picking up on the significant increase in mobile penetration, which of course becomes even more interesting in our context when leveraged as initiation channel for credits and debits (think m-SEPA!). The NPCI, responsible for all retail payment systems, looks to transform the ECS and to complement its functionality with mobile payments. The overall objective of creating a real-time payments environment is very much inspired by the UK Faster Payments Scheme, previously mentioned, which is a system that is running at a 24/7 rhythm (more or less). An interesting aside here is that the UK, in the Faster Payments project, did not include mobile payments within its scope as these were considered to be in the 'competitive space', hence not seen as relevant in the context of a collaborative network approach. However, the network effect is overall something that should not be ignored and in the case of India the potential benefits from including mobile into a countrywide real time processing environment are huge. The plan is to build a system that will tie individuals and mobile numbers to bank accounts, to enable customers to send and receive even if they do not have a bank account yet (a key measure for financial inclusion!).

In terms of standards, the ECS reengineering could be done on the basis of the ISO 8583 (for the payments part), which is the same international cards processing standard that has already been used in the Faster Payments UK context. One of the reasons for choosing the ISO 8583 could be the advantage of the small message size, which allows lesser bandwidth requirements to process transactions; larger messages such as the ISO 20022 XML may create a capacity problem for some banks as a good network infrastructure may not be available in all locations. Obviously, in the longer run the ISO 20022 XML should also be considered as a candidate. At the same time there is still a question as to which standard to choose to ensure the transmission of payment information. Again the ISO 20022 XML would be a potential solution, certainly in the longer run once the market has developed further.

From a legal perspective and similar to what we have seen in Europe and other regions, India has adopted the Payment and Settlement Act in 2007, which provides for finality of settlement in the context of the multilateral netting systems and security of electronic payments. This was a crucial move to establish the much needed legal basis for payment and settlement systems and will strongly support the growth of electronic and mobile payments, which will trigger significant overall efficiency gains, estimated at USD 10 billion in case all of India's physical payments were to transform into electronic ones.[8] In a move to promote electronic transactions, many banks in India have been installing core banking applications in recent years. The ATM capability is also growing month by month and there is an overall clear focus of the banking industry on promoting accessibility, social inclusion and reach across the country. Card penetration, even though only reaching around 200 million this year, has lately been growing in popularity and the current levels are a result of Indian debit and credit card market growth of a compounded annual rate of 128 + per cent between 2004 and 2010.

Overall, India's vision is to be able to connect all banks under one messaging standard. However, with a significant cross-section of banks – for example, the 155,000 Cooperative Banks across India – that have not yet implemented core banking systems, this will take time. The key focus will therefore be on expanding reach as much as possible first, before taking up the challenge of implementing a harmonised messaging standard similar to the European SEPA project. Nevertheless, NPCI is still open to looking at various message formats as part of the creation of the technology infrastructures for these various initiatives and so the ISO 20022 XML will not be forgotten.

With a size of Western Europe, albeit without quite the same level of political challenge that we face in Europe in terms of creating consensus, this massive project possibly represents the creation of the single largest payment system of its type ever attempted. Good luck!

Better WATCH out! – SEPA as an export hit

As I have hopefully now demonstrated to your satisfaction through the quick geographical tour we have just taken, many of the elements that make up SEPA and the wider EU payments harmonisation story are not confined to Europe alone and are manifesting themselves as key components of a number of *intra*-regional and country initiatives in various parts of the globe.

In the next stage of our exploration let's broaden out our focus still more widely and take a look at a particularly interesting case where it seems that the SCT rulebook is becoming something of a role model for the international cross-border payments arena – meaning that this time our focus is on the impact of the EU experiment on *inter*-regional payment flows.

The genesis of the initiative we are about to discuss lies in the argument being put forward by a mix of commercial and central bankers and infrastructure businesses that SEPA for Europe is a great thing, but only the first step. Why not replicate the idea of a pan-geographical ACH beyond the borders of Europe in order to create cheaper and more efficient ways for the execution of cross-border international payments?

This idea is, in many ways, the direct descendent of a much older concept. During the late 1990s a number of banks across the globe got together and crafted a plan to build a Worldwide Automated Transaction Clearing House (WATCH) – intended to be a low-cost electronic system that could support the exchange of international low-value payments. The WATCH was supposed to be a complex converter tool, allowing a bank in country A to initiate a number of file-based low value payments formatted under national (or internationally accepted) standards and provide this payment file to WATCH, where the relevant standards and format conversion would take place before sending the file in the local format of country B to the indicated beneficiary bank.

Having completed phase I of the project – the definition of the organisational governance structure plus the business requirements for the payment system – a press declaration announced the incorporation of WATCH including the election and first general assembly of the board of directors. However, soon after this seemingly rather positive step, the complexity of the project (and differences in the views of some of the participants) resulted in this particular WATCH slowing down and then coming to a standstill for good.

Bringing the story more up to date, a group of players recently got together, with similar goals to the original WATCH-makers, but with the huge additional opportunity to leverage all the work that has been done since then. The first exploratory discussions quickly crystallised into what is now known as the International Payments Framework (IPF) initiative, which essentially aims to leverage SEPA standards to develop cost-efficient ways for executing cross-border non-urgent payments between Europe and the rest of the world, initially starting with the US and using the Euro and the USD as the two currencies for such transactions. So, very much like the WATCH idea. In similar fashion one of the first tasks of this initiative (as with all inter-bank initiatives) was to sort out the governance arrangements, resulting in the creation of the IPF Association in early 2010.

The membership (which does not come for free) is currently composed of more than 20 banks and central banks (key here being the Fed as US counterpart), CSMs, software vendors and associations. One of the key driving forces behind the initiative is European infrastructure and processor Equens. Equens and the Fed consider themselves as pioneers in providing an international electronic payment bridge between the European and American continent, which in the longer run is envisaged to be replicated across as many geographies and currencies as possible. The idea is that the central IPF agreements will be supplemented by a web of bilateral agreements between members or members' networks as a way of building an overlay solution with broad coverage. While the IPF proposal is not the same as WATCH (something which the association is quite keen to point out), there is still considerable need for conversion/mapping between message formats – such as between the US IAT (International ACH Transaction) format and the core IPF ISO message taken from the SEPA CT scheme. As with the SEPA CT scheme, any FX conversion which needs to take place as part of a payment transaction is seen as falling outside of the IPF scheme rules.

The development of a shared low-cost international payment network – only very few global banks have managed to build their own network of direct connectivity with ACHs and RTGS systems across the globe – is of course an honourable goal. However, there seems to be a degree of initial wariness in some parts of the EPC community, not least as the IPF adopted so much of the SEPA rulebook.

There are in fact not that many differences between the approach adopted for SEPA CTs and the IPF's proposed approach. We even encounter a PSD-inspired rule that states that an IPF participant is not allowed to deduct a fee from the amount of a payment transaction (yes – our favourite full amount principle!). Where differences do exist, they seem reasonably logical in the context of the somewhat different objectives and scope. For example, from a regulatory perspective, things like the PSD or Regulation 924/2009 do not formally apply to IPF in a legally binding way and ECB oversight is limited to the Euro currency part of IPF. Also, IPF does not need to concern itself with all the issues that SEPA has to deal with in terms of how to break down the barriers between domestic and cross-border as it effectively looks at building a new cross-border international channel. The data sets vary slightly because IPF is using the SEPA 2006 Rulebook version. Also the IPF rulebook is not governed by the laws of an EU Member State, such as Belgian law for SEPA, but by US law.

In any event, the EPC community, encouraged by the ECB, has agreed to enter into a dialogue with the IPF in a European context, and therefore in some ways to play the role in Europe that NACHA – the National Automated Clearing House Association – is playing in the US. The EPC has also stated that it intends nevertheless to protect the Intellectual Property Rights (IPRs) of the SEPA CT rulebook – though arguably this is a slightly empty statement given that the IPF is already using large elements of the SCT rulebook freely and it is also a little hard to pin down exactly what it is within the SCT Rulebook that would be regarded as IPR anyway (and what would we do with the Egyptians then ...).

In terms of its next steps, the IPF is currently looking for more members and is in the position of having completed some initial test transactions. Before it can fully establish itself though, it will need to pass the close scrutiny of the Fed and other US regulators and government agencies who will wish to assure themselves that the planned operational processes meet all their various requirements.

SWIFT – the case of MT to MX

Now, that last reference to US regulators and government agencies may perhaps remind those readers who have been paying particularly close attention of the story that I highlighted at the very beginning of the Prelude, when I talked about the row between the US authorities and the EU regarding access to data from SWIFT, the industry-owned global standards body and financial messaging network provider. As mentioned earlier, this case that started in 2007 was finally settled when on the 9 July 2010 the European Parliament approved a new deal to allow US anti-terrorism investigators access to European banking data while at the same time providing safeguards to protect the privacy of European citizens. This decision will give the US access to European banking data starting from 1 August 2010.

With that thought firmly in mind, there is a certain symmetry in the fact that we are now about to close the final chapter of this final Title by reminding ourselves of the role that SWIFT has played in contributing to the SEPA initiative, but also by exploring the potential role that Swift now has to play in further supporting payments integration on a global level from the perspective of technical standards, linking us directly back to the four key forces of change we identified earlier in our tale of EU payments integration.

As we know, SWIFT was heavily involved in the definition of the SEPA subset of the ISO 20022 XML. Beyond that, as we touched upon earlier, SWIFT also has a specific role as the ISO Registration Authority where it acts as the guardian of ISO 20022's integrity at international level. As the ISO 20022 Registration Authority, SWIFT is at the heart of the development and maintenance activity with more than 200 messages delivered and over 300 in the pipeline. The Registration Authority has received approaches from more than 15 different organisations and is seeing a keen interest from a growing number of organisations (financial institutions and vendors) to integrate the repository components within their own applications and services.

A further example of SWIFT's involvement in this space comes from the world of corporate actions. Messaging for corporate actions is primarily exchanged among central securities depositories, intermediaries such as custodian banks, broker dealers and investment managers. There is a suite of message types covering various corporate actions for use by issuer companies, their agents, intermediaries and market infrastructures. ISO 20022 XML messages also exist to cover communication and processing between a central securities depository and issuer agents/registrars within a market. SWIFT has been working closely with DTCC (the US Depositary Trust & Clearing Corporation) to develop a 'taxonomy' complying with the ISO 20022 standard for financial transactions. All very exciting apparently if you are a corporate-action sort of person.

Anyway, returning to our main topic, all these examples serve to highlight the interesting and important question of what is happening generally within the SWIFT community to embrace these new standards, given that – as we learnt in Title VI – upgrading a bank's payments applications to ISO 20022 XML has great potential to facilitate faster and more efficient transaction processing, with the nirvana possibility of global compatibility, given that these standards are themselves global and non-proprietary.

Moving completely to XML-based messaging would have some obvious benefits, not least due to the greater simplicity involved in implementing and updating messaging applications. Benefits to the SWIFT community as a whole would include lower costs for all financial institutions to update their messaging solutions every year (and to be able to do so faster and with less risk); lower cost to update SWIFTReady applications – of great benefit to all service providers and their customers; and generally the likelihood of greater competition in the number of solutions in the market in both the open source and proprietary segments.

So what is the current position and ambition within the SWIFT community on this important topic then? Well, the good news is that the standards team within SWIFT has fully embraced the new world, and there are a number of ISO 20022 XML message standards operating in parallel with some of the key existing MT messages. Also of course from a user perspective there are emerging cases of national payment systems, such as the Zengin system in Japan starting to embrace the ISO 20022 XML approach, as the SEPA schemes have done already.

All very positive then, surely. Well, yes and no. Clearly the new standards needed to be developed first, before any migration could take place from the old MT world. However, rather like the migration aspect of our SEPA story, the key question is how long this 'operating in parallel' will continue in practice within the SWIFT network. At one point, not so very long ago, there were big plans to migrate all credit transfers passing across the SWIFT network from the MT standards across to MX (SWIFT's shorthand term for the exciting new world of XML standards). However, the current language being used to describe the state of play is the slightly less promising-sounding term (if you are a fan of rapid progress) called 'coexistence'. The issue seems to be that while everybody agrees that ISO 20022 XML standards now have centre stage in the search for efficiency gains and new business opportunities, different participants have diverging views on the value and business case for the SWIFT community migrating en masse to ISO 20022 XML versus a prolonged coexistence approach – whereby multiple standards could remain for an extended period. As a consequence of these competing voices within the community, the current stance is that while SWIFT remains committed to ISO 20022, it has for the time being moved away from the idea of a large scale and short-term mandatory MX adoption.

The issue here ironically is in some ways directly linked to one of SWIFT's greatest strengths – the size of its community (7000 plus banks) and its ubiquity as the financial messaging network of choice in most parts of the globe. Such a broad membership inevitably involves many different levels of sophistication when it comes to business and indeed

IT infrastructure requirements, and not all can adopt change at the same pace. This leads to a dilemma where SWIFT really needs a robust plan to fully embrace the MX world to keep current and competitive and to meet the needs of its biggest customers, but knows that if an attempt was made to force the change through too soon, or via a big bang approach, the inability for all to keep up would risk destroying the ability of the whole community to communicate through the network, which is the very essence of the collective.

Following the withdrawal of the original idea for a rolling 3-year migration plan and the move to a business-area by business-area approach to ISO 20022 migration, the SWIFT community has been unclear on the overall approach and divided on the merits of full migration to MX, meaning that coexistence is currently a fact of life for the financial community given the multitude of domestic and international standards in use today. Standards are starting to align at the level of business models and data dictionaries, but rapid migration to ISO 20022 XML messages at a community level is unlikely in the absence of a compelling collective business case.

Against this background, the current SWIFT approach is to continue to drive the gradual adoption of ISO 20022, through actions such as providing common models and dictionaries to facilitate interoperability between bank-to-bank message standards, hence helping to lower the costs of coexistence, while at the same time continuing to develop additional ISO 20022 XML messages in cases where no adequate existing standards are available. It will be important to ensure that the MT to MX project will not be a mere like-for-like replacement activity, but rather that the underlying business processes are being considered in response to the changing transaction banking landscape.

In a final neat circle back to our SEPA story, while it was SWIFT which encouraged and supported the EPC to make its bold selection of XML and ISO 20022 for the SEPA project, maybe it could yet turn out to be the case that setting an end-date for SEPA migration, which hopefully is now not too far away from being agreed, will give SWIFT the additional encouragement it needs to start examining again the possibility for working towards speeding up the migration from MT to MX.

Just as a final closing thought to ponder on here, let us not forget that SWIFT is a cooperative owned by its member banks and governed by what the community wants and asks for. If SWIFT isn't moving as quickly as the banks would like it to, whose fault is that?

Epilogue

Given that so many different elements have ended up being studied and discussed in this book under the general umbrella of 'payments integration' – and given that so many of these remain work in progress as I write – it is proving hard to accept that this is finally the moment to put down my pen ... at least for now.

That said, it is in fact exactly the right time to do so, as in the context of the EU payments integration story and in particular its interwoven central characters – our good friends PSD and SEPA – we are at the close of a major chapter, allowing us to pause, take stock of what has been achieved so far, celebrate a few successes and get prepared for the equally exciting developments which now lie ahead.

During the course of our journey we examined the EU regulatory machine room and explored the foundations of the Single Market for Financial Services, before slowly immersing ourselves in the unfolding events that marked the start of the EU payments integration endeavour.

Memories of the birth and early years of SEPA, the long hours spent negotiating the PSD with all its intrigues and surprises as well as the gradual steps that have been taken towards something rather noble and extraordinary – the harmonisation of payments at a fabulously large scale in Europe – have all been recounted.

So, in terms of the potential next chapter of our EU payments fairy tale, have we now arrived at the 'and they all lived happily ever after' stage? While it is certainly true to say that from a legal and standardisation perspective the critical building blocks are in place, the key question now is how quickly the building itself will be constructed, and whether it will meet with the approval of its chief architects, or more importantly of its users – namely, all of us.

The encouraging news as I write these conclusions is that despite – or maybe even because of – the financial crisis, the political momentum to push along the full realisation of the SEPA vision by providing a migration end-date now seems to have full buy-in from all key EU institutions. As ever, there will be challenges ahead in ensuring that the text of this crucial measure is sufficiently elegantly drafted to avoid the very real risk of unintended consequences. Right at this point in time we are awaiting receipt (in the spirit of PSD article 64 §2!) of the official EC SEPA Regulation proposal to Parliament and Council. This particular super-tanker is due to arrive in the autumn of 2010 and no doubt a new chapter of EU regulatory drama is bound to unfold.

What is already clear is that banks need to get a move on in building their XML SEPA capabilities and start responding to customers' requirements for harmonised and streamlined payments and receivables processing. To escape from today's jungle of legacy formats, characterised by individual formatting and usage rules that developed out of specific domestic needs, the common data sets of SEPA that are exchanged in a common syntax need to be fully embraced by the market. The real benefits to users – improved control, reduced errors, increased efficiency and lower cost – will only unfold when a critical mass of transactions is being exchanged via SEPA. For that to happen, SEPA connectivity for European businesses, whether big or small, needs to be in place. At the same time mandating legacy close-downs to give way to SEPA will be essential in advancing this necessary evolution. In the multinational corporate space, there is clear evidence of a growing adoption of ISO 20022 XML in the C2B domain, with some banks already supporting these customers across all key geographies of the globe and for a variety of payment instruments. So all we need is for Europe to fall into step. Once implemented and used properly and consistently by banks and other PSPs, the SEPA ISO 20022 XML will be the key to unlock the efficient future for customers and providers!

One final measure of the broader strategic significance of EU payments integration and all its facets is the great level of interest this has triggered in other communities across the globe. A number of the forces of integration seen in Europe are now firmly in action in other regions, with the potential long-term outcome of a much more joined-up world, at least from a payments perspective.

I hope that you have found the story told in these pages an interesting one. At the end of the Prelude I wished you all an informative, thought-provoking and hopefully enjoyable reading experience. Now I conclude by thanking you for staying the course and hope that at least one or better still *all three* of these wishes came true!

Appendix I

Table A1.1 PSD Implementation: Use of Derogations in Titles III and IV by EU/EEA Member States

Title III

Article 30 Paragraph 2

Application of information requirements to micro enterprises in the same way as to consumers

1) Usage of this derogation during national transposition

AT: option not transposed	FI: option not transposed	MT: option transposed
BE: option not transposed	FR: option not transposed	NL: option not transposed
BG: option not transposed	HU: option transposed	NO: option not transposed
CY: option transposed	IE: option transposed	PL: pending
CZ: option transposed	IS: pending	PT: option transposed
DK: option not transposed	IT: option transposed	RO: option not transposed
DE: option not transposed	LT: option to be transposed	SE: option not transposed
EE: option not transposed	LI: option not transposed	SI: option not transposed
EL/GR: option not transposed	LU: option not transposed	SK: option transposed
ES: option not transposed	LV: option not transposed	UK: option transposed

2) Details of any key implementation features in MS where this derogation has been used

Member State	Key Features
CY	Micro enterprises will be treated in the same way as consumers in relation to provision of information.
CZ	According to the Czech Act on Payment Services – article 75.2 – micro enterprises are treated the same way as consumers. Micro enterprises have to submit (on PSP's request) relevant documents proving their status as micro enterprise before being able to enter a framework contract (article 75.3). The Czech law does permit the use of the EU Commission definition of a micro enterprise as provided for by Recommendation 2003/361/EC.

(*continued*)

Table A1.1 Continued

DE	In German law micro-enterprises are not equivalent to consumers. Information requirements in German Law (§ 675 d chapter 1 German Civil Code) are however relevant for all customers. Under § 675e chapter 4 of German Civil Code a PSP has the opportunity to opt-out from the information requirements by agreement with the customer, if the customer is not a consumer.
HU	Republic of Hungary decided to put this derogation in the General Rules and in the Special Rules of Act No. 85 of 2009 on payment service (hereinafter: the "Act"). In the General Rules, the Act regulates this derogation via Article 3 Paragraph 2. PSPs are required to treat micro-enterprises and consumers in the same way in terms of information provision, framework and single payment contracts including changes thereof.
IT	This opt in has been fully used without any making any changes (e.g. scope extension or reduction) to PSD Article 30(2).
SK	PSPs can decide whether to treat microenterprises as consumers or not.
UK	Option used and extended to small charities with an annual income of less than £1million.

Article 33

Burden of proof on the payment service provider for information requirements

1) Status update on usage of this derogation during national transposition

AT: option not transposed	FI: option transposed	MT: option transposed
BE: option transposed	FR: option transposed	NL: option not transposed
BG: option not transposed	HU: option transposed	NO: option not transposed
CY: option transposed	IE: option not transposed	PL: pending
CZ: option transposed	IS: pending	PT: option transposed
DK: option not transposed	IT: option transposed	RO: option transposed
DE: option transposed	LT: option not transposed	SE: option not transposed
EE: option not transposed	LI: option not transposed	SI: option not transposed
EL/GR: option not transposed	LU: option not transposed	SK: option transposed
ES: option transposed	LV: option not transposed	UK: option transposed

(*continued*)

Table A1.1 Continued

2) Details of any key implementation features in MS where this derogation has been used

Member State	Key Features
DE	It is already an existing principle in German law that the bank has in such a case the burden of proof.
IT	This opt in has been fully used without any making any changes (e.g. scope extension or reduction) to PSD Article 33.
UK	Burden of proof will usually rest with the PSP. In practical terms, it will be assumed that the PSP is complying with the information requirements under Title III, unless a customer complaint to the contrary is substantiated.

Article 34 Paragraph 2 –A –

Reduction or doubling of the amounts for national payment transactions (low-value/e-money payment)

1) Status update on usage of this derogation during national transposition

AT: option transposed	FI: option transposed	MT: option not transposed
BE: option not transposed	FR: option not transposed	NL: option transposed
BG: option not transposed	HU: option not transposed	NO: Possibility to use this option later by means of Royal Decree.
CY: option transposed	IE: option transposed	PL: pending
CZ: option transposed	IS: pending	PT: option not transposed
DK: option not transposed	IT: option transposed	RO: option transposed
DE: option transposed	LT: option not to be transposed	SE: option not transposed
EE: option not transposed	LI: option transposed	SI: option not transposed
EL/GR: option transposed	LU: option transposed	SK: option not transposed
ES: option not transposed	LV: option not transposed	UK: option transposed

2) Details of any key implementation features in MS where this derogation has been used

Member State	Key Features
AT	Amounts doubled for national payments transactions
CY	Amounts doubled for national payments transactions

(*continued*)

Table A1.1 Continued

CZ	Amounts doubled (Czech article 76.4 a, b) for national transactions
DE	Limits in German law 30/150 Euro: 200 Euro for domestic payments
EL/GR	Amounts doubled for national payments transactions
FI	If the low-value payment instrument can be used only for national transactions, individual payment transactions may not exceed EUR 60, or, the spending limit may not exceed EUR 300
IE	Amounts doubled for national payment transactions
LI	Amounts doubled for national payment transactions
IT	Bank of Italy's secondary legislation provides that for national transactions: (i.e. between two PSPs located in Italy) amounts are doubled
LU	Amounts doubled for national payment transactions
NL	Amounts doubled for national payments transactions
UK	Amounts doubled for national payments transactions

Article 34 Paragraph 2 – B –

Increase of the amounts for prepaid instruments up to EUR 500 (low-value/ e-money payment)

1) Status update on usage of this derogation during national transposition

AT: option transposed	FI: option transposed	MT: option not transposed
BE: Possibility to use this option later by means of a Royal Decree (Art. 21 §2)	FR: option not transposed	NL: option transposed
BG: option not transposed	HU: option not transposed	NO: Possibility to use this option later by means of Royal Decree.
CY: option transposed	IE: option transposed	PL: pending
CZ: option transposed	IS: pending	PT: option not transposed
DK: option not transposed	IT: option transposed in Bank of Italy's secondary legislation	RO: option transposed

(*continued*)

Table A1.1 Continued

DE: option not transposed	LT: option not transposed	SE: option not transposed
EE: option not transposed	LI: option transposed	SI: option not transposed
EL/GR: option transposed	LU: option transposed	SK: option not transposed
ES: option not transposed	LV: option not transposed	UK: option transposed

2) Details of any key implementation features in MS where this derogation has been used

Member State	**Key Features**
AT	Increased to EUR 400 for pre-paid instruments.
CY	Increased to EUR 500 for pre-paid instruments.
CZ	The amounts for national prepaid low-value/e-payment transactions are increased up to EUR 500 (Czech article 76.4 c).
EL	For prepaid payment instruments, the amount will increase up to EUR 500.
FI	If the prepaid instrument can be used only for national transactions, the store funds may not exceed EUR 500. Otherwise the limit is EUR 150.
LI	For prepaid payment instruments, the amount will increase up to EUR 500 or the equivalent value in Swiss francs.
IT	Bank of Italy's secondary legislation provides that: that for prepaid instruments the limit is increased to 500 EUR.
LU	The amounts for prepaid payment instruments are increased to EUR 500.
NL	The amounts for prepaid instruments are increased to EUR 500.
UK	Increased to EUR 500 for pre-paid instruments.

Article 45 Paragraph 6

More favourable provisions on termination conditions for framework contracts

1) Status update on usage of this derogation during national transposition

AT: option not transposed	FI: option to be transposed	MT: option not transposed
BE: option transposed	FR: option not transposed	NL: option not to be transposed
BG: option not transposed	HU: option not transposed	NO: PSP must have justifiable basis to terminate contract with customer

(*continued*)

Table A1.1 Continued

CY: option not transposed	IE: option not transposed	PL: pending
CZ: option not transposed	IS: pending	PT: option not transposed
DK: option transposed	IT: option transposed	RO: option not transposed
DE: option transposed	LT: –	SE: option not transposed
EE: option not transposed	LI: option not transposed	SI: option not transposed
EL/GR: option not transposed	LU: option not transposed	SK: option not transposed
ES: not defined	LV: option not transposed	UK: option not transposed

2) Details of any key implementation features in MS where this derogation has been used

Member State	Key Features
BE	1. Exception for a period less than 12 months do not exist 2. Extension of the scope to saving accounts (article 17 §3)
DE	Under the General Business Conditions the PSU is allowed to terminate the contract at any time, if not agreed otherwise. The maximum termination period is one month.
DK	The period of 12 months is reduced to 6 months in the Danish transposition.
FI	Termination of contract is always free of charge.
IT	The termination conditions shall be without charge for the PSU, regardless of contract duration. Italian law already provides these favourable provisions for banking contracts.

Article 47 Paragraph 3 & Article 48 Paragraph 3

Provision of information to the payer on paper once a month free of charge

1) Status update on usage of this derogation during national transposition

AT: option transposed	FI: option not to be transposed	MT: option not transposed
BE: not defined. Possibility to use this option later by means of a Royal Decree (Art. 20§3)	FR: option transposed	NL: option transposed
BG: option not transposed	HU: option transposed	NO: option not transposed
CY: option not transposed	IE: option not transposed	PL: pending

(*continued*)

Table A1.1 Continued

CZ: option not transposed	IS: pending	PT: option not transposed
DE: option not transposed	IT: option not transposed	RO: option transposed
DK: option not transposed	LT: option not transposed	SE: option partly transposed
EE: option not transposed	LI: option not transposed	SI: option not transposed
EL/GR: option transposed	LU: option not transposed but as industry practice major retail banks provide information at least once a month.	SK: option not transposed
ES: not defined	LV: option not transposed	UK: option not transposed

2) Details of any key implementation features in MS where this derogation has been used

Member State	Key Features
AT	The PSP shall provide information to the payer once a month free of charge though an agreed channel; upon request by the payer banks are obliged to send the payer information on paper once a month free of charge.
EL/GR	Information is to be provided every three months.
FR	The PSP provides information to the payer once a month free of charge, through one channel (i.e. paper or internet) as contractually agreed. Thus, if the agreed channel is paper, PSP must provide free of charge.
HU	Republic of Hungary decided to put this derogation in the Special Rules of the Act in Chapter No. V (Payment order under the framework contract includes prior general information). If the PSU is a consumer, upon his or her request the PSP shall provide him or her once a month with paper based information in relation to payment transactions and related charges.
NL	Only on request of the payer. If a payer only makes use of internet banking and the information is provided by the website, PSPs will not be obliged to send the payer information on paper once a month free of charge.
SE	On request of consumers the PSP shall present information on paper once a month free of charge.

(*continued*)

Table A1.1 Continued

Title IV		
Article 51 Paragraph 2		
Non application of out-of-court procedures to enterprises		
1) Status update on usage of this derogation during national transposition		
AT: option not transposed	FI: option transposed	MT: option not transposed
BE: option transposed	FR: option transposed	NL: option transposed
BG: option not transposed	HU: option not transposed	NO: option transposed
CY: option not transposed	IE: option not transposed	PL: pending
CZ: option transposed	IS: pending	PT: option not transposed
DK: option transposed	IT: option transposed	RO: option not transposed
DE: option transposed	LT: option transposed	SE: option not transposed
EE: option transposed	LI: option not transposed	SI: option not transposed
EL/GR: option not transposed	LU: option not transposed	SK: option not transposed
ES: option not transposed	LV: option not transposed	UK: option transposed

2) Details of any key implementation features in MS where this derogation has been used

Member State	Key Features
BE	Out-of-court procedure is only applicable if the user is a consumer (art 75) (consumer = natural person acting for purposes other than his trade, business or profession)
CZ	According to Czech law a financial arbiter arranges only consumer's out-of-court complaint procedures (article 137).
DE	Out-of-court procedures are also open to enterprises.
DK	Consumers have the option to complain to The Danish Complaint board for banking services. This option is, however, not open to enterprises.
FI	Small enterprises have the possibility to make a complaint to the Finnish Financial Ombudsman Bureau.
IE	Out-of-court redress procedures are available to consumers and micro-enterprises only.
IT	Italian legislative decree provides application of out-of-court redress procedures to all PSUs, including enterprises. This was already in place before the arrival of the PSD.
LT	Only consumers, not enterprises, are to use the out-of-court dispute resolving procedures.

(*continued*)

Table A1.1 Continued

NL	An out-of-court complaint procedure will only be set up for consumers.
UK	Corporates do not have access to out-of-court redress procedures but micro-enterprises do as they are treated as consumers under UK implementation.

Article 51 Paragraph 3

Application of Title IV to micro enterprises in the same way as to consumers

1) Status update on usage of this derogation during national transposition

AT: option not transposed	FI: option not transposed	MT: option transposed
BE: option not transposed	FR: option not transposed	NL: option not transposed
BG: option not transposed	HU: option transposed	NO: option to be transposed
CY: option transposed	IE: option not transposed	PL: pending
CZ: option transposed	IS: pending	PT: option transposed
DK: option not transposed	IT: option transposed	RO: option not transposed
DE: option not transposed	LT: option not transposed	SE: option not transposed
EE: option not transposed	LI: option not transposed	SI: option not transposed
EL/GR: option not transposed	LU: option not transposed	SK: option transposed
ES: option not transposed	LV: option not transposed	UK: option transposed

2) Details of any key implementation features in MS where this derogation has been used

Member State	**Key Features**
CY	Under Cypriot law a micro-enterprise can be treated as a consumer.
CZ	According to the Czech Act on Payment Services – article 75.2 – micro enterprises are treated the same way as consumers. Micro enterprises have to submit (on PSP's request) relevant documents proving their status as micro enterprise before being able to enter a framework contract (article 75.3). The Czech law does permit the use of the EU Commission definition of a micro enterprise as provided for by Recommendation 2003/361/EC.

(*continued*)

Table A1.1 Continued

DE	In German law micro-enterprises are not equivalent to consumers. German Law title IV provisions are relevant for consumers and non-consumers. But under § 675e chapter 4 of the German Civil Code the bank has the opportunity to opt-out from the requirements of title IV (except article 73) by agreement with the customer, if the customer is not a consumer.
HU	Republic of Hungary decided to put this derogation in the Special Rules of the Act, article 34. For PSUs that are not consumers or micro enterprises parties may agree otherwise.
IT	Title IV applies to micro enterprises in the same way as to consumers, but parties may agree that articles 62, 63 and 66.3 shall not apply in whole or in part.
MT	The Central Bank of Malta Directive applies to micro-enterprises in the same way as to consumers.
SK	Upon decision of the PSP a micro enterprise could be treated as a consumer.
UK	Yes, although it has also been extended to small charities with an annual income of less than £1million.

Article 52 Paragraph 3

Interdiction or limitation of surcharging practices

1) Status update on usage of this derogation during national transposition

AT: option transposed	FI: option transposed	MT: option not transposed
BE: option to be transposed	FR: option transposed	NL: option not transposed
BG: option transposed	HU: option not transposed	NO: option not transposed
CY: option partially transposed	IE: option not transposed	PL: option not transposed
CZ: option not transposed	IS: pending	PT: option not transposed
DK: option partially transposed	IT: option transposed	RO: option transposed
DE: option partially transposed	LT: option transposed	SE: option transposed
EE: option transposed	LI: option not transposed	SI: option not transposed
EL/GR: option transposed	LU: option transposed	SK: option transposed
ES: option transposed	LV: option not transposed	UK: option not transposed

(continued)

Table A1.1 Continued

2) Details of any key implementation features in MS where this derogation has been used	
Member State	**Key Features**
AT	The PSP shall not prevent the payee from offering the payer a reduction for the use of a given payment instrument. However, the payee is not allowed to request charges from the payer for the use of a specific payment instrument.
BE	Surcharging (or reduction) is allowed (art 56 §3). But in order to encourage the use of efficient payment instrument, there is a possibility to limit or suppress surcharging by means of a Royal Decree.
BG	Article 49 (4) of the Law on Payment Services and Payment Systems provides that in case of payment transactions executed by means of a payment card or another similar instrument, the payee may not request from the payer to pay charges for the use of the instrument.
CY	Option partially transposed – will ban surcharging for two payment instruments: cards & internet payments
DE	Contractual flexibility allowed between merchants & acquirers to ban surcharging but no contractual freedom to ban discounting.
DK	In Denmark a merchant is not allowed to surcharge when the payment service user and the merchant are both physically present. If th payment card is issued outside Denmark the merchant is however allowed to surcharge. In e-commerce the merchant is allowed to surcharge no matter where the payment card is issued.
EL/GR	The PSP shall not prevent the payee from offering the payer a reduction for the use of a given payment instrument. The payee may not request charges from the payer for the use of a specific payment instrument.
ES	The additional charge when used should be limited to the actual cost incurred. Further limits might be defined by secondary legislation in order to encourage competition and promote the use of efficient payment instruments.
FI	Charges have to be appropriate and based on actual costs

(*continued*)

Table A1.1 Continued

FR	The transposition text reads as follows (FBF's translation): The payee cannot apply charges for the use of a given payment instrument. It can be derogated from this interdiction only under conditions set by secondary legislation ("décret"), enacted after consultation with the competition authority, taking into account the need to encourage competition and promote the use of efficient payment instruments.
IT	The option has been transposed as follows (N.B. ABI's translation): 1. The PSP allows the payee to offer to the payer a reduction for the use of a payment instrument subject to the present law. 2. The payee cannot apply charges to the payer for the use of a given payment instrument. The Bank of Italy may decide derogations with the aim to promote the use of efficient payment instruments.
LT	It is prohibited to payees to apply charges for the use of certain payment instruments. If for a given payment instrument, a beneficiary provides a discount, the payer should be notified in advance of the operation. If for a given payment instrument, a PSP or a third party requests a commission, the payer should be informed in advance of the operation
LU	Surcharging is prohibited.
SK	Surcharging is banned in Slovakia. The PSP shall not prevent the payee from offering the payer a reduction for the use of a given payment instrument. Payees cannot request charges from the payer for the use of a payment card.

Article 53 Paragraph 2 – A –

Reduction or doubling of the amounts for national payment transactions (low-value/e-money payment)

1) Status update on usage of this derogation during national transposition

AT: option transposed	FI: option transposed	MT: option not transposed
BE: Possibility to use this option later by means of a Royal Decree (art 21 §2)	FR: option not transposed	NL: option transposed
BG: option not transposed	HU: not transposed	NO: Possibility to use this option later by means of a Royal Decree

(*continued*)

Table A1.1 Continued

CY: option transposed	IE: option transposed	PL: pending
CZ: option transposed	IS: pending	PT: option not transposed
DK: option not transposed	IT: option transposed	RO: option transposed
DE: option transposed	LT: option not transposed	SE: option not transposed
EE: option not transposed	LI: option transposed	SI: option not transposed
EL/GR: option transposed	LU: option transposed	SK: option not transposed
ES: option not transposed	LV: option not transposed	UK: option transposed

2) Details of any key implementation features in MS where this derogation has been used

Member State	Key Features
AT	If the low-value payment instrument can be used for national transaction only, individual payment transactions may not exceed EUR 60 or the spending limit may not exceed EUR 300. Otherwise the limits are EUR 30 and EUR 150.
CY	The amounts for national payment transactions are doubled.
CZ	The amounts for national transactions are doubled (Czech article 76.4 a, b).
DE	Limits in German law 30/150 EUR; EUR 200 for domestic payments
EL/GR	For national payment transactions the amount referred to in paragraph 1 will be doubled.
FI	If the low-value payment instrument can be used only for national transactions, individual payment transactions may not exceed EUR 60 or the spending limit may not exceed EUR 300. Otherwise the limits are EUR 30 and EUR 150.
IE	The amounts for national payment transactions are doubled.
IT	Amounts are doubled, when both payee's and payer's PSPs are located in Italy. The Bank of Italy, transposing measures adopted by European Commission, may provide in secondary legislation different amounts.
LI	The amounts for national payment transactions are doubled.
LU	The amounts for national payment transactions are doubled.
NL	The amounts for national payment transactions are doubled.
UK	The amounts for national payment transactions are doubled.

(*continued*)

Table A1.1 Continued

Article 53 Paragraph 2 – B –		
Increase of the amounts for prepaid instruments up to EUR 500 (low-value/ e-money payment)		
1) Status update on usage of this derogation during national transposition		
AT: option transposed	FI: option transposed	MT: option not transposed
BE: Possibility to use this option later by means of a Royal Decree (art 57 §2)	FR: option not transposed	NL: option transposed
BG: option not transposed	HU: option not transposed	NO: Possibility to use this option later by means of a Royal Decree
CY: option transposed	IE: option transposed	PL: pending
CZ: option transposed	IS: pending	PT: option not transposed
DK: option not transposed	IT: option transposed	RO: option transposed
DE: option transposed	LT: option not transposed	SE: option not transposed
EE: option not transposed	LI: option transposed	SI: option not transposed
EL/GR: option transposed	LU: option transposed	SK: option not transposed
ES: option not transposed	LV: option not transposed	UK: option transposed

2) Details of any key implementation features in MS where this derogation has been used

Member State	**Key Features**
AT	Increased to EUR 400 for pre-paid instruments if the pre-paid instruments can be used for national transactions only.
CY	The amounts for prepaid instruments are increased to EUR 500.
CZ	The amounts for national prepaid low-value/ e-payment transactions are increased up to EUR 500 (Czech article 76.4 c).
DE	A limit of EUR 200 is set for prepaid instruments.
EL/GR	For prepaid payment instruments, the amount will increase up to EUR 500.
FI	If the prepaid instrument can be used only for national transactions, the storage of funds may not exceed EUR 500. Otherwise the limit is EUR 150.

(continued)

Table A1.1 Continued

IT	EUR 500 is the amount for prepaid instruments. The Bank of Italy, transposing measures adopted by European Commission, may provide different amounts as part of secondary legislation.
LI	For prepaid instruments, the amounts will increase up to EUR 500 or the equivalent value in Swiss Francs.
LU	The amounts for prepaid instruments are increased to EUR 500.
NL	The amounts for prepaid instruments are increased to EUR 500.
UK	The amounts for prepaid instruments are increased to EUR 500.

Article 53 Paragraph 3 (e-money)

Option not to apply the liability provisions for unauthorised transactions when the payer's PSP does not have the ability to freeze the payment account or block the payment instrument limited to accounts or instruments of a certain value

1) Status update on usage of this derogation during national transposition

AT: option transposed	FI: option not transposed	MT: option transposed
BE: option transposed	FR: option not transposed	NL: option not transposed
BG: option transposed	HU: option transposed	NO: option not transposed
CY: option not transposed	IE: option not transposed	PL: pending
CZ: option transposed	IS: pending	PT: option not transposed
DE: option transposed	IT: option transposed	RO: option transposed
DK: option not transposed	LT: option not transposed	SE: option not transposed
EE: option not transposed	LI: option transposed	SI: option not transposed
EL/GR: option not transposed	LU: option not transposed	SK: option not transposed
ES: option to be transposed	LV: option not transposed	UK: option not transposed

2) Details of any key implementation features in MS where this derogation has been used

Member state	Key Features
AT	Maximum threshold of EUR 400 defined for e-money.
BE	The liability of the payer's PSP is limited in case of prepaid instruments (storage value lower than EUR 150) and for instruments allowing only payments below EUR 30 (Art 57 §1).
DE	See § 675 i Abs. 2 BGB

(*continued*)

Table A1.1 Continued

ES	Arts 60 & 61 shall not always apply; the limits are to be defined by secondary regulation.
IT	EUR 500 is the amount defined as 'certain value'. The Bank of Italy, transposing measures adopted by the European Commission, may provide for different amounts via secondary legislation.
MT	Full implementation without any restrictions.
SK	UK regulation in line with the Directive.

Article 61 Paragraph 3

Reduction of payer's liability for unauthorised use of payment instrument taking into account the nature of personalised security features of the payment instrument

1) Status update on usage of this derogation during national transposition

AT: option transposed	FI: option transposed	MT: option not transposed
BE: option transposed	FR: option transposed	NL: option transposed
BG: option not transposed	HU: option not transposed	NO: option transposed
CY: option not transposed	IE: option transposed	PL: pending
CZ: option not transposed	IS: pending	PT: option transposed
DK: option transposed	IT: option transposed	RO: option transposed
DE: option not transposed	LT: option not transposed	SE: option transposed
EE: option not transposed	LI: option not transposed	SI: option not transposed
EL/GR: option not transposed	LU: option not transposed	SK: option transposed
ES: option not transposed	LV: option not transposed	UK: option transposed

2) Details of any key implementation features in MS where this derogation has been used

Member State	Key Features
AT	EUR 150 is the payers' liability for acts of slight negligence.
BE	Payer's liability for unauthorised use of payment instrument is limited to 150 EUR (Art 37 §1) except in case of fraud or gross negligence.
DK	The liability provision does not apply to e-money unless the PSP has the possibility of freezing the payment account.
FI	Payer is not liable if he has been careful. The EUR 150 liability applies in cases of minor negligence.

(continued)

Table A1.1 Continued

FR	The 150 EUR payers' liability does not apply when the payment instrument was stolen or lost and the unauthorised transaction occurred without use of the personalised security features. The 150 EUR payers' liability does not apply in case of misappropriation of the payment instrument or its personalised security features.
HU	Republic of Hungary decided to put this derogation in the Special Rules of the Act, under article 45 (2) and (3) with the same wording than we can find under article 61 (3) of the PSD.
IE	Payers' liability reduced to EUR 75. Payer shall bear no liability in relation to e-money payment transactions if the PSP cannot freeze the payment account of block the payment instrument.
IT	Italian legislative decree delegates Bank of Italy to reduce the payer's liability, in case of defined (and published) security features of payment instruments.
NL	The judge can limit the liability taking into account the nature of personalised security features of the payment instrument and the circumstances under which it was lost, stolen or misappropriated.
PT	Payer's liability is reduced to a maximum of Euro 150 according to article 72 of the Portuguese PSD.
SE	Firstly the "floor" is lowered from EUR 150 to EUR 120 for cases where a PIN-code has been used – irrespective of negligence on the part of the user (corresponding to about 1 200 SEK, in line with most other Nordic countries). Secondly there is a cap of EUR 1 200 introduced (corresponding to about 12 000 SEK) for cases of gross negligence).
SK	Reduction of the payer's liability decreased to EUR 100.
UK	Reduced liability to up £50.

Article 72

Shorter maximum execution times for purely national payment transactions

1) Status update on usage of this derogation during national transposition

AT: option not transposed	FI: option transposed	MT: option not transposed
BE: option transposed	FR: option not transposed	NL: option not transposed

(*continued*)

Table A1.1 Continued

BG: option transposed	HU: option transposed	NO: option transposed
CY: option not transposed	IE: option not transposed	PL: pending
CZ: option transposed	IS: pending	PT: option transposed
DE: option not transposed	IT: option not transposed	RO: option transposed
DK: option not transposed	LT: option transposed	SE: option not transposed
EE: option not transposed	LI: option not transposed	SI: option not transposed
EL/GR: option not transposed	LU: option not transposed	SK: option transposed
ES: option transposed	LV: option not transposed	UK: option not transposed

2) Details of any key implementation features in MS where this derogation has been used

Member State	Key Features
BE	Domestic electronic credit transfers: D if debtor and beneficiary are within the same bank D + 1 for transfer between two different banks
BG	According to Article 64 (3) of the Law on Payment Services and Payment Systems when executing payment transactions in Bulgarian levs between PSPs participating in a Real-time Gross Settlement System or a payment and securities settlement systems where the Bulgarian National Bank is the settlement agent, the PSP of the payer ensures that the amount of the payment transaction is credited to the payee's account on the same business day the payment order was received.
CZ	The maximum execution time is D+1. However the payer and the PSP of the payer can agree on D+2 for transactions where other currency conversions than those between EUR and CZK occur (until 1.1.2012 transactions with a currency conversion between EUR and CZK are also covered by this provision).
ES	Domestic electronic credit transfers: Until 1.1.2012 for purely national transactions maximum execution time, if agreed, should not be longer than 2 days.
FI	The maximum execution time for purely national payment transactions is D+1 (D+2 when payment order is given on paper).

(*continued*)

Table A1.1 Continued

LT	For credit transfers made in the national currency in Lithuania, the payer's PSP shall ensure that the payee PSP account is credited on the same working day if the payment order is received before 12 am. If the payment order is received after 12 am, the PSP shall ensure that the payee PSP account is credited not later than the next business day.
LU	Industry practice: major retail banks apply an execution time for intra Luxembourg payments of D+1
PT	For transfers within the same bank branch/PSP the execution cycle is same day (article 83 of Portuguese PSD).
SK	D+0 for transaction within the same bank branch/PSP and RTGS.

Appendix II

Table A2.1 PSD Implementation: Examples of cases of gold-plating, non-conforming transposition and other interesting transposition features at Member State level

Details of cases where Member States have extended (or are believed to be planning to extend) the application of Titles III and IV (or some of their provisions) to one-leg transactions and/or non-EU/EEA Currencies

Member State	Details
AT	Provisions related to unauthorised transactions and information requirements have been made applicable to all transactions and all currencies.
BE	Provisions relating to responsibility in the event of non-authorised transactions have been extended to one-leg transactions. Additionally, provisions related to responsibility in the event of non-authorised transactions have been extended to all currencies. Furthermore, the possibility to extend other provisions to one-leg transactions has been extended by means of a Royal Decree (article 3 §1).
BG	Chapters III and IV of the Law on Payment Services and Payment Systems – which transpose Titles III and IV of the PSD respectively – have been applied to transactions in any currency, not just those of EU/EEA Member States.
CZ	According to the three first articles of the Czech law, the law is "a priori" applicable to all types of payment transactions, including payment services for both two-leg and one-leg transactions and those in non-EU/EEA currencies – but with possible exceptions as defined in the Czech article 75, para (1). It has been made possible (if contractually agreed between the parties) to exclude the application of the Czech law in relation to the following PSD articles. These are: 37 (1) b) to d); 38 c) and d); 42 (2) e) and (3) a); 46; 52 (2); 59 (2); 60 (1); 62 and 63 if the provider informs the user about the risk associated with the way of granting a consent and the use of payment instrument; 67; 68; 69; 75 (1) sub-para 2 to 4 and (2), noting though the provider however may not contractually exclude its general responsibility for an unauthorised or incorrectly executed transaction.
CY	The one-leg option has been used for all currencies and all articles, except for article 43.

(*continued*)

Table A2.1 Continued

DE	The provisions relating to PSD articles 54 to 61, articles 64 to 66 and articles 74 to 78 have been made in principle applicable also for one-leg transactions, but with the possibility for a PSP to vary this by contractual agreement with its PSU.
DK	The provisions in the following PSD articles have been extended to cover one-leg transactions: 34 para 1 (a); 36; 37 para 1 (a)(c)(d), para 2; 38; 41; 42 para 1, para 2(a-d) (e-f), para 3–7; 43; 44; 45 para 1–4; 46; 47; 55–63; 65–66; 73. The provisions in the following PSD articles have been extended to cover transactions in currencies other than those of Member states: 34 para 1 (a); 36; 37 para 1 (a)(c)(d), para 2; 38; 41; 42 para 1, para 2(a-d) (e-f), para 3–7; 43; 44; 45 para 1–4; 46; 47; 55–63; 65–66.
EE	The law has been generally made applicable for all transactions, albeit some specific provisions (execution time, availability of funds) have not been extended to one-leg transactions or transactions made in non-EU/EEA currencies. Additionally, it has been made possible for a PSP to vary the terms in relation to these two types of transactions by contractual agreement with its PSU.
ES	The law has generally applied the PSD's Title III and IV provisions to one-leg transactions, with the exception of provisions relating to charging options and amounts transferred, and Section 2 of Chapter III in Title IV.
FI	All PSD articles have been applied to one-leg transactions and transactions in non-EU/EEA currencies with the following exceptions: 52(2); 62–64; 58; 69(1); 69(3); 67; 75(1)(1–3); 75 (2)(1); 75(3); and 77; and all information requirements regarding execution time and charges payable by the PSU. Additionally, articles 69(2) and 71 have been applied only to EU/EEA-currencies.
FR	Some provisions in Titles III and IV of the PSD have been extended to one-leg transactions and transactions in all currencies.
IT	The whole of Title III of the PSD has been applied to one-leg transactions and transactions in all currencies, as was previously the case for transparency rules in Italy, which applied to all services offered by any intermediary located in Italy and irrespective of currencies.
LT	The application of Titles III and IV of the PSD has been extended to payments made to or from non-EU/EEA countries denominated in Member State or non-EU/EEA currencies. However, PSPs and PSUs may agree, in whole or in part, not to apply these provisions with the exception of the provisions on value dating and the availability of funds.

(*continued*)

Table A2.1 Continued

MT	All PSD provisions have been applied to one-leg transactions and payments in non-EU/EEA currencies, with the exception of articles 49.2; 52.2; 53; 59; 62; 63; 67–71; 75–78; and parts of 28.
NO	In general all articles have been extended to apply to one-leg transactions, with the exception of articles regarding execution times (article 69) and charges levied on payer and payee (article 52 §2). Additionally the application of article 73 has been extended to apply to any currency, but only for transactions within the EU/EEA.
SK	Some provisions have been extended so as to fully apply to one-leg transactions and/or payments in non-EU/EEA currencies: e.g. articles 32; 38; 52; 54; 55; 56; 57; 61; 64; 65; and 66. Some other provisions (e.g. articles 59; 69; 73; and 74) have been partially applied to these types of transactions (i.e. regulation of rights and obligations has partly been provided by the Slovak Payment Code and partly has been left to individual contractual agreement).

Additional points of interest regarding individual implementations at Member State level

Member State	**Details**
AT	The termination of a framework contract concluded for a fixed period exceeding 12 months or for an indefinite period has been required to be free of charge for the user.
BE	With regard to the management of direct debits there is an obligation to ensure that the mandate refers to the initial contract (mandatory information according to Belgium law article 29).
EE	Some provisions have been extended to apply also to savings accounts. These cover the obligation to provide in formal language and on durable medium information about interest rates, account credit and debit operations and to give customers the option to appeal to the supervisory authorities.
FI	A provision has been incorporated making the payment service user not responsible for unauthorised payment transactions if the payee (merchant) has not made sure that the user is the legitimate cardholder. It has been permitted to exclude via consumer terms and conditions a PSU's liability for consequential damages in relation to the execution of a payment order (only).

(*continued*)

Table A2.1 Continued

IT	The legislative decree provides for the continued validity of existing direct debit mandates with reference to their usage in the context of national collection instruments that are upgraded to conform to PSD provisions and for SDD. Notification of refusals should be only 'provided' (not 'made available') and the way this is to be 'provided' can be agreed between the PSU and PSP The law transposing article 60(1) provides that a PSP, in case of high suspicion of fraud, may stop the refund, notifying the PSU. Furthermore, a PSP can prove after the refund that the payment transaction was authorised. In this case, the law provides for the right of the PSP to obtain the return of the refund from the PSU. The maximum execution time may be agreed between PSP and PSU, also referencing the execution time established in SEPA rulebooks. After 1st January 2012, the maximum execution time is limited to D+1 even for paper-initiated payment transactions under article 68(1). Issuing electronic money is regarded as falling within the application scope of Titles III and IV. The decree included some transitional provisions: a) PSPs were given until 30th April 2010 to communicate changes or new contractual provisions of existing contracts to their clients, with a 'silence-means-consent' approach being permissible. b) National direct debits were given until the 5th of July 2010 to become PSD-compliant. c) Payment services to public authorities to be adjusted upon the issuance of an ad-hoc Decree by the Ministry of the Economy, in agreement with the Bank of Italy.
MT	Whilst Article 52.3 was not initially transposed, card issuing banks were requested by the Central Bank of Malta to amalgamate their proprietary POS networks on the basis that otherwise Article 52.3 would be transposed (it was not included in the initial transposition). Article 33 has been transposed in such a way that it not only covers Title III but also Title IV and parts of Title I, II, V, and VI. Article 28.2c was been omitted from the Central Bank of Malta transposition of the Directive, although the rest of Article 28 has been transposed.
NO	It has been included as a requirement that for purely national transactions, the debiting of the payers account and the crediting of the payees account must be on the same day.

Notes

II EU Financial Regulation Explained: 'The Powers and the Pitfalls'

1. http://europa.eu/legislation_summaries/institutional_affairs/treaties/treaties_ecsc_en.htm
2. Absolute majority (in the European Parliament): A majority of the members who comprise Parliament. In its present configuration (with 736 MEPs), the threshold for an absolute majority is 369 votes (Note: In the elections in June 2009 which took place on the basis of the Nice Treaty, the number of MEPs was reduced to 736. With the entry into force of the Lisbon Treaty on 1/12/2009, the number will be increased to 754 once the new arrangements have been completed and reduced to 751 for the elections in 2014. Consequently, the numbers necessary to reach an absolute majority will thus change to 378 and 376 respectively). Under the co-decision procedure, an absolute majority is necessary in plenary session when voting on a second reading in order to reject the Council position at first reading or to adopt amendments.
3. The subsidiarity principle states that action at EU level (except for areas of exclusive EU competence) will not be taken if there is a more effective way of action that can be taken at national, regional or local level.
4. http://ec.Europa.eu/codecision/stepbystep/text/index_en.htm
5. W. Heisenberg, 'Über den anschaulichen Inhalt der quantentheoretischen Kinematik und Mechanik', Zeitschrift für Physik, 1927.
6. For further information on the European EC Better Regulation Policy, see: http://ec.Europa.eu/governance/better_regulation/index_en.htm
7. J. B. Wiener, 'Better Regulation in Europe', AEI-Brookings Joint Center for Regulatory Studies, September 2006, p.5.
8. EC, 'Communication of the EC to the European Parliament, the Council the European Economic and Social Committee and the Committee of the Regions – Implementing the Community Lisbon programme (COM/2005/0535 final): A strategy for the simplification of the regulatory environment', See: http://eur-lex.europa.eu/LexUriServ/LexUriServ.do?uri=CELEX:52003DC0071:EN:NOT
9. EC, 'Communication from the EC – Towards a Reinforced Culture of Consultation and Dialogue – General Principles and Minimum Standards for Consultation of Interested Parties by the EC (COM/2002/0704 final)', 11 December 2002. http://eur-lex.europa.eu/LexUriServ/LexUriServ.do?uri=CELEX:52002DC0704:EN:NOT
10. C. M. Radaelli, 'What does Regulatory Impact Assessment mean in Europe?', AEI-Brooking Joint Centre for Regulatory Studies, January 2005, p.6.
11. L. Allio and M. H. Fandel, 'Making Europe Work: Improving the Transposition, Implementation and Enforcement of EU Legislation', European Policy Centre Working Paper No. 25, June 2006, p.31.

12. EC, 'Impact Assessment Board', See http://ec.europa.eu/governance/impact/iab/iab_en.htm
13. EC, 'Impact Assessment Board', See http://ec.europa.eu/governance/impact/iab/iab_en.htm
14. J. B. Wiener, 'Better Regulation in Europe', AEI-Brookings Joint Center for Regulatory Studies, September 2006, p.61.
15. J. B.Wiener, 'Better Regulation in Europe', AEI-Brookings Joint Center for Regulatory Studies, September 2006, p.3.
16. UK Better Regulation Task Force, 'Routes to Better Regulation – A Guide to Alternatives to Classic Regulation', December 2005, p.11.

III SEPA: A Reaction to EU Regulatory Activism: 'A New Hope'

1. D is the day the customer payment order is accepted by his bank. Accordingly, "D+5" in this context meant that the payment could take up to 6 business days to reach the beneficiary bank.
2. http://www.ebaclearing.eu/EURO1-N=EURO1-L=EN.aspx
3. The MT 103+ message is one of the "100 series" of SWIFT's MT message types, which are used by PSPs for making customer transfers.

IV PSD – A Parallel Universe to SEPA: The Odyssey from the First Ideas to the Final Text

1. EC, 'Working Document on a Possible Legal Framework for the Single Payment Area in the Internal Market', MARKT/208/2001 – Rev.1, 2002.
2. EC Communication, 'Retail Payments in the Internal Market', COM (2006) 36.
3. EC, 'Communication form the Commission to the Council and the European Parliament concerning a New Legal Framework for Payments in the Internal Market', COM (2003) 718 final, Brussels, 2 Dec 2003.
4. FATF/GAFI, 'Special Recommendation VI: Alternative Remittance', (1996 updated in 2003).
5. The ECB is competent to deliver an opinion in relation to EC legislative proposal, when those proposals touch upon the area of payment systems or prudential supervision of credit institutions and the stability of the financial system, based on Article 105(4) first indent and Article 105(2) as well as Article 105(5) of the Treaty establishing the European Community.
6. The ECOSC participates in the decision making process as a consultative body and is, among other areas, consulted in relation to internal Market legislative proposals (Treaty Article 95). The legal basis of the ECOSOC itself is established under Treaty Articles 257 to 262 as an advisory body.
7. ECB, 'Comments on the Communication from the Commission to the Council and the European Parliament concerning a New Legal Framework for Payments in the Internal Market', P/PSP/04/086, 19 Feb 2004, p.1.
8. EESC position on the 'Communication from the Commission to the Council and the European Parliament concerning a New Legal Framework for Payments in the Internal Market', INT/227 – CESE 951/2004, expert supporting Rapporteur: Ruth Wandhöfer, Brussels, 30 July 2004.

9. For information on the EC Better Regulation Policy, please see the EC website: http://ec.europa.eu/governance/better_regulation/index_en.htm
10. Corrigendum to Regulation (EC) No 1781/2006, 08 Dec 2007, OJ, L 323/59
11. The PSMG and the PSGEG were created in 1992 by a Commission decision. These groups were considered informal and as such lacked clear terms of reference or membership criteria. In 2009 the Commission chose to replace the PSMG with a revised and more formal body called the Payment Systems Market Expert Group (PSMEG) and the PSGEG with the Payments Committee (the latter body being established by virtue of a requirement in the PSD). The author of this book became a member of the PSMG in 2004 and was subsequently selected to be a member of the PSMEG in 2009.
12. EC, 'Proposal for a Payment Services Directive', COM (2005) 603 final 2005/0245 (COD), Brussels, 1 Dec 2005
13. EC, 'Impact Assessment Guidelines', SEC (2005) 791, Brussels, 15 June 2005, revised in March 2006, p.4.
14. EC, 'Impact Assessment – Annex to the Proposal for a Payment Services Directive (COM (2005) 603 final)', Brussels, 01 Dec 2005, p.26.
15. Institute of International Finance, 'Proposal for a Strategic Dialogue on Effective Regulation', Washington D.C., December 2006, p.13.
16. EC, 'Impact Assessment – Annex to the Proposal for a Payment Services Directive (COM (2005) 603 final)', Brussels, 01 Dec 2005, pp.26–7.
17. EC, 'Impact Assessment – Annex to the Proposal for a Payment Services Directive (COM (2005) 603 final)', Brussels, 01 Dec 2005, p.17.
18. EC, 'Impact Assessment – Annex to the Proposal for a Payment Services Directive (COM (2005) 603 final)', Brussels, 01 Dec 2005, p.10.
19. EC, 'Impact Assessment – Annex to the Proposal for a Payment Services Directive (COM (2005) 603 final)', Brussels, 01 Dec 2005, p.26.
20. EC, 'Impact Assessment – Annex to the Proposal for a Payment Services Directive (COM (2005) 603 final)', Brussels, 01 Dec 2005, pp. 110–23.
21. EC, 'Impact Assessment – Annex to the Proposal for a Payment Services Directive (COM (2005) 603 final)', Brussels, 01 Dec 2005, p.26.
22. EC (DG MARKT), 'Payments Newsletter 05 Dec 2007', 2007, p.2.
23. EC, 'Working Document on a New Legal Framework for Payments in the Internal Market, Version 4.0 of 06.08.2004', Confidential document intended for discussion with PSMG and PSGEG, p.3.
24. NB: the EC here actually means the issuing and acquiring of 'payment transactions' as opposed to payment instruments. This was confirmed by the EC in their first response to the banking industry's PSD Expert Group in April 2008.
25. NLF Version 3 of 12 May 2004, Article 3 Definitions, 'payment service provider'.
26. NB: The EEA countries traditionally adopt EU financial market legislation as part of the EEA Joint Decision 154/2003.
27. PSE consulting, 'Can We Make SEPA Cash Displacement a Reality?', IFB Conference, Lisbon, 01 Feb 2008.
28. See FATF Special Recommendations:http://www.fatf-gafi.org/document/4/0,3343,en_32250379_32236920_43755076_1_1_1_1,00.html
29. EC, 'Proposal for a Directive on payment services in the internal market', COM (2005) 603 final, 2005, p.22.

30. EC, 'Impact Assessment – Annex to the Proposal for a Payment Services Directive (COM (2005) 603 final)', Brussels, 01 Dec 2005, p.56.
31. ECB, 'Opinion of the European Central bank of 26 April 2006 on a Proposal for a Directive on Payment services in the Internal Market (CON/2006/21)'
32. ECB, 'Opinion of the European Central bank of 26 April 2006 on a Proposal for a Directive on Payment Services in the Internal Market (CON/2006/21)'
33. In 2006 around 100 enterprises operated as 'payment institutions' in Poland. The absence of proper supervision and capital requirements resulted in numerous failures of those institutions, including for example: Grupa Finansowo-Handlowa 'Nova, 'Futura Capital', Agencja Finansowa 'MM', Agencja Pośrednictwa Finansowego 'VIGO', 'Płatnik', Agencja 'Meritum', Agencja Finansowa 'Grosik', the latter representing one of the biggest failures with 150 service points all over Poland and many thousands of customers.
34. EC, 'Proposal for a Payment Services Directive', Brussels, 1 Dec 2005, COM (2005) 603 final 2005/0245 (COD), Article 10 'Activities'.
35. Article 16(2) of the PSD clarifies that "Any funds received by payment institutions from payment service users with a view to the provision of payment services shall not constitute a deposit or other repayable funds within the meaning of Article 5 of Directive 2006/48/EC". Directive 2006/48/EC relates to the "taking up and pursuit of the business of credit institutions".
36. EC, 'Directive 2007/64/EC on Payment Services in the Internal Market', Brussels, 13 Nov 2007, Article 16 (2) 'Activities', p.16.
37. The BIS paper on 'General Principles for International Remittance Services' supports this argument.
38. EC, 'Directive 2007/64/EC on Payment Services in the Internal Market', Brussels, 13 Nov 2007, Article 9 (1a) Safeguarding requirements, p.14.
39. S. M. Seyad, 'A Critical Assessment of the Payment Services Directive', *Journal of International Banking Law and Regulation*, 23/4 (2008), p.13
40. HMT, 'Payment Service Directive: A Consultation', (2008), p.27.
41. Maximum thresholds defined in Article 21 of the proposal and Article 26 of the Official Version. The Official version sets a maximum of transaction volume of €3 million/month.
42. S. M. Seyad, 'A critical assessment of the Payment Services Directive', *Journal of International Banking Law and Regulation*, 2008, p. 19.
43. Member State derogations in the Official text 2007/64/EC include Articles 30 §2, 33, 34, 45 §6, 47 §3 and 48 §3. The list of Member State derogations provided by the EC can be found in Table 5.1 of this book.
44. EC, 'Financial Services Policy 2005–2010, White Paper', COM (2005) 629 final, Brussels 1 Dec 2005, p.8.
45. Micro-enterprises and Small and Medium Sized Enterprises are defined in the Annex of Commission Recommendation (2003/361/EC) of May 2003, Title I, Articles 1 and 2 (1).
46. Key opt-out options cover the burden of proof of PSPs in relation to authentication and execution of payment transactions, PSU liabilities for unauthorised payment transactions, refund rules, irrevocability of a payment order and rules regarding non-execution or defective execution.
47. The concept of gross negligence is for example not recognised under English law.

V From Publication to Transposition: The Directive Dilemma: 'The Road to Nowhere'

1. C. Persson and M. H. Fandel, 'Better Regulation: a regional perspective', European Policy Centre Issue Paper No. 53, May 2007, p.15.
2. HMT, 'Payment service directive: a consultation', 2008, p.23.

VI SEPA: From Design to Launch: Finding Your Way through the SEPA Jungle

1. SWIFT stands for Society for Worldwide Interbank Financial Telecommunications, TWIST stands for Transaction Workflow Innovation Standards Team, IFX stands for Interactive Financial eXchange Forum and OAGI stands for Open Applications Group.
2. Capgemini Consulting (2007), 'SEPA: Potential Benefits at Stake', p.4.

VII Postlude: The Future for European Payments in a Global Context: The Emergence of a Global Agenda

1. This percentage indicates the share of SCTs in the inter-bank domain as a percentage of the total volume of credit transfers – that is credit transfers in the 'old' as well as in SEPA format. These statistics are complied by the ECB and based on figures are based on aggregated data from the following clearing and settlement infrasructures/systems located in the euro area: CEC, RPS, Dias, Iberpay, SIT/CORE, BI-COMP, JCCTransfer, Equens, Step.at, SIBS, Bankart, GiroClearing and STEP2. (see: http://www.ecb.int/paym/sepa/about/indicators/html/index.en.html
2. ECOFIN Council Conclusions of December 2009: http://www.consilium.europa.eu/uedocs/cms_data/docs/pressdata/en/ecofin/111670.pdf
3. European Parliament Resolution on SEPA: http://www.europarl.europa.eu/sides/getDoc.do?pubRef=-//EP//TEXT+TA+P7-TA-2010-0057+0+DOC+XML+V0//EN
4. For further information on SACU please visit: http://www.sacu.int/
5. CLS Bank provides the largest multi-currency cash settlement system, eliminating settlement risk for over half the world's foreign exchange payment instructions. www.cls-group.com
6. 'India Needs World Class Payment Systems', report in *The Business Line*, 19 October 2006.
7. 'Payment Systems in India Vision 2009–2012', see: http://rbi.org.in/scripts/PublicationReportDetails.aspx?UrlPage=&ID=573
8. Mahadevan Balakrishnan (2009), 'Improving Payment System Efficiency in India: Next Steps', *Journal of Payments Strategy and Systems*, vol. 3 no. 4, 7 October 2009, p. 379.

Index

F

G

H

I

J

K

L

M